Shaker Textile Arts

Shaker Textile Arts

Beverly Gordon

Published by the University Press of New England
with the Cooperation of the Merrimack Valley
Textile Museum and Shaker Community, Inc.
Hanover, New Hampshire and London, England

The University Press of New England

Brandeis University	Tufts University
Brown University	University of New Hampshire
Clark University	University of Rhode Island
Dartmouth College	University of Vermont

Library of Congress Cataloging in Publication Data

Gordon, Beverly.
　Shaker textile arts.

　Bibliography: p.
　Includes index.
　1. Textile fabrics, Shaker.　　I. Title.
NK8912.G67　746'.0974　78-69899
ISBN 0-87451-158-5
ISBN 0-87451-242-5 (pbk.)

Contents

Illustrations

COLOR ILLUSTRATIONS
(following page 170)

FIGURES

Preface

Despite world-wide attention to Shaker furniture and architecture, Shaker textiles have received little public notice, even though they are ubiquitous in the Shaker environment. This lack of recognition is unfortunate but hardly surprising. Domestic textiles do not, on the whole, receive much attention anywhere. Textile work was usually done by women, and its status was generally low. We are far removed from textile processes today, and we are not taught to look for their subtle decorative and aesthetic qualities, as we are taught to look for these qualities in painting and sculpture. We pass by textiles almost as if they were invisible.

The quality of Shaker textiles is particularly subtle, and it is necessary to delve more deeply than usual to understand fully their beauty and integrity. It is worth while to do so, for Shaker textiles are as much a reflection of the Shakers' ideas, beliefs, and attitudes as any of their other work, and the same aesthetic characteristics are found in them.

This book is a comprehensive study of the textiles of the Shakers. Though it is written for a general audience, some technical information is introduced, and patterns, recipes, and construction details appear in the Appendixes for readers with specific interests.

The following people gave me invaluable help: all of the Shaker sisters for their cooperation and hospitality; John Ott, Amy Bess Miller, June Sprigg, and Sandra Scace of Hancock Shaker Village; Charles Thompson and his staff of Canterbury; Theodore E. Johnson, David Serette, and Steven Foster of Sabbathday Lake; Robert F. W. Meader, formerly of The Shaker Museum at Old Chatham, New York; James Thomas, Edward Nickels, and Helen Jo Trisler of Shakertown at Pleasant Hill; Dee Dee Hall and Julia Neal of Shakertown at South Union; Joseph Meany of the New York State Museum; Kermit J. Pike and Virginia Hawley of Western Reserve Historical Society; Frank H.

Somer and Beatrice Taylor of the Winterthur Museum Library. I would also like to thank Mary L. Richmond, Helene Von Rosenstiel, Katherine Koob, Philip Lief, and Kate and Joel Kopp for their advice; Anthony Carlotto, Paul Rocheleau, and Linda Moore for their help with photography; Gail Giles for her drawings; and Steven Vedro for his unflagging support.

Northampton, Massachusetts   B.G.
July 1978

Shaker Textile Arts

Chapter One
Who the Shakers Were

 One of the most interesting and most studied of America's religious communities is the United Society of Believers in Christ's Second Appearing, more commonly known as the Shakers. The sect was founded by Ann Lee, an English factory worker who, after a series of visions, came to see herself as the female manifestation of Christ. Mother Ann, as she was known, emigrated to America in 1774 with eight loyal followers. After an initial period of hardship and persecution, she was able to establish a religious society which at its peak in the 1840's had close to 6,000 members in eighteen separate communities. Membership began to decline seriously after the Civil War, when agricultural America was transformed by increasing industrialization and mobility. As a celibate sect with a comprehensive utopian vision, however, Shakers were remarkably hardy, and the Church survives to this day, with nine living Shaker women in two functioning communities.

The Shakers believed that they could experience God and His love directly, and that in their striving for perfection they could live as if the kingdom of heaven was already manifest on earth. In their worship services the Shakers often went into ecstatic raptures, or trances; their religious dancing and shaking was responsible for the name Shaking Quakers, or Shakers.

Shakerism developed with several guiding principles: celibacy, equality of the sexes, separation from "the world" (isolation), communality of goods, and a hierarchy of authority. Shakers lived in isolated communal groups where men and women were separated from one another in their daily lives and where all activities were geared to the good of the community as a whole.

The first two of these guiding principles were formulated as a direct result of the visions Ann Lee experienced when she was still in England. It was revealed to her that God has both a masculine and a feminine nature, with both components always present and perfectly balanced. Both men and women, then, had full access to the word of God. The sexes were kept apart because of the further revelation that purity and righteousness had been lost in the carnality, or original sin, of Adam and Eve, and only those who kept themselves free of any carnal activity could remain worthy of the kingdom of heaven.

To the Shakers, men and women were separate but equal. Although their work was different, their respective jobs were considered equally important. Leadership, both temporal and spiritual, was shared: there was always an eldress for every elder, a deaconess for every deacon. Women supervised women, and men supervised men.

The attempt to establish and maintain a "pure" life was also the principle behind the idea of separation from the world. It was felt that Believers would be better able to follow the tenets of the special life they had chosen if they were kept free from any external influence. When people became Shakers, they left behind all ties to their former lives. They consecrated both themselves and their belongings to their Church. Pooling their resources and possessions, Church members became a strong, relatively self-sufficient group that was better able to remain apart from the world.

In each community subgroup, or "family," large multilevel dwelling houses were established. Men lived on one side and women on the other, with several people sharing a single "retiring" room. Downstairs there were communal dining halls where the men sat at one side of the room and the women at the other. No nuclear family units were allowed to remain intact, and when a husband and wife joined the Shakers they were required to relinquish their matrimonial relationship completely. Children who were brought into the community as part of these families were put into the hands of "caretakers" and were no longer to have any special relationship with their parents. (By the second quarter of the nineteenth century there were a fair number of children in Shaker communities, for the Society also took in orphans and children whose parents could not care for them.)

The relationships of men and women (and boys and girls) with one another were effectively summed up by the terms used as forms of address: "sister" and "brother." Affection and mutual responsibility were assumed, but no deeper bonds were permitted. A true sister or brother was an adult who had willingly and consciously signed a covenant and become a full-fledged member of the Church. All Shakers were converts. No one was "born a Shaker," and even children who were raised in the Society had to choose whether to join when they reached maturity.

The Shakers had an elaborate hierarchical legal and social structure. The central headquarters of the Church was in New Lebanon, New York, about thirty miles east of Albany. Under this central ministry there were several bishoprics, each comprised of several communities in a relatively coherent geographical area. Communities varied in size but might have anywhere from 250 to 800 people at the peak of the Shaker movement. Communities were in turn divided into families of up to 100 people, and families were organized as orders—for example, novitiate, junior, and senior. The number of orders and families varied according to the community, but there was always a Church Family where the most trusted and respected members lived, including the spiritual leaders and the temporal leaders (trustees, who handled legal, financial, and business matters; and deacons, who were in charge of the internal workings of the community). Each family was overseen by two elders and two eldresses, who were appointed by the ministry and usually served a lifelong tenure. The chart of the organization of the Hancock community in Appendix I illustrates this hierarchy.

Shaker communities operated, then, as extended families. Each had its own dwelling house and workshops, and day-to-day tasks were carried out by family members. The sisters saw to the maintenance of the dwelling, the preparation of meals, the laundry, and the upkeep of community clothing and household goods. In addition, they usually operated a dairy, an herb and seed industry, and spinning, weaving, and sewing shops. The brethren did the heavy labor: they worked the fields, tended the animals at the farm, and ran such small community industries as tanneries, blacksmithing shops, and furniture manufactures.

Young people, who lived together (boys with boys and girls with girls) in the Children's Order, were given special duties of their own. From a very early age their caretakers taught them such activities and skills as they could master, and children's products were fully integrated into community life. Formal schooling, limited to certain times of the year (the summer for boys, the winter for girls), was overseen by the Believers themselves. Children worked side by side with their elders as soon as they were skilled and mature enough to do so.

On a typical day Believers would be awakened early by a bell. After dressing and straightening their rooms, they would attend to morning chores, then, after a brief prayer meeting and breakfast, turn to the main work of the day. Jobs were assigned by deacons and deaconesses, who tried to keep in mind both the good of the community and the good of the individual. Certain tasks were routinely shared by everyone on a rotating basis; every sister, for example, would take a turn at kitchen or laundry duty. Believers who were highly skilled or proficient in certain areas, however, were encouraged to spend much of their work time at those activities. Work was geared first to community needs, and second to trade with the outside world. Thus a cobbler's task was to make shoes for fellow Shakers, but if there was a demand from the "world's people" for Shaker-made shoes, he might make additional pairs for sale.

Work also varied according to the time of year. Agricultural tasks, of course, followed seasonal patterns much as they would on any family farm, and indoor work was usually done in the winter. For special projects the labor of the whole community could be mobilized. In the spring, for example, several days might be given over to refurbishing the dwelling: windows would be cleaned, walls given a new coat of whitewash, and floors painted.

The Shakers were industrious and productive, but they were never hurried or pressured in their work. Since they believed that they were manifesting God's kingdom—a perfect society filled with heavenly love—all of their everyday activities were considered to be consecrated acts, and care and patience were expected at every step. Mother Ann told her followers to "put your hands to work and your hearts to God," and to "work as if you had a thousand years to live and as if you were to die tomorrow." Superior quality and craftsmanship in Shaker products was a result of this conscious attitude.

Because of their uniformly high quality, Shaker-made items were highly respected by people in the outside world, and there was always a market for them. Sale items varied from community to community and changed over the course of time, but in most cases they were sold in special Shaker stores or by mail. Dealings with the world were generally handled by trustees and deacons, who were in charge of both the goods purchased by the Shakers and the items made for sale. The average Believer, at least until the second half of the nineteenth century, seldom needed to interact directly with the people of the world. Money earned in any shop went back to the general family fund. Careful records of all expenses and income were kept in every shop.

Many people believe that the routine, celibate, and constricted life of the Shakers was rigid and joyless, but the Shakers themselves felt that they were the most blessed people on earth. It is true that their lives were controlled and limited on a daily, temporal level, but it is also true that all of their needs were met and they had no individual worries. As they saw it, their ordered existence gave them time and space for spiritual development. They gave up carnal love, but were able to receive a higher, cosmic love. The Shakers were at peace with themselves and their world, and they lived lives of quiet fulfillment.

Chapter Two
The Textiles Overall

 Shaker textiles were not dramatically different from those of their contemporaries in the outside world. The Shakers were always a part of the changing traditions in America, and although their relative isolation and religious beliefs led to characteristic products, these products reflected the work of the world's people in many ways.

In the early years of the sect, this was especially true. Edward Deming Andrews, an outstanding Shaker authority, remarked that "in a very true sense, the early Shaker community was but an enlarged colonial household."[1] Men who joined a community as carpenters brought their knowledge of carpentry to the Shaker shop, and women who knew how to spin, weave, and sew brought their training, work habits, patterns, and ideas into the sisters' shops. That there were continual converts meant that there was continually fresh external influence. An ongoing trade between Shakers and non-Shakers also provided constant exposure to worldly products and changing worldly styles.

It is sometimes difficult, in fact, to identify a particular textile as "Shaker," for many objects made in the outside world were brought into the communities and used there. Special items were as prized and well-loved inside the community as out. A touching example, in the collection at Hancock Shaker Village, is a small white linen cloth with an indigo blue monk's belt design. Inked across the cloth are the words "1777 Weding [Wedding] Linen, Lovica Slawson." Clearly, Lovica treasured this piece, and although she became a Shaker many years after her marriage, she saved it and perhaps even passed it on to other sisters.

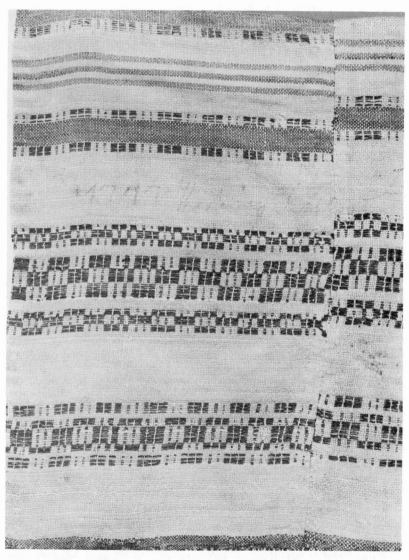

FIGURE 1. *This small scrap (7-1/2 x 11 inches) was a highly treasured piece of wedding linen. It is hand spun and woven with a dark blue monk's belt design. Lovica Slawson was fifteen years old in 1777. (Hancock Shaker Village)*

Despite constant interaction with the outside world, characteristic Shaker features evolved. An inward-looking community with shared attitudes and values was bound to mirror these values in the objects they produced. The most striking thing about the textiles, and indeed about all Shaker work, is a sense of order. In most cases this is achieved through a structural rather than decorative design, simple lines, symmetry, and regularly repeating patterns. There is also careful attention to detail and a subtle but rich use of color. In addition, many textiles are finished with some sort of border around them, and often the borders are as important to the design as the central area; they act as frames which complete the pieces and affirm that they are finished statements. Shaker textiles, like all Shaker products, are practical, functional, and comfortable, and have a consistent aesthetic integrity.

Structural Design and Simple Lines

Structural design is design that emerges from the inherent characteristics of the materials, shapes, or processes used. The characteristics can be fully exploited and dramatized, but there are no additional embellishments. In a woven piece of cloth this means that the pattern is loom controlled: it is a function of the way the loom is set up and manipulated. No finger-manipulated effects or decorative embroidery are part of the design. In a handsewn item such as the sewing case shown at the left in Figure 2, the design results from positioning the striped cloth so as to form a decorative edging. In the case shown at the right, the printed cottons are also positioned carefully for a decorative effect.

This emphasis on structural design is related to the Shaker emphasis on simplicity and practicality in every aspect of life. Unnecessary adornment was considered frivolous and fussy, unsuitable for the purity of their "heaven on earth;" smooth, uncluttered lines were more appropriate. In this regard the contrast between Shaker and non-Shaker textiles is less dramatic than the contrast between Shaker and non-Shaker furniture or architecture, but it is still valid as a general principle.

The uncluttered, clean look does not mean that Shaker textiles

FIGURE 2. *Two similar sewing cases from the first half of the nineteenth century. The blue-and-white striped cotton, seen at left, is also used on the outside of the case at right. This is one of the materials that the brethren's trousers were made out of shortly after 1800. Note how the stripe is used as a border on the folded case; it is cut on the bias and carefully angled so as to form a decorative edging. These small, subtle details make Shaker textiles special. (Hancock Shaker Village)*

FIGURE 3. *A "caterpillar" rug from Pleasant Hill. Note the four borders that frame the circular motif.*

were simply or easily made, or that a tremendous amount of effort did not go into them. On the contrary, details were well planned and meticulously carried out. Because the Believers were under no pressure to work quickly, they had the freedom to produce items that were unusually complicated or involved. In the case of the poplar cloth that they made after the Civil War, for example, eighteen separate operations were necessary just to prepare the materials for weaving (see Chapter 3, below). With the bed covering shown in Figure 44, the subtle plaid is achieved by gradual color changes—dark red to medium red to light red; light green to gray to dark gray; and so on. Only people who had a cooperative, labor-intensive work situation could afford the luxury of this kind of craftsmanship.

FIGURE 4. *A woven rug from one of the northeastern communities, with the character-istic diagonals formed by plying two or more colors together. Two heavy braids encircle the rug. (The Shaker Museum at Old Chatham)*

Symmetry and Repeating Pattern

Most Shaker products are symmetrical, and in many cases they are bilaterally symmetrical—that is, the two halves are mirror images of each other. All of Shaker life was permeated with this kind of parallelism. There were an equal number of elders and eldresses, of deacons and deaconesses. Each dwelling had a staircase for men and an identical staircase for women. There were shops for the brethren and shops for the sisters. No element of daily life, and no individual person, was more important than any other.

This balance and overall unity pervades the textiles. In the rug illustrated in Figure 3, for example, every element of the design on the right is reflected on the left; there is a central point and a design radiating out from it. Patterns in Shaker textiles also tend to be repeated again and again, and the repetition perpetuates and accentuates the sense of order and containment. This is illustrated by the rug in Figure 4, which has a regularly repeating sequence of horizontal stripes. Both of these rugs also illustrate the phenomenon of concentric borders which act as framing devices and bring the pieces together visually.

Color

Many people assume that, given their emphasis on simplicity and modesty, the Shakers used only dull, dreary colors. Though it is true that they avoided flashy colors, at least until late in the nineteenth century, they never set out to be drab. Early in the history of the sect, Believers were told they might use any color they could dye themselves, and Shaker dyebooks, mostly dating between 1830 and 1840, include recipes for various shades of red and scarlet, orange, brown, beige, rust, blue, gray, slate, yellow, lavender, and purple.

By the 1820's and 1830's there were general guidelines for colors that could be used on certain items. As Andrews points out, the guidelines evolved primarily out of a practical concern for regulating the nature of pigments, dyes, and paints, and to establish a degree of uniformity throughout Shaker communities.[2] They were not intended to exercise complete control over the colors in Shaker life. The Millennial Laws, written in 1820, contained the only formal written color restrictions, and these referred to the furnishings in retiring rooms. According to the Laws, bedsteads were to be painted green; curtains were to be white, blue, or green; and outer bed coverings were to be blue and white.[3] The restrictions, an attempt at standardization, were never completely effective. It was stipulated in the first place that bedcovers already in use could be allowed to wear out. Even in the 1820–1830 period, then, other colors were in use; and as time went by, the restrictions were adhered to less and less stringently, even for new covers, particularly in communities that were geographically removed from the Church center in New Lebanon.

Until the twentieth century, color was fairly uniform in clothing, mostly because the cloth that went into the clothes was made or purchased in large quantities. Permissible colors changed over the years. White, dark (indigo) blue, deep butternut (reddish) brown, gray, drab color, and low-key reds were most significant in the nineteenth century. Rose-pink was a favorite for such clothing accessories as silk kerchiefs and collars. Generally, the colors the Shakers used were in keeping with colors used by the world's people at the same time.

There is some question whether yellow was restricted. Recipes can be found for yellow dye, and a mustard yellow paint was popular for exterior building walls; with the exception of some of the fibers found in rugs, however, there was very little yellow in Shaker textiles until the twentieth century. There was no lack of availability; many native plants yielded dependable and bright yellows, and yellow cloth was available in many stores. No existing records specifically prohibit the color, and the Shaker sisters still living do not know of any ban on its use, but since so little is to be found in the earlier textiles, it may have been discouraged at one time.

Later in the nineteenth century and certainly in the twentieth, color restrictions disappeared completely. Synthetic (aniline) dyes were discovered in 1856, and by the end of the Civil War a whole new range of bright, almost garish colors were generally available. The Shakers, like everyone else, loved the new and vibrant royal blues, purples, roses, pinks, greens, and reds, and there was never any question that they could use them. Many Shaker household textiles from the latter part of the nineteenth century were made with brilliantly colored fabrics and yarns, but the early synthetic dyes, not very colorfast, have faded badly.

Both the earlier naturally dyed pieces and the later chemically dyed ones indicate the Shakers' strong sensitivity to color. Interesting color combinations were used, and colors were frequently blended subtly together. As we shall see in Chapter 3, this was done in a number of different ways: by mixing different colors of wool before spinning, plying different colors of yarn together, mixing colors in weaving, and juxtaposing subtle gradations of color in woven and knitted items. Color blending can be seen as another reflection of Shaker attitudes and ideals. Mixing several colors to create a new, composite color is a dialectical, integrative process. The Shakers found joy in routine aspects of daily life, and believed that the world was an integrated manifestation of divine order. Synthesis in blended colors is in keeping with this overall synthesis in Shaker life.

Comfort and Aesthetic Integrity

The Shakers were always practical, and everything was designed with maximum usability in mind. That the items were practical, however, did not preclude their comfort or attractiveness. Chair seats covered with narrow woven cloth strips, for example, were extremely durable, but they were also pleasing to look at and comfortable to sit on.

Although the impression is common that Shaker life was rigid and severe, even totalitarian, in many ways it was surprisingly flexible. Within a highly disciplined and structured framework, there was room for comfort and even some luxury; also, individuals found ways to express their personal tastes and their love for beautiful things.

The nature of this personal and communal expression of beauty and comfort is subtle, almost elusive. To understand how pervasive it is, we must look with Shaker eyes. Texture, stitching, and fabric were carefully juxtaposed to create certain effects. If any one of these small details was changed, the overall feeling was lost. The sewing case illustrated in Figure 2 is a good example of this subtlety. There are also many parts of Shaker clothing, in particular, which have wonderful details the Shakers knew about but which were not seen by anyone

FIGURE 5. *Detail of a chair seat covered with handwoven tapes. These are woven around the chair in a basketweave pattern. (Hancock Shaker Village)*

FIGURE 6. *Neck lining detail on a Shaker dress, late nineteenth century. The shiny outer cloth is wool which has been treated for wrinkle resistancy. The checked lining is cotton. This lining was not visible when the sister was dressed; there was a kerchief or bertha worn over it. (Hancock Shaker Village)*

FIGURE 7. *View of a typical (brother's) retiring room. Note the woven rug, the white half-curtains at the window, the plain bedcover, the towel rack with plain and checked towels, the checked wall cloth behind the bed, and the straw hat and tailored coat hanging on the wall. (Hancock Shaker Village)*

else; some of the brethren's collar bands, for example, were made with three or four different kinds of silk, all rich and luxurious. Dress linings were made from decorative cotton prints—sometimes more than one. Details like these were clearly included solely for the Shakers' own enjoyment.

Textiles in the Lives of the Shakers

The Importance of Textiles

There were an enormous number of textiles in a Shaker village. The retiring rooms in a typical dwelling house contained mattresses, sheets, pillowcases, blankets, quilts, and coverlets; window curtains; floor rugs and runners; chair seat tapes and chair seat cushions. Splash cloths protected the walls behind the washstands, and large wall cloths protected the walls around the beds. There were towels for both personal use and cleaning, as well as mops, washcloths, laundry bags, napkins, and table mats. The kitchens contained assorted dishcloths, potscrubbers, breadcloths, and strainers of various types.

Great quantities of cheesecloth were required in the dairy, and ironing cloths and nets for holding small items during washing were used in the laundry. There were also bandages, garden sheets, feed sacks, horseblankets, rags, and workbags of all kinds.

FIGURE 8. *View of the ironing room, North Family, New Lebanon. On the left is a round stove, set up to hold and heat many "sad" irons at once. There are window shades at the right. The man in the rear is operating a clothes press.*

Added to household, workshop, and farm textiles were the myriad types of clothing that people wore. Surprisingly, each Shaker had a great deal of clothing—far more, in fact, than many of their contemporaries outside the sect. Everyone had work clothes, regular clothes, and dress clothes, a complete set of each for summer, winter, and the transitional season.

Obviously, an enormous amount of time went into the preparation, creation, and upkeep of all these textiles. On the whole, textile work was the domain of the women. The brethren built and repaired the equipment (looms, spinning wheels, and so forth), worked in community mills, and in some instances did weaving or helped sell the textile products. With the exception of tailoring, however, the hand work was done by the sisters. They were responsible for handspinning, handweaving, dyeing, sewing, knitting and crocheting, and the endless tasks of mending, darning, washing, ironing, and generally keeping the textiles in good order. Each sister was responsible not only for her own clothing and personal linen, but for those of a particular brother as well; she was assigned by the ministry to look after him and make sure that his personal furnishings were clean and in good repair. When the Shaker mills were in operation, some women also worked in them.

A huge proportion of the sisters' time went into this textile work. Journal entries indicate that some of them worked in the textile shops as many as five or six days a week, resting on the Sabbath and perhaps taking a turn in the kitchen or laundry, or working in some facet of the herb industry, or occasionally taking a day or two off for a special excursion.

Textile-related activities were important both for the internal workings of the community and for community income. This was true throughout Shaker history. Items were made for sale from the beginning of the nineteenth century, and when the number of Shaker men declined in later years, the sisters' sewing, knitting, and "fancy goods" industries became especially important as a source of cash.

The Record and Journal of the Sisters, written in the First Order at Watervliet, New York, in 1838, conveys a feeling for the proportion of time and the enormous amount of work accomplished. The following were produced for community use:

510   runs* of tow and linen spun
1826 runs wool and worsted yarn [spun]
800   pounds sheared wool
1342 yards woven [cloth]
1270 yards tape woven
          made 48 pairs trousers, and 10 jackets

Items made for sale in the same year were:

29   runs glove thread
1030 palm leaf bonnets
5½   dozen palm leaf baskets
40   dozen braided sashes
26   dozen big mops
40   pair stockings knit
65   pair footings knit
52   pairs gloves knit
53   yards cloth [woven]
30   runs stocking yarn [spun]

Even the children worked extremely hard, and spent much of their time at textile activity. The following excerpt is also taken from a Watervliet journal. The girls' caretaker, or supervisor, Catherine Damph, summed up the work done in the Girl's Order in 1845:

Spun caretaker and all 479 runs. Wove 14 yards of towel loops, 180 yards of carpet bindings, spooled 960 runs of yarn, girls quilled [wound the bobbins for the weaving shuttles] for nearly all the falls weaving, bordered 40 nets, knit 10, made 17 shifts, 4 pressed aprons, 7 checked aprons, 27 collars, 5 petticoats, 12 gounds [i.e. gowns] sleaved knit 11 pair of stockings, footed 4 pair, made 13 waistcoats, 10 pocket handerchiefs, two nightcaps, foulded the close and ironed every week, and sometimes the older girls ironed twice a week, knit 22 pairs of sail [i.e. sale] footings, bottomed 15 chairs with list and bindings. All this besides innumerable chores, their mending, working in the kitchen, tending to their school lessons, went to school three months and a half.

*A "run" is approximately 1600 yards.

We had 8 girls in the order, the oldest 12 years, the youngest 4 years old.[4]

Work Habits

Textile activities, as we have seen, followed natural seasonal patterns. Dyeing, for example, was usually done in the summer, and out of doors when the weather permitted. Preparation of flax, used for both fine linen and rough tow (for feed bags, rope, twine, and so on), was most often done in March and April. On March 19, 1845, in one northeastern community, Sister Anne Williams wrote, "we card [comb] the rest of the tow without brakeing the weather being too cold to brake any more."[5] Palm-leaf fiber, used in bonnets, was generally woven in May and June. Even while a seasonal occupation was carried on, however, many other activities relieved the tedium. An anonymous dyer reports in her journal that during June, July, and August she worked at haying, cutting onion seed, cutting carpet rags, "picking out" stitches, and "attending to the gift of cleansing and sweeping"—all in addition to dyeing.[6] *

No single individual had to be proficient in all textile activities. Everyone was doubtlessly encouraged to become familiar with different processes and techniques, and all women were expected to be able to spin (at least until the latter part of the nineteenth century), sew, and knit, but there were specialists in some areas. Sisters who were good weavers spent much of their work time at the loom. Others who were competent seamstresses were often responsible for developing new features and styles in the clothing (subject to the approval of the ministry). And there were expert dyers, rugmakers, and other specialists.

When a task needed many hands, spontaneous work "bees" or "frolics" were held. We are told of spinning frolics where there would

*The "cleansing and sweeping" may well have been more than regular housekeeping. In the 1840's there was the phenomenon of "Mother Ann's Sweeping Gift"; a day was set aside to thoroughly rid the entire premises of "evil spirits." In addition to actual cleaning and sweeping, a few chosen individuals marched through the village chanting and moving "spiritual brooms."

be "music in the wheels," and of times when corn was husked in a gathering of the whole community on moonlit summer nights.[7] Bees were also held in honor of something special; it is reported, for example, that after a dinner celebrating Eldress Molly's fiftieth birthday in New Lebanon, the group held a spinning and weaving bee in which 120 runs were spun and 40 yards were woven.[8] Another sort of bee was mentioned on April 23, 1872, by New Lebanon Sister Polly Ann Reed: they "had a bee at the ironing room to starch, iron, and draw up the sisters new grenadine caps with a thread drawn in."[9] Mutual cooperation of this sort was a matter of course in the communal Shaker environment.

Individuals also willingly helped another on a one-to-one basis, and there seems to have been a relaxed, casual interchange. In an 1860 journal from Harvard, Sister Mary Babbitt wrote that "M. finished off her gown and cut one for the Elder sister and worked on it in exchange for her helping on the carpet." Believers visited back and forth between families and nearby communities, and stayed to help when it was necessary. New Lebanon sister Selah Draper went with two other women to visit Hancock in 1833, and she stayed when she found it was necessary to "learn them [the Hancock sisters, presumably] to knit socks."[10]

Types of Textile Activities and Accouterments

Textile activities varied considerably over the course of Shaker history. People often think the Shakers were completely self-sufficient, making all of their own products and tools from scratch. This is not true. They were pragmatic, forward-looking people, and they always followed the most practical course of action. When it was cheaper or more sensible to buy goods or services from the outside world, they did so. Their products were highly respected and sold well, and money earned from sale items was in turn used to buy necessities and materials for other Shaker products.

Fiber processing and cloth production was done by hand as long as it was necessary but was mechanized as soon as possible. For example, Shakers raised their own sheep but sent their wool out to nearby carding and spinning mills as soon as they were opened. In many communities they later built and operated their own mills; these were small "family" operations run by a few Believers on a seasonal basis, where cloth was produced primarily for community use rather than for sale.

Handspinning continued well into the nineteenth century, and handweaving into the twentieth, but handmade yarns and cloth were used only for certain items. Handspun linen (flax was still prepared by hand) was used for household sheets and toweling, agricultural sacking, and rough clothing. Handspun wool went into such knit items as gloves and mittens. Handwoven cloth was sometimes used for clothing (shirts, trousers, frocks, aprons, even shoes) but was especially important as tape (for chair seats, rug bindings, and many other items), blankets (for both people and animals), towels, dishrags, cheesecloth, meal (feed) bags, and other household and community furnishings. Rugs were handwoven as late as 1940, and palm leaf, straw, and poplar strips were handwoven into special cloth for bonnets, hats, and fancy boxes until about the same time.

These specialty items became the most important products of the handlooms after the middle of the nineteenth century; Andrews says that handweaving in New Lebanon ranged from 1,500 to 2,000 yards per year before 1851 but had decreased to 581 yards by 1861.[11] By the end of the Civil War most communities had also abandoned their mills. After a mill fire in 1866 in Hancock, for example, it was decided not to rebuild because of intense competition from non-Shaker industry.[12]

At all times in Shaker history a great deal of cloth was purchased from the outside world; a large proportion of the items the Shakers bought, in fact, were textile related. Journal records of products bought and sold in specific years provide insight into Shaker give and take with the outside world. An account book of 1845–1850 from an unidentified community (probably Enfield, Connecticut) listing items the Shakers purchased in Hartford shows that during 1840 they bought close to 500 yards of cotton cloth. In February 7 skeins of silk, 17 papers of needles, 1 gross of buttons, 1 pound of Irish linen thread, and 6⅜ yards of flannel were among the items purchased; in March the list included 1 pound of linen thread, 3 yards of white plaid cambric (a soft cotton), 152¼ yards of fulled cloth (probably wool), 4½ yards of satinette, and a large quantity of dyeing supplies (17 pounds of indigo, 25 pounds of madder, 10 pounds of copperas, 25 pounds of alum, and 29 pounds of glauber's salts); and in May, they bought 100¾ yards of sheeting.

The list of purchases during 1845 included 354 yards of sheeting, 122 yards of blue striped cloth (probably cotton), 91 yards of twilled cotton, 109 yards of checked cotton, 48 yards of cambric and muslins, 41 yards of merino (fine wool), 55 yards "flannel of baize," 75 yards of cotton, 10 yards of flannel, 18 yards of oil cloth, two pairs of blankets, 10 yards of table linen, 14 yards of alpaca, thread, tape, ribbon, scissors, pins, thimbles, buttons, and 10 pounds of harness twine. Silk, velvet, and cotton batting were also common purchases. In exchange, the articles sold included 250 pounds of broken rags, 66 pairs of socks, 25 yards of diaper (fine handwoven linen), unspecified numbers of gloves, mittens, and stockings, and an unspecified amount of mixed yarn for knitting.

Decisions about what items to buy were made by the deacons, but individual Shakers put in personal requests for things they wanted. The Millennial Laws specify that "when brethren and sisters want anything bought, or brought in from among the world . . . they must apply to [the deacons and deaconnesses] for whatever they desire."[13] When small quantities of an item are listed among the purchases, it is probably safe to assume that a specific sister had asked for it; "two yards of silk ribbon,"[14] for example, was probably needed to complete a special task. Certainly by the late nineteenth century, individuals were working on special projects on their own initiative. In the 1872 diary of Polly Ann Reed, a New Lebanon sister, the November 29 entry reads, "I asked Ann to look in Philadelphia and see if she could not find some brussels lace for us."

Shakers are known for their inventiveness, and besides looking to the outside for new textile products, they of course developed and improved products themselves. As we will see in Chapter 3, Believers in Kentucky developed an unusual system of separating the flax fiber from the plant without previous retting, or rotting, to decompose the stalks.

Small but immensely helpful furnishings such as steps and "thrones" were developed to make every facet of textile work more efficient and pleasant. Thrones were platforms about one foot high placed under windows, allowing the person sitting on them to benefit from the maximum amount of daylight while she worked. Sewing steps were another example of Shaker practicality described by Irene Zieget, a visitor to the Shakers in 1929. She explained that "every woman crosses her legs when she hems but with these steps she doesn't have to; for close work she puts her foot on the second step [and] if it isn't so close, on the first."[15]

Another Shaker "invention" was a method of making cloth wrinkle-resistant (the forerunner of permanent press). They put cotton or wool fabric into a special press with paper that had been treated with zinc chloride, and applied heat and pressure. The resulting fabric was shiny and smooth on one side (the top) and was also water resistant. This press was first developed in Sabbathday Lake, Maine, in 1824, and many of the dresses, trousers, and outer garments of the nineteenth century were made in Maine from material so treated. The other Shaker communities provided the Sabbathday Lake community with their own products or with cash in exchange for the treated cloth.[16] (This was not unusual; Shakers sold many products from one community to another, and in the mid-nineteenth century exchange was particularly important for clothing material. With the large cloth output possible in the mills, greater standardization of clothing was made possible. Communities that had no mill purchased Shaker-made cloth from those that did.)

Dyeing was an important textile activity as long as cloth was Shaker-produced. As the list quoted above shows (pages 25–26), a great deal of dyeing material was needed. All of it was used for natural dyes. By the time chemical dyes were in general use, shortly after the Civil War, the Shakers were relying almost exclusively on cloth purchased from the outside world.

Sewing and knitting were perhaps the most important activities in the lives of the Shaker sisters. They were not seasonal activities but were carried on all the time. Knitting, in fact, was pick-up work, and when there were a few spare moments, knitting was indeed picked up. A Hancock butter churn on rockers can be worked with the feet, and it is said that the rockers left the sisters' hands free to do something else—in most cases, probably knitting. At certain times, knitting was the major occupation of the day. Polly Ann Reed wrote in her 1872 journal that she "went to the shop and knit all day—finished off [her] sixth neckerchief."[17]

FIGURE 9. *This press, still in its original location at Sabbathday Lake, was used to make clothing water repellent and wrinkle resistant. The cloth was placed between the wooden boards.*

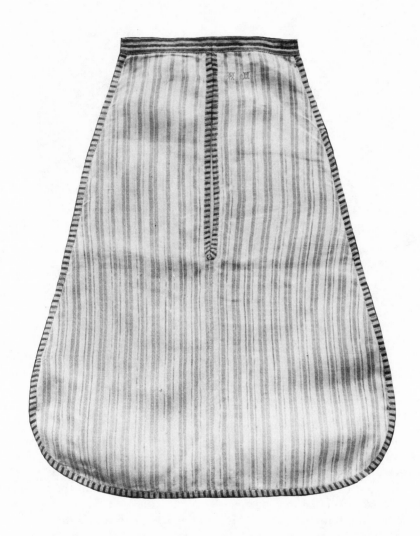

FIGURE 10. *A handspun and handwoven linen "pocket" from the eighteenth or early nineteenth century. These pockets were used for holding sewing equipment—threads, spools, and so forth. They were worn under the skirt, which had slits in the side so that the pocket could be reached easily. (Hancock Shaker Village)*

FIGURE 11. *Handcarved spools and spool holders, Hancock Shaker Village. New Lebanon Brother Henry De Witt wrote in March 1835: "I have been getting my timber ready for turning bobbins . . . I got out willow enough for 19 more spools. I turned out 52 warping spools [similar, though larger than these] by 4 o'clock."*

The importance of sewing is reflected in the many pieces of sewing equipment and accessories which have been found. Handcarved spools and threadholders, sewing cases, purses, pouches, pockets, and boxes of all shapes abound in Shaker collections. A great many were made for sale, but many show signs of heavy use and initial markings —an indication that they belonged to a particular individual and were used in the community itself. Most of this equipment, with the exception of such wooden items as carved spools, was made by the sisters.

Journal entries indicate that the sisters gave one another sewing accouterments as gifts: specially made emeries, spools of thread, papers of pins, waxballs. (They also exchanged scarves, handkerchiefs, and other personal accessories.) [18] A deep sense of pride permeated the giving of these objects, and they were made with loving, careful attention.

Sewing of one sort or another was in effect the life work of many sisters. In a personal journal (as opposed to a family record book) written in Harvard by Sister Mary Babbitt, there are many entries along the lines of "sewing as usual."[19] In all cases where women left the Shakers to make their way in the outside world, they were given sewing equipment (for example, "1 box and contents thread, silk, thimbles, needles, etc.") and cloth and/or yarn. In the same situation, men were given tools, such as hammers and saws.[20] The sewing necessities were literally the tools of the sisters' trade.

Shakers were among the first people to use sewing machines; in Harvard "the Dorcis sewing machine was brought to the sister's shop" in 1857,[21] although it was not in common use elsewhere before 1865.[22] All communities apparently had sewing machines by the 1870's, and they were welcomed as an extremely important labor-saving device. They had an enormous impact on the lives of the sisters who used them. In the November 9, 1877, journal entry of an anonymous Canaan, New York, sister the sentence "our new sewing machines have come" was significant enough to be underlined twice. According to Eldress Bertha Lindsay, the Canterbury, New Hampshire, records from the same year contain the following: "Brother Benjamin went to Concord for a sewing machine, but finding he could get two for $88 he brought the two home and it was all that it was said to be. Sister Julia had one of these machines in constant use for 39 years."[23]

Girls were taught to knit and sew at a very young age, and as we have seen in Catherine Damph's record of the Watervliet Girl's Order, (pages 22–23) much of what they worked on was actually used in the community and sold to the outside. There are still some examples of samplers stitched by girls who lived with the Shakers, used primarily as a vehicle for learning to stitch well and to mark initials; it was considered less important (at least until late in the nineteenth century) that girls become accomplished embroiderers.

Almost all women sewed their own clothes. Those who were particularly good seamstresses helped others to sew theirs, or made clothes for them. Sometimes they made clothes for the men, too,[24] but there were male tailors who specialized in this. Many of the tailors

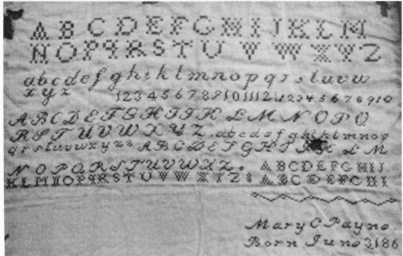

FIGURE 12. *The sewing room, North Family, New Lebanon, c. 1880–1890. The sisters are probably sewing white shirts. Note that all adult sisters are wearing white caps, although two young girls are bareheaded. Some sisters are wearing the typical kerchief over their bodice, but the two on the far left are wearing berthas.*

FIGURE 13. *Linen sampler stitched by Mary C. Payne, born 1860. Mary lived at the Shaker community in Pleasant Hill, Kentucky. Note that all of the letters are embroidered in cross-stitch.*

FIGURE 14. *Umbrella swift (expandable skein winder) made at Hancock. Note the adjustable clamp at the bottom and the cup for holding a ball of yarn at the top. (Hancock Shaker Village)*

earned reputations even outside the Shaker community for their meticulous workmanship; they believed that tailoring was an exact science.

Textile sale items, as we have seen, were important from early in Shaker history. One of the first community industries was the painstaking job of setting the wire teeth in the hand cards used in processing woolen fiber, an industry developed late in the eighteenth century. The brethren also made other kinds of textile equipment for sale to the outside world. Spinning wheels and skein reels or winders were important sale items early in the nineteenth century, and table swifts (expandable skein winders that clamped to flat surfaces) were a major industry at Hancock as late as 1875.

Different communities specialized in producing certain items, and huge quantities of textile-related items were made. In Watervliet, New York, for example, 1,606 bonnets were made in 1836; 1,550 in 1837; 1,030 in 1838; and 1,200 in 1839.[25] They were made with imported palm leaf that was woven on a loom and fashioned over a bonnet mold. Fans were sold as early as 1835 and were a particularly important industry at Harvard.[26] Although they were not used by the Shakers, they were popular with the world's people, and they sold well. Between 1840 and 1849, small items like emeries, pincushions, table mats, and chair mats became sale items in New Lebanon. Knitted stockings and needlebooks were sold in the 1850's, and rugs and chair seat cushions were available in large numbers by the 1860's. In New Lebanon, white cotton shirts were made by the hundreds once the sisters had sewing machines.[27]

By the turn of the century, fancy goods were the major source of income for all remaining communities. Even today, Shaker sisters who are still able spend some of their time with needle in hand and produce knitted, crocheted, or stitched articles for sale.

Chapter Three

Production of Textiles

Fibers and Fiber Preparation

Flax (Linen)

In the eighteenth century linen and wool were the fibers of primary importance in the northeastern United States, where the Shakers had settled. Flax (called linen when it is spun) was grown in all communities up to the middle of the nineteenth century. For the most part, flax was processed the same way in a Shaker community as it was anywhere else. It was sown in the spring and harvested in July. The seeds were removed from the plant, and the stalks were then rotted, or retted, so that the husk and inner pith would decompose. The strong linen fiber was not affected by this process. Once the retting had softened the chaff, the flax stalks were "broken" in small bundles; hard pounding in a flax break (also spelled "brake") would break the softened husk and pith, leaving the fibers unharmed. Hetcheling, or hackling—a combing process—followed breaking. The long, unmatted fibers that emerged from the hetchel were used for fine linen thread, while the shorter, tougher fibers (called tow or "toe") were made into rough sacking material, work clothes, mopheads, and rope.[1]

In most communities this work was done by hand. The sisters were usually the ones who processed the flax, and records from the sisters' shops include entries like "Today we begin to hetchel,"[2] or "This spring and winter there has been 304 pounds hetcheled."[3]

In the first part of the nineteenth century in the northern communities, flax processing was usually done in early spring; many references are made to it in March and April. This would mean that the previous summer's crop was stored through the winter, and the linen woven in any year would not have been from the most recent flax crop.

In the western and southern communities during the nineteenth century, flax was an especially important crop, for these communities were heavily oriented to agriculture and agricultural products rather than to manufacturing. In North Union, Ohio, the flax and hemp crops were second in importance only to corn.[4] In Pleasant Hill, Kentucky, flax processing was so basic to the life of the community that it was mechanized to a certain extent; the famous Shaker inventiveness is revealed in the following excerpt from a description of Pleasant Hill in an article in the Richmond *Inquirer* of May 3, 1825, "Letters of Inquiry on the Condition of Kentucky":

> . . . Their flax is broken and "swingled" by machinery and without previous rotting. By this machinery they can break 4,000

FIGURE 15. *Flax hackle, or hetchel. The hackle would be bolted to a table, and the flax would be drawn through a succession of hackles, each finer-toothed than the last. (Hancock Shaker Village)*

weights* of flax a day. The operation is performed by means of three iron rollers, about the size, and form of the common apple mill, and like it, these rollers are fluted and run into each other, being placed horizontally, and one on top of the other: it is actuated by a two-horse power: the swingling is done by means of a wheel six feet in diameter with six or more wooden knives fastened to the rim, this is united by a band to the other machinery; the rollers which I have described, are cast in segments, and fastened on a wooden cylinder.

Pleasant Hill and North Union also had special mills for pressing linseed oil, made from the seed of the flax plant.[5]

By about 1840 most Shaker flax was primarily used for tow rather than for fine linen. Hand processing was extremely time-consuming, and linen and cotton were commercially available at reasonable prices. Fifteen years later it was not sensible to produce even rough tow cloth by hand. In 1856 Elder Isaac N. Young of New Lebanon summarized Shaker history in a handwritten document: "A Concise View of the Church of God and of Christ on Earth Having Its Formation In the Faith of Christ's First and Second Appearing." The Shakers, Young wrote, "formerly manufactured considerable tow cloth, but of late tow and linen are pretty much [entirely] displaced by cotton."[6]

Even when it was no longer used for fabric, however, tow was put to use in mops and other items. The tow was broken and then put through a carding machine. This must have been a fairly rough process, and the mops were referred to as being made of "raw tow."[7] On April 21, 1851, Eliza Ann Taylor noted that the sisters in her New Lebanon shop "commenced hatcheling, have 400 lb. of Flax very coarse not very good." On April 26 she said that they

> finished the Mops and Tow. Two sisters have carded 213 lb. at the Machine. . . 6 sisters and all the little girls have carded on last years tow. 6 hands have spun the Mops, 253. 77 are for sale of Swingle Tow. All the first Hatcheling is spun in Mops and carpet binding, the second hatcheling is carded into rolls and put by.

---

*I have been unable to determine the modern equivalent of one weight.

Wool

All Shaker communities had their own sheep, and wool production was very important until at least the middle of the nineteenth century. Little information is available about the type of sheep kept by individual families or the comparative size of the flocks at various times in their history, but we know that flock size varied considerably from community to community. The only specific reference to the subject indicates that in the 1840's the total number of sheep in the New Lebanon communities was between 1200 and 1500, "mostly Saxon and Merino."[8] Canterbury was also known for its large, prize-quality flock of sheep; Believers there often traded wool for products or services from other Shaker communities.[9]

Wool also was processed by hand at first. The sisters scoured (washed) the fleece and carded it with hand cards made by the brethren. (Carding straightens and aligns the fibers so that they will run perpendicular to the finished yarn. Carded wool produces woolen yarn, as opposed to worsted yarn, which is produced from combed wool and in which the fibers run parallel to the tightly spun yarn.)

As we have stated, the New Lebanon community even had a spare-time business of putting wire card teeth into leather backings. This activity began late in the eighteenth century. According to the Shaker *Manifesto* of August, 1890:

> During the continuation of the [hand card] business, all the available help of the first family was secured. Even the farmers and teamsters would eagerly catch every spare opportunity to assist in the setting of the card teeth. All the family were very much interested in the work and their mornings and evenings and even the few minutes while waiting for their meals was utilized in this employment.[10]

Setting teeth grew less profitable during the War of 1812 and was completely unnecessary by 1815, when a machine was developed (in the world) to set them automatically.

There were several other developments in wool processing in the same period. About 1800 the New Lebanon Shakers invented a device to speed up sheep shearing. The shears were attached to a water-driven belt so that they did not have to be manipulated by hand.[11]

In the outside world, wool carding machines were also introduced around the turn of the century. The metal teeth that straightened the fleece were mounted on two drums, driven by water power, which rotated against one another. Numerous mills were opened.

At first the Shakers, like everyone around them, sent their fleece to nearby carding mills for processing, but by 1809 the New Lebanon community had purchased a Scholfield carding machine of its own.[12] As soon as they found it feasible, other communities also built or purchased carding machines and set up their own mills. There were mills in Hancock, Sabbathday Lake (where the machine was made by the brethren), Canterbury, Pleasant Hill, South Union, Kentucky; and North Union and Union Village, Ohio. There may also have been mills in other communities (Watervliet, New York; Watervliet, Ohio; Enfield, Connecticut; Enfield, New Hampshire; Alfred, Maine).[13]

The term "carding mill" can be misleading. Often several processes and activities were done in one mill. A description written in 1853 by Canterbury Elder Henry Blinn, who was visiting the Hancock community, contained the following:

> The east family own a carding mill which is situated on a stream a few rods west of the north family. It contains two double carding machines which have been in use for many years, also two looms and some other machinery. In the case of the failure of water they have a small steam engine, which help through the dry season.[14]

The term "fulling mill" was used to cover more than the fulling process (technically, removing grease from a finished woven cloth, then brushing and napping it). An 1815 advertisement for the fulling mill at South Union, Kentucky, for example, included instructions for preparing fleece for carding. The Believers were concerned with the complete process of cloth preparation. Occasionally the Shakers used the term "woolen mill"; a woolen mill might carry on all the operations of carding, spinning, weaving, and fulling.

All of these mills were small "family" operations which employed four or five Believers on a seasonal basis. In general they were intended only for community use, but there were exceptions. Outsiders used the fulling mill at South Union[15] and the carding mill at Sabbathday Lake.[16] It was also common for Believers at one community to take their work to another community. Wool produced in New Lebanon was spun at Hancock for several years,[17] for example, and the Sabbathday Lake families often used cloth made in nearby Alfred.[18]

Wool combing (for worsted yarn) was done by hand for a much longer time. Isaac Young explained in 1856:

> In early times the sisters did the combing of the worsted, from the first till 1792, after which the brethren did it for several years; then the sisters did more or less. The brethren continued to comb a part of several years and then left it to the sisters, and of late, for a few years it has been hired done by the world.[19]

In the "Holy Orders of the Church" written in New Lebanon by Father Joseph Meacham in 1841, there was an admonition against processing wool in anything but a Shaker family. This rather strong edict was not seriously adhered to for long. It is interesting, however, to see how important the Church considered good wool processing to be:

> (Sec. 7)
> 1. Ye shall not take woll, that is raised among yourselves to any factory or to any other place whatever to be manufactured, carded, spun, woven or dressed by the hands of the wicked; unless your own clothier or carding works should meet with some accident, or from some other extraordinary cause. . . .
> 3. But if ye have not woll enough to make all the cloth ye need, ye shall buy cloth instead of woll. . . .[20]

Cotton

Cotton is a sturdy, versatile fiber, but it was not used by the Shakers to any great extent until the last years of the eighteenth century. The cotton plant did not grow in the cold climate of the north, of course, but its product was available in local stores. The difficulty of processing it (removing the seeds and spinning the short fibers) discouraged its use until Eli Whitney's invention of the cotton gin in 1793 revolutionized fiber usage in America. By the very next year, cotton had been introduced to the Shakers in New Lebanon,[21] and the sisters were preparing cotton yarn. In the words of Elder Isaac Young:

In early times in the Church the sisters carded and spun all their cotton by hand. But in the forepart of this [the 19th] century, cotton factories began to be established in America, and the Church soon began to purchase their cotton yarn, and to weave it into cloth to suit themselves, and finally entirely gave up carding and spinning cotton, but continued to weave all their cotton cloth for several years. Next they began to purchase the cotton cloth ready wove, increasing in this way till about the year 1834; since which the greater part of their cotton cloth has been purchased at the dry goods store, as also the linen.[22]

The situation was similar in some other communities. In North Union, Ohio, for example, raw cotton was sometimes purchased and cotton was occasionally spun, but, as community members put it, cotton was "mostly bought on bolts."[23]

The story was a little different, however, in the southernmost communities. Believers in South Union, Kentucky, for example, went to nearby towns to learn about cotton processing in 1813. By 1822 they had purchased their own cotton gin, and with this machine they were able to prepare about 200 pounds of cotton for spinning every hour.[24]

Silk

The Shakers in many communities tried to raise silkworms, but the industry was most successful in the relatively warm climate of Kentucky and southern Ohio. The Kentucky Shakers, in particular, developed a viable silk industry that lasted from the 1820's through the Civil War. By the 1830's there was enough silk produced at South Union to furnish every community member with a silk kerchief. On New Year's Day, 1832, the sisters all appeared at meeting in neckerchiefs that had been made from their own silk supply. The brethren were impressed, and on New Year's Day of the following year the sisters presented each brother with a silk neckband and tie (Figure 104).[25] An enormous amount of work went into preparing silk. Mulberry trees were carefully grown for silkworms to feed on, and "Brother Elisha raised both kinds of mulberry trees necessary to the cultivation of silk" at North Union, Kentucky, in 1838.[26] A report from the North Union, Ohio, community said that children were in charge of picking the leaves, while the eldresses handled the "crop" of cocoons.[27] The diary of Eldress Nancy E. Moore of South Union, Kentucky, reported that

> Eldress Betsey's worms began to hatch this morning. . . . Today [June 1, 1863] we picked the silk balls from the brush of our scrap stand. We had in all 4,890—3,615 marble sulphur balls, and the rest yellow peanuts.[28]

When reeled (unwound into long continuous fiber), the product of these several thousand cocoons amounted to two pounds, six ounces of "good reeled silk."[29]

The exact number of cocoons required to produce one pound of silk apparently varied considerably, depending on the condition of the mulberry and how well the silkworms had fed that year. Eldress Betsey's crop was of poor quality, since it was from the scrap stand. In another crop of apparently higher quality, 805 cocoons were used for one pound of silk.[30] In 1843, Sister Ann Buckingham of Watervliet, New York, mentioned that "300 silkworms have hatched out; silkworms have begun to wind the second time—[we] reel silk."[31] The amount of silk thread produced in this northern community, then, must have been negligible.

Although we are told that the peak of production in North Union, Kentucky, was in 1840, when eleven thousand silkworms were raised,[32] the overall height of the Shaker silk industry was probably in the 1850's or 1860's. By the time of the Civil war silk production at South Union was high enough to sell a small amount to the outside world. Production declined drastically, however, after the general devastation of the war.

Reeling the silk was a tedious process. The cocoons were placed in boiling water to melt the natural adhesive the silkworm had secreted when winding the fiber around and around into a ball. If the cocoon was undamaged and carefully handled, the one loose end could be found, and the fine thread could be unwound in a single continuous strand. Strands from several cocoons would be unwound simultaneously and reeled, or wrapped around a winding frame. One silk thread was composed of the reeled fiber from four or five silkworms.[33] A silk reeling machine was invented by Abner Bedell of Union Village, Ohio, in 1837.[34] No information is available about how this machine worked, but presumably it helped wind the silk mechanically. In any event, the reeling still required a great deal of careful attention. Prudence Morrell, a Shaker from New Lebanon, described her visit to Union Village in 1847. She noted on July 16 that the "sisters reel between 50 and 60 runs [of silk] in a day on one reel; but it takes two hands to tend it, or in other words, one to reel and one to tend the balls."[35]

The silk was woven by hand. On the same visit, Prudence Morrell saw the sisters weaving silk handkerchiefs. "They were a plain white cloth," she reported, "with a twill'd border. They are very handsome, and better than they can buy to wear to meeting."[36]

Other Fibers

The Shakers also worked with some unusual fibers, although never on any grand scale. Such local game animals as raccoons, opossums, rabbits, and beavers were occasionally caught and skinned, and their fur was incorporated into yarn or felted fabrics. Raccoon fur was mixed with silk to produce a delicate, soft, warm novelty yarn, ideal for winter gloves that were popular with the people of the world. Andrews reports that the brethren and sisters worked together to pick and pull apart the skins. In 1898 it took three weeks for all available help in the New Lebanon Center and Church Families to remove the fur from 200 coonskins.[37] One sister is said to have knitted 47 pairs of these gloves in 1891, and in March of the same year an anonymous sister wrote in her journal, "Mary . . . feels that to use up some prepared silk we must get some more fur."[38] Cat hair and rabbit fur were also mentioned in New Lebanon records from 1872.[39]

Unusual plant fibers, both local and imported, were used for special Shaker products. Palm leaf was imported from Cuba and made into fans, table mats, and—most important—bonnets.[40] The leaf was

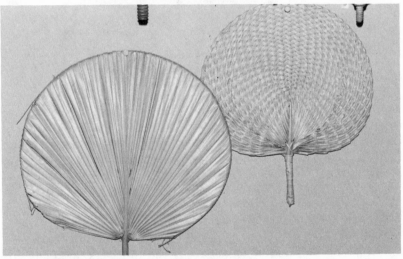

FIGURE 16. *Gloves made from coonskin and silk in the late nineteenth century. The label at the lower left reads:*
> The only GENUINE
> COON FUR AND SILK GLOVES *made by the*
> Shakers at Mount Lebanon. Sam'l Budd, Madison
> Square, N.Y. Sole agent for the U.S.

(The Shaker Museum at Old Chatham, New York)

FIGURE 17. *Two round palm leaf fans. The handles are the natural stems of the leaves.*
(Canterbury)

folded ("turned under") for fans and mats, and inserted as strips into a loom for woven bonnet cloth (see Chapter 5, below), but the leaf was not processed in any way.

When palm leaf became difficult to import for political reasons, rye and oat straw, grown on Shaker land, were used as substitutes. The straw was gathered about mid-August. Two or three sisters usually went out into the field to do this all-day task, sometimes bringing a light lunch for their midday meal. They took a small hand cart outfitted with several long baskets which were lined with sheets that could be folded over the straw to keep it from blowing away. Wearing white gloves to keep the straw clean, the sisters cut the stalk at the second joint, then cut off and separated the seed heads. These were later used for cattle feed.

Back at the village, the straw was taken to the laundry, where it was boiled for about fifteen minutes in a large kettle of water. Strand by strand, it was then laid on the lawn and allowed to bleach in the sunlight for one or two full days. It had to be watched carefully and taken in if the weather became damp. After bleaching, the stalks were stripped of the outer husks and returned to the kettle for a second scalding and a second sun-bleaching, this time for about three or four days. A sulphur bleach followed. The straws were placed in rows on a wooden box having upright slats. A small iron kettle under the box was filled with hot coals, and a little sulphur was added. The fumes wafted up into the box and were confined to it. This treatment took about twenty-four hours.

After the final bleaching, the oat straw was rinsed in light suds, to prevent dark spots from appearing later when the straw was exposed to heat.

The straw was placed on long tables to dry. Each stalk was then dampened once again and opened with a pin, to be split later with a special splitting device into a narrow strip. A full-sized oat straw is usually less than half an inch wide when it is opened, and the pieces used in Shaker bonnets were a fraction of that. Finally, the straw was ready for use.[41]

At about the time of the Civil War, the Shakers developed a method of cutting the wood of the poplar tree into thin strips which they wove into a fine, paperlike cloth, used primarily for covering boxes of various shapes. Poplar was not good for firewood or furniture, and this process allowed the Believers to put an otherwise idle resource to good use.

Poplar cloth was woven in Maine, New Hampshire, New York, Massachusetts, and Connecticut (but not in the western communities in Kentucky and Ohio). Although it is claimed that the cloth-making process was developed in Enfield, Connecticut, around 1860,[42] the most intricate poplar work was done in the northernmost communities in New Hampshire and Maine.

Preparation of poplar strips was a laborious process. It was winter work, for when the wood was kept frozen it did not splinter easily. The brethren cut trees from moist land on community property and brought the logs to the Shaker sawmill, where they were cut into lengths of approximately two feet, stripped of their bark, and split. One description tells of splitting the log into eighths, making sticks about 24 inches long and two to two-and-a-half inches square;[43] another refers to "quartering" the cut logs.[44]

If the wood began to thaw out, it was put outdoors and covered with water, so that it refroze. Smooth, accurate planing, or shaving, was easier to achieve with frozen wood.

Each stick was tied to an upright plane and shaved by hand; the thickness of the strip was determined by the amount of pressure applied. Strips were beveled on one edge, and they were always discarded if the grain was marred or split in the shaving process. The planed pieces were only a fraction of an inch thick—about the thickness of two pieces of heavy construction paper. They were tightly curled when they fell from the plane into a waiting basket (Figure 18). Several sisters sitting at a long table at one side of the room would straighten them by drawing them quickly through their hands.

The straightened sheets were then transferred to the ironing room for drying, and since rapid drying resulted in whiter poplar strips, this process was done as quickly as possible. The humidity was high from the intense heat of the stove and the moisture from the drying poplar, but the sisters tried to do the drying in one session. The time required depended, of course, on the amount of poplar being processed. Elder William Dumont reported that in 1872 when he first helped with the task at Sabbathday Lake, 17 logs were processed; at the peak of the industry shortly after the turn of the twentieth cen-

FIGURE 18. *Sisters in Sabbathday Lake straightening curled poplar strips with their fingers.*

FIGURE 19. *Straightened poplar strips laid out to dry, Sabbathday Lake. This is Sister Prudence Stickney.*

tury, the same community cut and processed three or more cords of poplar.[45]

The planed sheets were cut into strips, about one eighth to one sixteenth of an inch wide. This step was originally done by hand, but mechanical devices were soon invented. In 1872 Sabbathday Lake mechanic Granville Merrille perfected a steam-operated cutting machine.[46] Later models were run by electricity. The machine was a hollow, leather-covered wheel with a three-inch-wide steel lip embedded in it. The lip clamped the poplar sheets into position while a lever fitted with rows of close-set sharp knives was brought down on them by hand. As the wheel made one revolution, the knife cut the poplar into thin strips, which were automatically ejected from the wheel. The poplar strips were then ready for use. Poplar cloth and poplar items are discussed in Chapter 6, below.

Spinning

In the eighteenth century, when Shaker communities were first established, spinning was a skill that almost every woman had mastered. Most female converts to Shakerism, then, were already accomplished spinners. The early Shakers as a matter of course hand-spun their own wool, flax, and sometimes cotton thread.

The first Shaker spinning house was erected in New Lebanon in 1791.[47] Other communities had similar shops. The brethren made spinning wheels—both small treadle (flax) wheels and large walking (wool) wheels—for the sisters and people of the outside world.

"Jennies," which expedited the spinning process by multiplying the number of spindles, were purchased soon after they were available at the beginning of the nineteenth century. In New Lebanon,

> A small spinning Jenny of 24 spindles was purchased; after which [the sisters] spun the woolen yarn on the Jenny, the wool being carded into rolls, and the rolls spun into what was called roping on the "Roper," at the Carding Machine. They continued for a number of years to spin their wool on the Jenny, occasionally getting some spun and made into cloth, among the world, till the year 1851, when the Jenny was wholly laid aside. . . .

FIGURE 20. *Miscellaneous weaving and spinning equipment in the Sisters' Shop, Hancock Shaker Village. In addition to the full-size loom at the left, a floor swift and a wool wheel are visible.*

The sisters have from the first manufactured all the fine worsted and cotton-and-worsted. They spun all the worsted on a "big wheel" till about 1834, when there was a great improvement, by what was called a "Pleasant Spinner," used to the present day [1856] for spinning worsted.[48]

Other communities also had thriving spinning industries. An 1847 visitor to the West Family of Union Village, Ohio, mentioned that they had 140 spindles, and fifty to seventy pounds of wool were spun each day.[49] In the North Union, Ohio, woolen mill spinning jacks of 160 spindles were operating on the third floor in 1854; by 1873, 200 spindles were in use there. Most of the yarn produced was used to knit stockings.[50] In the Hancock woolen mill in 1860 there were 60

FIGURE 21. *Detail of a spindle post on a Shaker wool wheel. The initials "EA" stand for the trustee under whose auspices the wheel was made. (Hancock Shaker Village)*

spindles in operation, and 300 pounds of wool yarn were spun during the three months of the year that the mill operated. No cotton appears to have been spun, though it was woven there at that time.[51]

Many Shaker mills had machines for "twisting," or plying. The plying may sometimes have been done on the same spindles as the spinning; whether it was or not, plying was of particular importance where wool was used for stocking yarn. There were twisting machines in Canterbury and Enfield, New Hampshire, New Lebanon; North Union, Ohio; and Union Village, Ohio. In North Union it was reported that the "brethren do the carding and spinning and the sisters the twisting."[52]

Stocking yarn was manufactured long after weaving and spinning were "hired out to the world." A catalogue from Canterbury indicates that stocking yarn was sold even in the twentieth century. Some of the spinning and plying machines must also have remained in the communities long after the industry was thriving. The journal of an unidentified New Lebanon sister on June 16, 1891, has the following entry:

> I go to the factory, take a set of 200 bobbins, make two threaded [i.e. 2-ply] yarn for caps and wristers. The twisting is quite a task for old eyes.[53]

Weaving

Weaving is an activity that has spanned Shaker history; the earliest converts to the faith spent much of their time at the loom, and even today rugs are woven at Sabbathday Lake. Weaving was usually a job that fell to the sisters, but there were exceptions. Isaac Young reported that

> During several years in early times of the Church [at New Lebanon] there were several weavers among the brethren, who did chief of the weaving, and the sisters the spinning, and in those times there was very little cloth purchased from the world. After a few years the weaving devolved more and more upon the sisters, so that since 1830 [until 1856] the brethren have done little weaving.[54]

The cloth that was woven on Shaker handlooms in the early days was fairly typical of cloth woven elsewhere in America. A description of a visit to the Harvard Shakers in 1795, for example, mentioned that blue-and-white handkerchiefs, linens of different kinds, muslin, and diaper were being woven.[55] Blue and white was perhaps the most common color combination in early America, partly because indigo, used as blue dye, was a dependable, long-lasting dyestuff. Linen, as we have seen, was important as a basic fiber, and a great deal of household linen was needed. Diaper, fine cloth with a diagonal pattern, was made usually of linen but sometimes of cotton. The Shakers produced linen diaper in great quantities and made enough to sell to the outside world as early as 1810.[56] (Two diaper patterns are included in Appendix 3).

Patterns in handwoven cloth tended to be very simple. Plain and twill weaves (twill produces the diagonal effect found in blue jeans) were most common, and cloth used for clothing was woven exclusively in one of them. A simple check or stripe was the most typical design. There was no standard stripe or check proportion; considerable variation is seen in woven items of the same period. Two colors were most typical, but three-color stripes or twill checks sometimes appeared.

A twill variation pattern, such as Goose-Eye or Bird's Eye, might be woven on a blanket or bedcover. The pattern was usually done in only two colors, typically white with blue, brown, or red. Although most household linens were perfectly plain, fine pattern weaves were not uncommon in small linen towels. Huckaback and M's and O's variations, both of which produce a heavily textured, absorbent cloth, were often worked in fine bleached linen.

All of these patterns originated in the outside world, and the Shakers adopted them.[57] Overshot patterns (where weft floats pass over two or more warp yarns) were sometimes used on blankets or coverlets, but they were not as common as the simpler twills. They may have been more common in the southwestern communities (notably Pleasant Hill) than in the northeastern; the Dogwood pattern, in particular, may have been indigenous to Pleasant Hill and may in fact have been the one pattern that was uniquely Shaker (see Figure 26 and Appendix 3).[58]

Although the weaving patterns themselves were not special, certain elements of the weaving were unusual and noteworthy. One was the

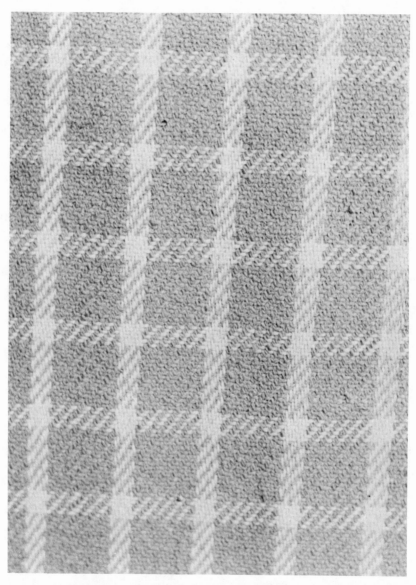

FIGURE 22. *Detail of a simple twill blanket. The white yarn is cotton; the dark yarn is a naturally dyed buff-colored wool. (Hancock Shaker Village)*

FIGURE 23. *Detail of a handwoven coverlet. The brown-wool pattern thread is worked into a white-wool base. (Hancock Shaker Village)*

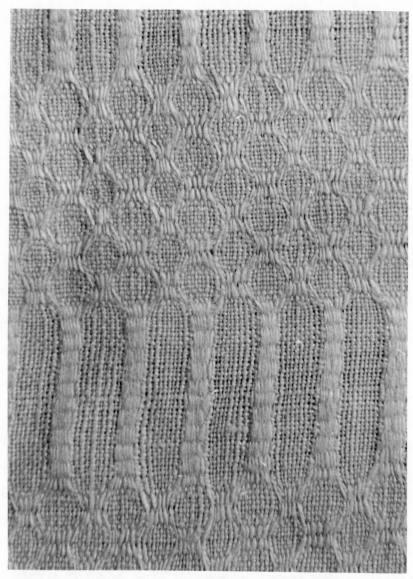

FIGURE 24. *Detail of a handwoven bleached linen face towel, M's and O's pattern. (Hancock Shaker Village)*

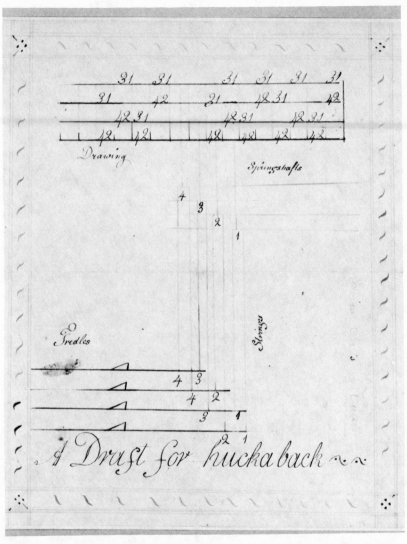

FIGURE 25. *Pattern draft for huckaback. The name "Elvira Curtis Hulett" is on the draft; she was probably a sister from New Lebanon. There is no date, but it was probably written early in the nineteenth century. (Edward Deming Andrews Memorial Shaker Collection, Winterthur Museum)*

FIGURE 26. *The "Dogwood" pattern, probably indigenous to Pleasant Hill, is worked into a white coverlet. (Pleasant Hill)*

use of color. As we have seen, colors were often created by mixing different yarns or dyed fibers. One color would be used in the warp (the vertical or supporting threads), while a second color was used in the weft or woof (the horizontal or crosswise threads). For example, a rich and subtle purple-cast fabric was created by mixing cochineal or madder red with indigo blue. The blended color was never solid, but was made up of many small specks of red and blue. The specks picked up and reflected the light in different ways, creating a rich, almost iridescent effect. Butternut (rich sienna brown) was mixed with blue in this same way, creating a dark color that varied depending on the depth of both the blue and the brown. Green and blue were also combined. In the silk cloth made in the southwestern communities, especially beautiful iridescent effects were created by this same color mixing. White and red was a particularly popular combination; pink kerchiefs were well loved by Shakers in all communities.

In fabrics other than silk there was often a mixture of textures as well as colors; in brown and blue cloth, for example, the blue was typically a cotton yarn and the brown was a worsted.

Extensive use of this sort of blended color was not typical at the time, and the cloth was highly admired outside of the Shaker community. In 1935 Sister Emma Neale told students from the Darrow School in New Lebanon that a skirt made by the Shakers from their iridescent cloth was "so fascinating that children followed the wearer in an attempt to touch it, asking if it were leather."[59]

Another color-mixing technique the Shakers used was yarn plying: two or more different colors were twisted, or plied, together, creating a diagonal candy-canelike striped yarn. In weaving or knitting, these yarns created a multicolored slanting design. Plied yarn was used most consistently in rugs, but it also appears again and again in unexpected places—sewing bags, chair seat cushions, and the like (Figure 27). Conscious use is made of the design possibilities of this technique. At times the plied yarns are used in one area only and are contrasted against a plain, single-color background; at other times several sets of plied yarns alternate with one another. In many items, instead of literal plying, two or three colors have been used together as if they were one, creating a similar though less regular effect.

Another common practice was to create colors by blending dyed and undyed fleece before the yarn was spun. "Parker mixed," a cloth popular around 1870, was named after David Parker, a trustee at Canterbury, who originated it. Ninety percent of the unspun wool was dyed a deep indigo, and the remaining 10 percent was left white. The overall effect of the yarn and the cloth woven from it was a speckled gray.[60]

Color gradation, the final type of color blending, was particularly popular in Shaker weaving of the late nineteenth century. Wool blankets and rugs made in that period show a careful arrangement of color—several shades of red blending into several shades of brown, for example (see the bedcovering and the rug in Plates 4 and 8).

The characteristic border in many Shaker textiles is actually woven in. Kerchiefs usually have a thick border stripe running around all four sides. In colored kerchiefs the border might be of a contrasting

FIGURE 27. *Plied cotton yarns create a subtle, small-scale diagonal effect in the cloth of this drawstring bag. (Hancock Shaker Village)*

color; in plain white kerchiefs it is often a fancy twilled area set against a plain woven field. Borders are also sometimes set apart by textural relief—perhaps thick cords running through a flat background.

In all aspects of their weaving industries the Shakers tried to be practical, efficient, and consistent. The *Weaver's Ready Reckoner*, by Pauline Springer of Alfred, Maine (undated, but probably written in the first quarter of the nineteenth century) was intended as a reference for all Shaker weavers. It told a weaver how to calculate exactly how much spun yarn would be necessary to make a specific piece. If the weaver had 42 runs of yarn, the *Reckoner* would tell how to calculate what length and width could be woven with them; columns were set up on both a horizontal and vertical plane, and the weaver simply found the correct figures on the charts.

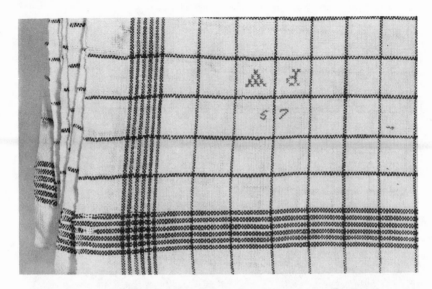

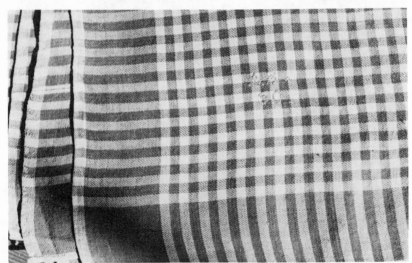

FIGURE 28. *Green and white cotton-twill kerchief. Note the border emphasis and the embroidered initials (center of photograph). (Hancock Shaker Village)*

FIGURE 29. *A cotton kerchief in the Hancock Shaker Village collection. The regular checks are formed by indigo-dyed yarn.*

An enormous amount of cloth was made on Shaker looms in the early years. If, as Isaac Young indicated, very little cloth was purchased from the world, the Believers in the first part of the nineteenth century were producing almost all of the fabric for their clothing, domestic linens, household textiles, and agricultural needs (grainbags, horseblankets, and so on).

In *The Community Industries of the Shakers*, Andrews summarizes Sister Joanna Kitchell's weaving account book from New Lebanon:

> In 1835 a total of 1205 yards of cloth was woven for frocks, surtouts, flannel shirts, habits, trousers, drawers, bags, garden sheets, serge, worsted serge for shoes, drugget gowns, drugget linings, drugget trousers, jackets, jacket linings, worsted linings and wash aprons. In 1836, 1337 yards were woven for many of the above purposes, besides such additional uses as tow and linen frocks, barn frocks, boys' trousers, coarse flannel, linen ironing cloths, cotton and wool blankets, and narrow cotton and wool sheets. In 1837, 78 yards of horse blankets (wool with a cotton warp) were woven on the same loom, and 99 yards of checked linen "pocket hankerchiefs." In this year is the first mention of the characteristic red and blue cotton and worsted cloth. . . . Other items listed are cotton and linen "open frocks," "fine towels linen and tow," coarse strainers, drab habits, under coats, wide ironing cloths, scrub aprons, and cotton and wool, red and blue deacons' frocks. The total for this year was 2334 yards. Horse blankets of "doubled and twisted tow" were woven in 1838; also 51 yards of white linen handkerchief cloth, cotton check aprons, light striped gowns for the ministry, blankets for the ministry, "coppras" (copperas) aprons, butternut drawers and 120 yards of window curtain. Linen for stair carpets was woven in 1840, besides 43 yards of "crape," 30 yards of cheese straining cloth, 90 yards of rag carpeting, 19 yards of cloak head-linings, 54 yards of kitchen aprons, besides many [other] materials.[61]

In the next ten years, blue lasting for shoes and cotton bibs, "butt" flannel drawers, meat strainers, linen wash house bags, linen table "clothes," cotton and wool "bread clothes," and dish cloths are also mentioned.[62]

Joanna Kitchell's records do not show clearly who did all this weav-

FIGURE 30. *Rug-weaving on a large loom in Enfield, Connecticut, early twentieth century. Brother George Clark is in the rear; the sisters are unidentified.*

ing. She probably recorded the work done by the sisters in one family. Other weaving may have been done by a Girl's Order, and certain products may have been woven exclusively in other families. No chair seat tape, or "listing," for example, is included, though a great deal of tape was woven in the 1830's (see Chapter 4, below). Some of the yardage listed was probably woven on a fly shuttle or semiautomatic loom (pages 64, 71), and it is also conceivable that some was woven on a mechanized loom. No distinction is made in Shaker account books between hand and mechanized spinning, and this probably also holds true for weaving.

In the 1830's a great deal of cloth was also purchased from the outside world. The figures listed above only partially represent the amount of woven cloth used by the Shakers in any one year, as we saw in Chapter 2.

Andrews calculated that between 1841 and 1851 a total of 24,234 yards of material were woven in Joanna Kitchell's community. He also noted that the annual output ranged from 1,500 to 2,000 yards before 1851 but was only 581 yards in 1861.[63] This dramatic decrease reflects the fact that by this time good quality commercially manufactured cloth was available at a competitive price. Isaac Young reported in 1856 that "the increase of factories in the world enables us to purchase cloth cheaper than we can make it among ourselves, though the cloth generally is not so durable as home made, though it looks and feels more agreeable." He lamented, however, that

the world is so little to be relied on, so fickle and fluctuating, in their colors and fashions of cloth, and their factories are so changeable and liable to failure, that Believers are much afflicted to get such kinds of cloth as they want, which prevents their maintaining the uniformity among themselves that they otherwise would.[64]

Shortly after Isaac Young wrote these words in New Lebanon, a Shaker woolen mill was operating in nearby Hancock, and it is probable that the New Lebanon families were able to get at least some of their cloth there.

The mill operated for three months in the spring, when rivers were running high and there was ample water to drive the belts on the looms and wheels. A steam engine was available for dry periods. In 1860 two men and six women worked in the mill, and in addition to the 300 pounds of wool that were spun, 766 yards of wool cloth and 650 yards of cotton cloth were woven. The mill was apparently considered vitally important, for $4,000 was invested in it that year. This was twice as much as was invested in any other Hancock industry at that time.[65] Even so, the Hancock elders decided in 1869 that it was not worth while to rebuild the mill when it was gutted by fire. Competition was fierce by that time from a plethora of local mills, and the volume of the Shaker factory was not high enough to make it a profitable enterprise.

When it was no longer necessary or profitable to produce cloth for everyday use, the Shakers concentrated on handweaving special items that were popular with the world market. By about 1860 shag chair-seat cushions and mats were being made in New Lebanon. The poplar cloth industry developed a few years later and was in full swing by the 1870's. The production of rugs made for sale also evolved in the Victorian period. (See Chapters 4 and 6, below.)

Textile Equipment

Although it is not the purpose of this book to discuss the tools of Shaker industries in great detail, a brief description of the type of equipment used in Shaker spinning, weaving, and sewing shops seems appropriate. The looms, wheels, and accessories are models of the same excellent proportion, design, and craftsmanship as all Shaker furniture and crafts.

Most equipment used in manual textile production was made by Shaker brethren, although there are occasional references in account books to buying a loom or wheel. Most likely, Believers would have been willing to buy a well-built loom if they happened to find one at a good price when they needed it. More typically, one or two brethren in each community who were specialists in the carpentry shop turned out equipment as it was called for.

Henry De Witt was such a carpenter in New Lebanon. From 1827 to 1845 there are various references in his journal to making spinning wheels and scarnes, turning "about 40 wheels for clock reels," and making different kinds of looms. De Witt apparently made equipment as it was needed, and he made it to suit the particular people who would use it. In 1833, for example, he wrote that he made "little spools for to weave tape with. Made the barrels of tin and heads of pewter."[66] In March 1834 he wrote:

> I have been about four weeks making this spring shuttle loom.*
> I took my new loom over to the spinshop and set it up for weaving—beamed on about 30 yards of coarse linen. Betsey Crossman wove some and it went well.[67]

*Spring shuttle looms are discussed below, p. 71.

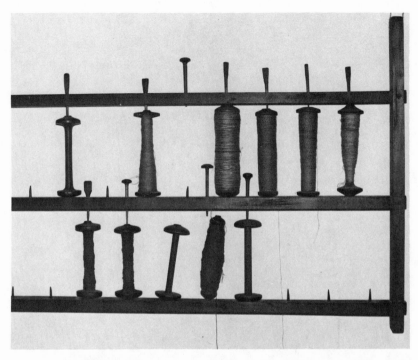

FIGURE 31. *Wool spool holder or "scarne." Yarn was wound from these spools on to a loom. Note the removable wooden pins that hold the spools in place. The spools are not uniform because they are all individually turned and carved. (Hancock Shaker Village)*

Brother De Witt and others like him made some equipment for sale. This was more common in the early years of the Church, of course, since the demand was greater at that time for domestic textile equipment. There was a large market for spinning wheels in particular even as late as the 1830's and 1840's; according to Pennington and Taylor in *A Pictorial Guide to American Spinning Wheels*,[69] some of the brethren made as many as 700 of them for sale.

The spinning wheels they made were not very different from others of their day, except that in the Shaker tradition they usually had a minimum of turned and decorated wood (though some made in the western communities are an exception). Large wool wheels (also called "high wheels" or "great wheels") were made both with and without

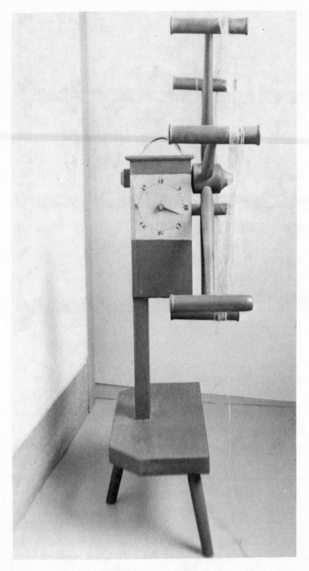

FIGURE 32. *Clock reel ("weasel") in the Hancock Shaker Village collection. Each revolution of the wheel moved the dial one digit. In the standard skein the reel would revolve 200 (5 x 40) times.*

Minor's heads (devices to make the spindle turn faster). Flax or treadle wheels were made with and without distaffs. Quill wheels, or bobbin winders, had boxes for bobbins and spools under the spindle.[70]

Wheels were typically marked with the initials of the trustee who had overseen their manufacture (Figure 21). Wool wheels made in New Lebanon between 1780 and 1830 under Elder David Meacham, for example, were marked "DM," and flax wheels initialed "SR AL" were made in Alfred under Deacon Samuel Ring. The initials assured the purchaser that the product was of such high quality that the trustee was willing to vouch for it. Pennington and Taylor feel that wheels without initials were made for home use.[71]

Looms were made in a variety of sizes, as indicated in carpenter De Witt's journal. Tape looms, for weaving narrow bands for chair seat webbing, rug binding, and other assorted items, ranged from simple slot-and-heddle looms that either fit on the lap or were free-standing, to table looms with movable harnesses, or floor looms with overhead beaters.

The bonnet loom mentioned by De Witt was probably of the type invented in 1837 by Brother Abner Bedell of Union Village, Ohio.[72] This was a floor loom about 20 to 25 inches wide, equipped with two (or sometimes four) harnesses. The back upright beams slanted at an angle of about 70 degrees from the top of the overhead swinging beater to the floor (Figure 34). Ratchets were usually made of iron. These looms were used for weaving the palm leaf or straw fabric for bonnets and, later, for weaving poplar cloth.

Full-size floor looms were similar. They were counterbalance looms with two or four harnesses that worked on pulleys and had overhead beaters. Their rear upright beams often slanted back to the floor—perhaps because this form resulted in a very stable loom that could withstand a good deal of heavy beating. Some had sectional warp beams and some had built-in weaving benches, but free-standing tall weaving stools were also common. These usually had a seat angled down to the loom, and a storage drawer under the seat.

Many large Shaker looms have a system whereby the weaver can pull a lever or pulley to release the back brake and then work a warp-advance mechanism, all without getting up from the weaving bench. It has been said that the Shakers invented this system, but there is no conclusive evidence to this effect.

FIGURE 33. *A free standing slot-and-eye, or rigid heddle, loom from Pleasant Hill, Kentucky. Alternate threads are drawn through either the eye (hole) or the slot of the loom. Threads that are in the holes remain "rigid," in the same position. Threads that are in the slots can be either raised above or drawn below (as shown) the threads in the rigid position, thus creating two alternating layers of threads.*

FIGURE 34. *A two-harness floor loom made expressly for weaving tapes. (Hancock Shaker Village)*

FIGURE 35. *Detail of the advance mechanism of an 1834 Shaker loom used in New Lebanon. The lever was worked by the right foot. (Hancock Shaker Village)*

As Henry De Witt's journal indicates, many looms were equipped with fly (spring) shuttle attachments. These made weaving rapid and semiautomatic; by pulling a lever in the center of the loom, the weaver could send the shuttle carrying the weft thread across the piece automatically.

Equipment used in Shaker mills—carding machines, spinning jennies, power looms, and so on—was usually purchased from the outside. The Shakers could have made some of these themselves in their own machine shops, but it was generally cheaper and most practical to buy them ready-made.

Accessories for handweaving and spinning were as important as the basic equipment. The brethren made shuttles (both handcarved boat shuttles and large netting type shuttles for rugs), spools, scarnes (for holding spools), weaving needles for working with straw and poplar, winding reels, temples or templates for keeping the woven web taut, warping boards and reels, niddy-noddies for winding yarn, numerous wheel pulleys for the looms, bamboo reeds, and umbrella skein winders, or swifts. Small spools and spool stands for holding fine threads were the last textile equipment made by the brethren; they were popular items in Shaker fancy-goods stores in the early part of the twentieth century.

Dyeing

Dyeing, like spinning, was a skill that women in early America learned as a matter of course. Shaker dyeing processes were consequently not special, and Shaker dye recipes, like Shaker weaving patterns, were not very different from others of their period.[73] The way the Believers incorporated dyeing into their communal structure is, however, unique and interesting.

A few sisters were assigned to do the community dyeing. They usually worked at the wash house, or laundry, although a special dye house was erected in some communities. The work was seasonal, usually running from April or May until the end of the summer, and was quite varied. Fiber preparation was actually part of the same job. A journal kept by Sister Eliza Ann Taylor of New Lebanon makes nu-

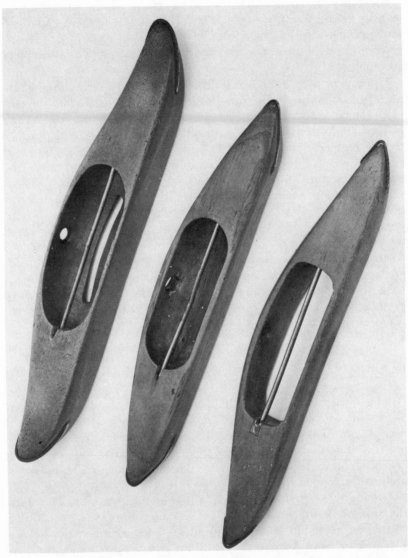

FIGURE 36. *Three boat shuttles in the Hancock Shaker Village collection. Note that each shuttle is slightly different. The tips are reinforced with steel wire; these shuttles could have been used in a fly shuttle loom.*

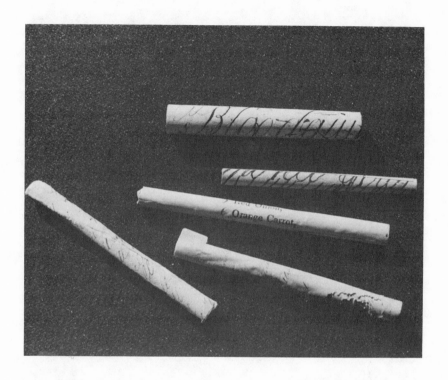

FIGURE 37. *Rolled paper "quills" used for holding weft yarn in boat shuttles. The Shakers used miscellaneous pieces of scrap paper for these quills. Some came from the schoolroom and have lessons repeated over and over on them; others were shopping lists or papers from seed packets. (Hancock Shaker Village)*

FIGURE 38. *Detail of a hand-carved "squirrel cage" yarn winder. (Hancock Shaker Village)*

merous references to "getting out" runs of yarn, "fixing" tow, cotton, and linen yarn, hatcheling, "carding last year's tow," and spinning mop yarn. It is logical that most of these tasks should have been carried out by the sisters who were engaged also with dyeing, since coloring and fiber processing had to be coordinated.

When raw wool was sent to the mills, the sisters knew exactly how all of it was going to be used. Eliza Ann Taylor's journal specified what would be done to the wool to be carded in 1842:

> White Wool to be spun and coloured blue for filling and the warp red cotten No. 14 for Aprons. 17 lbs. when sent to the machine spun 4 runs to the lb. This wool was the fine short such as has formerly been taken for fine flannel and we took of the same to fill the brethren's drugget jackets. It is also suitable for footings, stockings, etc.

Much of the wool was sent to be combed and made into worsted yarn. Elizabeth Lovegrove specified how 138 pounds would be used in 1840:

11	lbs. for stockings, grey and some white
36	for linings and fine crape white
9	for common crape Butternut
6	for Cloak head linings do fine
15½	fine worsted trowsers butternut
9	for linings for blue jackets, to fill on cotton
20	for Serge trowsers
12	for drugget trowsers
7½	for fine drugget gowns
7	for quality and sewing thread
6	for backings[74]

After the fiber was prepared, a butternut dyebath was usually started in June. Butternut, popular in all Shaker communities, was the most important local dyestuff. A great deal of cloth was colored with this dye. In 1840 in New Lebanon 60 yards of cotton cloth were dyed for frocks and trousers, and 60 more yards were dyed for linings.[75] The sisters at Watervliet, New York, "brought home 111 pounds of butternut bark."[76]

Butternut dye recipes are not common in Shaker receipt books,* probably because they were not needed: butternut was relatively easy to use and understand. The bark was usually taken while it was still green, broken into small pieces, and set to soak. Typically, the material to be dyed would be put in the dyepot and scalded, and no additional additives were necessary.† The brown color could be varied by adding copperas (iron sulfate) to the bath after it was exhausted, or by using dry rather than fresh bark. On occasion, butternut hulls were used instead of bark.

A variety of other dyestuffs were used during the remainder of the summer. Some were gathered or procured locally (purslain, hemlock, beech bark, sorrel, sumac), but most were purchased from chemists. A wide range of dyestuffs and chemical "assistants" is mentioned in Shaker account and receipt books. Cochineal, madder, indigo, and logwood were very common dye purchases; and alum, cream of tartar, copperas, and vitriol were common setting-agent, or mordant, purchases. Other dyestuffs—aleppo galls, camwood, brazilwood, fustic, annato, redwood, catchetu, weld, and woad—are also mentioned.

Dye recipes were freely shared among Shaker communities and even with members of the world. Often the same recipe appears in the receipt books of several communities, and sometimes they are even credited to a particular sister. Letters containing recipes and advice were sent from one community to another. An Englishman, residing at Tyringham (presumably in the Shaker community), came in 1850 to teach the sisters of the New Lebanon Church Family about "bleaching and colouring," and Sister Elizabeth Lovegrove "wrote [down] 33 receipts from his own mouth."[77]

At times the Shakers dyed fabric for people of the world. An anonymous sister wrote a treatise on "The Method of Colouring Blue, practiced by the Society of Believers in Kentucky." Apparently written for the benefit of the sisters in other communities, the treatise was well circulated. The following excerpt describes how the dyeing business paid for itself and explains the procedure:

*"Receipt" was a nineteenth-century term for "recipe." The Shakers used the two forms interchangeably.

†One recipe for dyeing with butternut is included in Appendix 4, below.

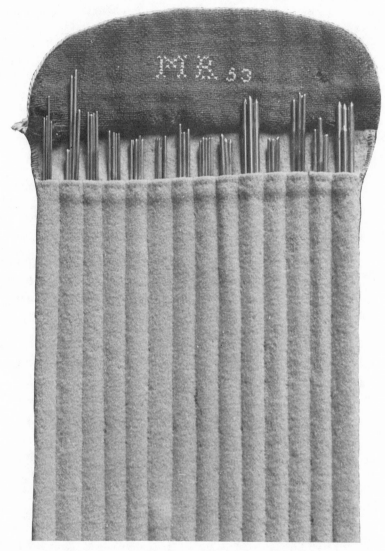

FIGURE 39. *A knitting-needle case from Hancock Shaker Village. The outside is dove-grey wool; the inside is red flannel. The case is 5 x 9 inches.*

We obtained [our] method of colouring chiefly by trying experiments in which we have had great success. We have had little or no trouble with our dyes, and they have always been in a prosperous situation. Two young sisters is the most strength that has ever been applied to them and a part of the time only one; and the income of their work for the world, besides colouring for all the Believers, who make a very extensive use of blue, has supported their shop with all kinds of stock, and even paid for all their tubs and kettles, and enough to support themselves besides; so that the Society has been at no expense whatever for all their blue.

For sometime past the colouring has been taken care of and done by two active girls; the one that has the chief management is about 15 years of age. She manages her own dyes and keeps them in good order, keeps her own books, sets down her own accounts, receives the yarn etc. from customers, delivers it to them again in good order and well dyed, receives her pay for it, and gives good satisfaction, both to Believers and the world; and thus by the labour and earnings of these two children, the Society is supported in all their blue besides supporting themselves. What colour then can be cheaper than this?

When the business was first set up, the Trustees of the Society desired that a strict account might be kept of all the outgoes and incomes of it, which accordingly has been done, and with which they are much pleased, and think it a very profitable branch of business. They think a blue is cheaper than even a bark colour, especially if the root bark is used.

We experience none of the difficulty so much complained of keeping dyes in order; a child can be taught to do it, and yet the colour, we believe, is as good as any made in America, if not in the world. Our shop is in high credit and great demand. The people of the world say they never saw such blue for duration before, they reject all other shops about here and come to ours.

Believers were told they might use any color they could dye themselves, and dye books indicate how broad that color range actually was. Besides the popular (and practical) blue and the butternut shades, recipes for red, black, "lead or mouse color," salmon, pink, yellow, green, drab, brown, purple, crimson, lavender, scarlet, orange, buff, blue-black, and slate are given. Yellow was not used extensively, and the number of dye recipes for yellow is proportionately low. There are a great many recipes for red shades, and, interestingly, recipes for the brightest colors (orange, bright green, purple) are often specified for dyeing on silk.

Recipes are usually given in very large quantities, as would be appropriate for a large community. In Mary Ann Gill's Receipt Book from Canterbury in 1857, for example, instructions are given for "setting up a woad vat capable of holding 40 barrels." Six hundred pounds of English woad, 300 pounds of French woad, one bushel of bran, five pounds of madder, 20 pounds of indigo, and up to 35 quarts of lime are called for. Other recipes give instructions for yellow on 100 pounds of flannel or yarn, blue-black on 100 pounds of wool, fast prussian green on 176 pounds of wool, spruce green on 170 pounds of greasy wool, and snuff brown on 164 pounds of clean wool. Clearly, these receipt books were important references for sisters who may have learned their dyeing skills in quantities appropriate for a family of five or ten people. Interestingly, receipt books almost always included both dyeing and cooking recipes. Whether the sisters who worked in the dye or wash house used these books for their own reference when they worked in the kitchen, or whether the books were used by the whole community, is not clear.

Modern-day dyers who use natural dyestuffs will be interested that a great majority of Shaker recipes combine several dye elements. A "blood red" on silk, for example, was achieved with aleppo galls and brazilwood and with alum and cream of tartar as mordants; "scarlet on silk" was achieved in a copper vessel with annato and brazilwood with perlash. Black, in one recipe, was the result of fermenting sorrel and adding logwood. Other black recipes call for sumac berries with clamoniac* and copperas, or for witch hazel and maple barks, copperas, and logwood. Green could be achieved on cotton with one pound of logwood, two pounds of fustic, and one ounce of blue vitriol for every pound of yarn.[78]

The receipt books also include instructions for washing and household preparations, as well as "painting cloth for table coverings, car-

*Clamoniac may well be sal ammoniac, or ammonia salt.

petings, etc."; putting gloss and stiffness in silk; making oil cloth; washing with sal soda; and the like (see Appendix 4).

In addition to producing "Parker mixed" gray by combining 90 percent blue wool with 10 percent white wool (see above, page 58), the Shakers made other shades by mixing other percentages of different-colored wools. Elizabeth Lovegrove's journal states, in 1837, that, "surtouting [should be] 4/5 blue. 2/3 of this should be colored dark as you have patience too." Fine frocks should only be one half blue, but coarse frocks should be two thirds blue. Footings should be "7 oz. to the lb. blue," and stockings should be "6 oz. to the lb. blue." She completes her instructions with the words, "color the blue several shades," and "weigh the wool when prepared for the [carding] machine."

As indicated by the sister who reported on the Kentucky method of dyeing blue, the Shakers were always willing to experiment with new recipes and procedures. Elizabeth Lovegrove's entry for September 1, 1847, illustrates an experiment that was not completely successful:

> Coloured red for horse blankets with Nicwood and red wood, putting the yarn and chips in the kettle together, but long before we got cleaned up we promised ourselves never to do so again.[79]

The goals they hoped to achieve by continued experimentation were, of course, more satisfactory and efficient working conditions and products. Traditional work habits and customs were not eschewed; on the contrary, as long as they were still appropriate, they were maintained. Elizabeth Lovegrove or Eliza Ann Taylor (it is not clear which one) wrote the following, "Concerning Wool:"

> As there are on this earth many people and as all these people have a mind of their own it seems impossible for anyone to suit all these very nice and peculiar notions. I have taken pains to select as many rules from Sister Tippora as she can reccollect for the manufacture of wool etc. Many of these rules were established by Father Joseph and Mother Lucy and practiced without deviation when the Church was first gathered.[80]

The dye industry of the Shakers declined drastically in the 1860's and 1870's. The amount of yarn and cloth the Shakers produced was greatly diminished by the end of the Civil War. In addition, there was a rapid conversion to synthetic coloring agents after the discovery of aniline dyes in 1856. Dyeing with these agents was relatively simple. By about 1875, most cloth and yarn used by the Shakers was purchased, already colored, from the outside world.

The last reference to dyeing that I have come across in Shaker manuscripts is from 1892, when 200 pounds of wool—probably to be woven into rugs—were sorted, cleaned, and dyed "in the old fashioned indigo blueing tub" in the North Family in New Lebanon.[81] It is unclear if the wool was being dyed with indigo or with a synthetic dye, but the dyepot itself was already far out of date at this time.

Knitting and Crocheting

Knitting was an integral part of the lives of the sisters throughout Shaker history. They knitted all of the community members' socks, stockings, gloves, and mittens, and most of their undergarments; and they made many of these items for sale. In later years, hats, washcloths, facecloths, sweaters, potholders, toys, rugs, and other items were also knitted and sold in Shaker stores.

At first, all knitting was done by hand, and by any standards Shaker hand knitting was exceptionally fine. Knitting needles, or "pins," were purchased locally, and all were less than size oo in the measuring system we use today. Knitting-needle cases were made of wool flannel cloth. Since many look exactly alike, they were most likely made according to a specific pattern, and embroidered initial markings indicate that the cases belonged to individual sisters. As many as 35 or 40 needles would fit into one 5-by-9-inch case.

Stocking knitting frames were in use in New England as early as 1790, and knitting machinery was well developed by the middle of the nineteenth century. At least some, and possibly most, of the Shaker communities purchased knitting machines and put them to heavy use. Canterbury had a special knitting shop where the machines were kept. Great quantities of sweaters and stockings were turned out by machine, but all were finished by hand. Sweater sleeves and bodices, for example, were machine-knit, but cuffs and edgings were hand-knit. Stockings were knitted as tubes on the machines, but footings were knitted by hand.[82]

Crocheting became an important activity in America in the Victori-

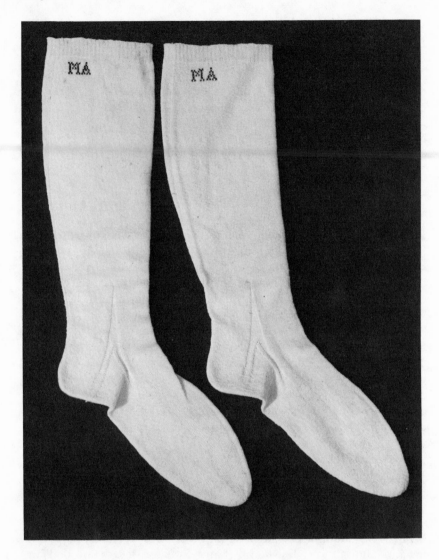

FIGURE 40. *Knit cotton stockings from Hancock Shaker Village. The Shaker heel detail, called a gusset, was famous even beyond the Shaker community. Note the initials "MA" embroidered near the top.*

FIGURE 41. *Fine fingerless gloves, or "mitts," from Hancock Shaker Village.*

an period, and the Shakers took it up just as their contemporaries did. In the Shaker Museum at Old Chatham, New York, there are two large sample books of crochet stitches which date from this period, and the variety of patterns they include is as great as any that could be found in the world.

Little girls were taught to crochet soon after they were taught to knit. One woman who was raised in the Watervliet, New York, community recalls that she could crochet a "nice flat doily" by the time she was eight.[83] Another woman who grew up with the Shakers remarked that, try as she might, she could not learn to crochet well. She was not pressed to continue, but was given other tasks.[84]

Crochet hooks, like knitting needles, were purchased from the outside world, and these were also very fine.

Shawls, mantillas, doilies, "tidies," hats, toys, potholders, and belts were among the crocheted fancy-work items that were sold in Shaker stores around the turn of the twentieth century.

Chapter Four
Household Textiles

Household Linens

In a community that at its height included perhaps several hundred people, a great deal of household linen was needed. It was no small task to keep in good repair an adequate supply of the mundane textiles used day in and day out by every Believer. Careful attention and a good deal of work went into their production and upkeep.

The mattresses used by the Shakers in the early days were probably made of straw, much as in any farm home. Later, cotton mattresses were purchased from dry goods stores in the outside world, and mattress covers were hand made from common blue-and-white cotton ticking, also purchased.

Bed linens were cotton or linen and were perfectly plain. Well after the middle of the nineteenth century, flax was hand-processed into linen and handwoven into sheets in the sisters' shops, usually in its natural color but occasionally bleached; the weave was plain or twill. Cotton sheets were rarely handwoven, but when they were, a plain weave was used. More commonly, cotton sheeting was purchased by the bolt and cut into appropriate lengths. Both cotton and linen sheets were hemmed by hand with a very fine blindstitch, or, later, by machine.

Blankets were occasionally bought ready made. Bolts of plain woolen cloth (perhaps from the Shaker mills) were also cut up into blanket lengths; almost without exception these were solid blue, white, or gray, with no special pattern or adornment. Handwoven blankets, which were done in plain weave or twill or twill variation weave, tended to be a little livelier. The most typical design was a check of some kind—most often blue, black, or red on a white background.

FIGURE 42. *A typical wool blanket. The check is a dark blue, and the pattern is a point (diamond) twill. (Hancock Shaker Village)*

Although the Millennial Laws specified that only two colors should be used on bed coverings, several more elaborate examples have a third or fourth color brought into the check. Sometimes pattern and color schemes were worked in together; in one blue-and-white piece, for example, a diamond pattern appears only in the blue checks. Blankets, like sheets, were hemmed on all sides and generally did not have fringe.

Designs on Shaker blankets are all of the structural type discussed above (page 10). They are determined by the geometric patterns made possible by the loom, and no further decorative embellishment, such as embroidery, is added. (Non-Shaker contemporaries often added decorative embroidery to plain blankets; many, for example, have embroidered designs in each of the four corners; and checks or plaids are sometimes softened and made less angular by an embroidered motif in some or all of the checks.)

In addition to blankets, the Shakers had special bedcovers (coverlets) and quilts. It is difficult to determine whether beds in early Shaker communities were always covered with an extra spread, but it is clear that at least part of the time they were. When Sarah Potter left the Watervliet, New York, community in 1827, a coverlet was among the necessities she was given to make her way in the world.[1] The record of the Children's Order in the same community shows that in 1846 the girls pieced nine quilts and quilted thirteen.

The Shaker coverlets that remain today are often surprisingly elaborate. It is impossible to assign specific dates to the pieces, but some were dyed with natural materials, which probably date them before the Civil War. There are numerous fragments and some complete pieces (notably in the Shaker Museum at Old Chatham, New York, and at Shakertown at Pleasant Hill) which have intricate overshot weaving patterns. These coverlets may have been considered very special; they have been preserved with great care. It is altogether possible that plain coverlets were much more usual, but wore out more quickly from heavy use or were cut up into rags or reused in other ways.

A beautiful bed cover made in Canterbury in 1880 is now on display at Hancock Shaker Village. It is handwoven, completely of wool. The top was carefully planned to fit on a large bed, with a central gray-green color area surrounded by a multicolor plaid section that falls

FIGURE 43. *Detail of an overshot coverlet (indigo blue wool and white cotton) found at Pleasant Hill.*

FIGURE 44. *Detail of a handwoven tufted bedcover, made in Canterbury in 1880. Several shades of red, green, and grey blend into each other gradually, and multicolored wool ties attach this cover to a red flannel lining at regular intervals. (Hancock Shaker Village)*

on the side of the bed when the cover is in place. Typical Shaker color gradations appear in the plaid area: for example, several shades of red bleed out from one another. The top is tied (tufted) to a solid red flannel backing, or lining, into which cloth handles for lifting and carrying have been sewn. The complete piece wonderfully embodies many characteristics of Shaker textiles—order, balance, symmetry; subtle color blending; repeating pattern; borders within borders; and interesting lining details.

Photographs taken at Canterbury during the 1880's include other large textiles similar to this coverlet, also having plaid designs of gradated colors and evenly spaced tufts of a darker colored yarn. They may all have been made by the same sister, or they may be examples of a Canterbury "style" of coverlets in the Victorian period.

Very few early quilts remain, and there does not seem to be anything consistently Shaker about them except for the usual fine workmanship. Single-color linsey-woolsey quilts have been found, as well as various pieced and patchwork designs. To my knowledge, no nineteenth-century Shaker appliqué quilts have been identified.

There are at least two Shaker crazy quilts in existence, both made around the turn of the twentieth century. Both are in keeping with other Victorian quilts of this type, but one, made and used at Hancock Shaker Village, has an airy quality that is not quite of the same mold as its contemporaries (Plate 14). The two-inch-wide border is a cheerful pink rather than the more typical crazy-quilt black, and there is none of the characteristic spider webs, insects, or other macabre images. Furthermore, some of the patches are made from Shaker silk scarves, and one is complete with a Shaker blessing. A small piece of white silk was slipped into a typewriter in Harvard, Massachusetts, in 1910, and the following was inscribed:

> Dear Annie Bell Tutle,
>   I cannot find a truer word
>   Nor fonder to caress you.
>   Nor song nor poem have I heard
>   Is sweeter than God Bless You.
>
>   Josephine Jilson.

FIGURE 45. *A silk crazy quilt made at Hancock about 1910. This is a double-faced quilt. (Hancock Shaker Village)*

FIGURE 46. *A detail of Figure 45. The flower is a special decoration that was sold for just this sort of application. Note the different types of stitches joining the patches.*

Household towels, like blankets, were both purchased and hand-woven. Purchased towels were made of cotton, while handwoven towels were usually linen—sometimes natural unbleached linen, but most often bleached, white linen. Towels were usually done in the same plain weave and twills used for blankets, often in the same blue-on-white check, though sometimes more elaborate weaves, like variations of huckaback, M's and O's, or diaper, were used (Figures 24 and 25). None of these patterns was peculiar to the Shakers; fine pattern weaves were popular everywhere for towels because their textured surface increased absorbency.

In the late nineteenth and early twentieth centuries, towels were important as sale products. Design on the sale towels, contrary to the design on those the Shakers used themselves, was not solely structural; decoration was added freely. Ready-made towels were purchased in the world, and embroidery was added in corners, or crocheted edgings were attached on two sides.

Washcloths, at least in the later days of the nineteenth century, were knitted or crocheted of cotton or linen, and typically had a simple checked or striped pattern. They were both sold as fancy goods in Shaker stores and used by the Believers.

Shaker linens and textiles, like other textiles used in eighteenth- or nineteenth-century households, were almost always marked, usually with embroidered initials. In the outside world marking was important, because linens were used on a rotating basis so that they would wear evenly, and number markings were helpful in determining which pieces were used when. The owner's initials were also marked on the pieces, probably more for proprietary reasons than for avoiding confusion. In Shaker textiles there were always initials, which stood either for an individual's name (for example, "HB" for Henry Blinn) or for a particular family ("CH" for Church family, "E" for East family, and so on). Numbers on textiles usually referred to rooms in the dwelling houses—each room had a number above the door—and sometimes to the year in which the piece was made. Thus, a Shaker towel marked CH
18
32
probably belonged in room 18 of the Church family, and was made in 1832. The placement of letters and numbers (numbers centered un-

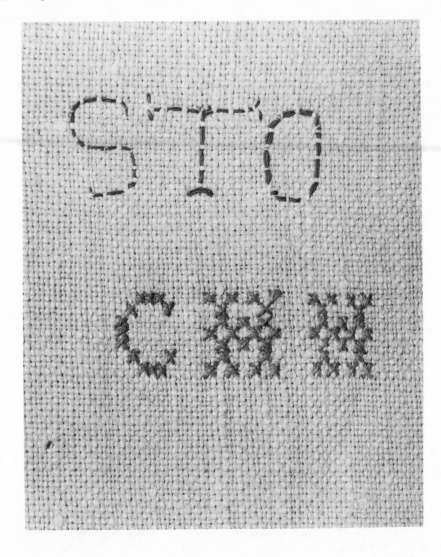

FIGURE 47. *The markings on this towel indicate that it belonged to an individual with the initials "STO," who lived in the Church family. (Hancock Shaker Village)*

der letters) was conventional, adapted from markings of the outside world.[2] Originally, markings were embroidered in fine linen, wool, or silk thread (usually blue) in tiny cross-stitches (embroidery of this type was specified in the Millennial Laws),[3] but later markings were embroidered in other colors or, sometimes, written in ink.

In some if not all communities, wall cloths were hung from pegs in the area around the beds in retiring rooms (Figure 7). When the temperature and humidity changed markedly (at the time of the spring thaw, particularly), the walls could become damp. The wall cloths absorbed this moisture and protected the sleeping inhabitants from it. They also provided a certain degree of insulation and were easier to clean than white walls. Small splash cloths, hung behind washstands, protected the walls from water. Both wall cloths and splash cloths were often made of a blue-and-white-checked cotton material, though sometimes plain or striped cotton was used.

Although people often have the impression that windows in Shaker dwelling houses were bare, window curtains were used almost universally. They were most often plain white linen or cotton, but sometimes they were blue or green—the three "colors" specified in the Millennial Laws. Red, checked, striped, or flowered curtains were specifically prohibited.[4] For curtains the specifications in the Laws appear to have been followed. Many curtains covered only the lower half of the windows and were starched and pleated. Curtains were no doubt made from handwoven material at one time, but I have not found any. White window shades were sometimes used in the shops instead of window curtains (Figure 8).

Rugs and Floor Coverings

Floors in Shaker buildings were covered by all sorts of rugs—braided, woven, hooked and hooked-type, sewn, knitted, and crocheted. Handmade rugs were one area where Shaker love of color and design truly blossomed. Other than a generalized ban on representational imagery, there were very few restrictions or guidelines about how rugs were to be made or used.

Floor rugs of various types did not become popular in America until about 1830,[5] and the earliest known Shaker rugs probably date from about that time. Woven rag rugs were certainly in use by the 1840's. The hooked-type, shirred, and sewn rugs that were indigenous to western communities in Kentucky were probably made in the same period. In the Victorian era in the later nineteenth century, hooked rugs, shag mats, and knitted and crocheted rugs were also made, and a distinctive rag-rug style had evolved. Linoleum became popular about the turn of the twentieth century, and rug production decreased markedly around that time, although it did not die out completely.

Rag Rugs

When one hears the term "rag rug," a certain image comes to mind: a thick woven rug with many short pieces of rag placed haphazardly, in random color combination, into a thick cotton warp. The impression is that the rug was put together with endless little household scraps that had accumulated from worn-out clothing and textiles, or that the rags were purchased by the bale from a factory.

The image applies in some degree to Shaker rag rugs. Since Shaker communities were comprised of many people, they did, in fact, accumulate a good many fabric scraps, particularly in communities that operated their own textile mills. In the first half of the nineteenth century (and even into the twentieth), these scraps were probably woven into the type of hit-and-miss rug described above. By the Civil War period, however, a particular style of Shaker rag rug had evolved. It was subtle but inventive, and a sense of unity, order, and balance was inherent in it. Most rag rugs made in the world were practical but not particularly aesthetic devices to cover floors; the majority of Shaker rag rugs, however, were of excellent design as well.

They had four salient characteristics. First, there was an all-over repeating design, most frequently seen as a repeating sequence of bright and cheerful colors. Second, the rug-makers created rhythm and direction by plying or twisting together rags and yarns of different colors in the weft. They held several different strands and twisted them together on a spinning wheel or plying machine—a process essentially the same as spinning except that it joined yarn rather than raw fiber. The resulting plied yarn was strong (appropriately for rugs)

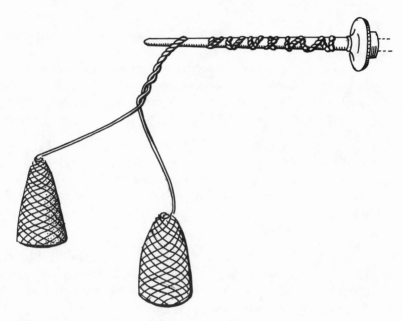

FIGURE 48. *Plying yarns.*

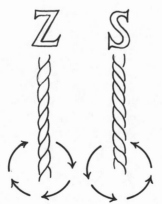

FIGURE 49. *S and Z twist.*

and had a candy-cane diagonal stripe created by twisting contrasting colors. If the yarns were plied in a clockwise direction, there was a "Z" twist, or if counterclockwise, an "S" twist. The Shakers used a conscious juxtaposition of S and Z twists and color combinations to create interesting and complex patterns.

A third characteristic is that the rag rugs were frequently finished with borders or bindings on two or, more often, four sides. Often thick and heavy, the borders were made of tape or braid. They created a sense of framing, a final statement that the rug was a complete entity to be looked at as an object worthy of attention. Borders within borders, used at times, reinforced this sense.

Fourth, despite the thick edgings, many rugs were made with weft shots (a "shot" is one row) of fairly narrow strips, usually one half to three quarters of an inch wide, so that the overall effect was not bulky —a decided contrast to the typical heavy rag rug.

Rag rugs of this style were woven primarily in the northeastern Shaker communities (Maine, New Hampshire, Massachusetts, New York, and Connecticut). Floor runners were undoubtedly also used in the western communities of Kentucky and Ohio—in Shakertown at Pleasant Hill, carpeting hooks are still visible on the Center Family dwelling-house stairs—but I have not seen any rugs with these characteristics known to have been made there. Although more of the western textiles have been lost because those communities were dismantled earlier, it is likely that if large numbers of rag rugs of this style were made in Kentucky, we would have found more of them. The sisters may have made plainer ones and put more of their creative energy into their smaller hooked, shirred, or sewn mats (see below).

The first mention of rag carpets in the Shaker manuscripts and journals I have examined is from 1832. On May 10 of that year, the Watervliet sister who kept the records for her shop mentioned that they "cut and sewed 33 pounds of rags for Eldress Ruth's carpets, eleven in number."[6] Extensive work on rag carpets may not have been typical this early in Shaker history, however. It is mentioned that the Groveland, New York, community sold its rags for cash in 1844 and 1846—100 pounds on one occasion, and 156 pounds on another.[7] There are a few other scattered journal references to rag carpets— Harvard sister Mary Babbitt made one in 1859,[8] and a New Lebanon

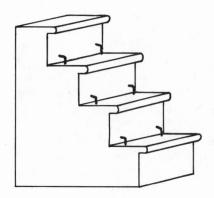

FIGURE 50. *Carpet hooks on the stairs at Pleasant Hill.*

eldress began to cut her rags on April 25 and completed her rug on April 30, 1860[9]—but it is conceivable that large numbers of them were not made until the 1860's and 1870's. In 1872 the Mount Lebanon community bought rags from a factory in Albany,[10] and it seems safe to assume that rags were in greater demand by that time.

Because most of the rags and yarns in the rugs remaining today were dyed chemically, they can be dated after the Civil War. Indigo dye was used on fiber in many of the rugs, but this does not necessarily imply an earlier date, for indigo was still used as late as 1900. Extensive use of bright velvets also puts the rugs in the Victorian period, roughly the last quarter of the nineteenth century.

Sizes of Shaker rag rugs vary a great deal. Some completely finished rugs, as small as 27 by 38 inches, were used at interior doorways as footwipes; Charles Nordhoff, who visited the Shakers of New Lebanon in 1875, observed that "mats meet you at the outer door and at every inner door."[11] It is also quite possible that the smaller rugs were in demand as sale items. Photographs of Shaker shops taken around the turn of the century include pictures of sale rugs that appear to be about 36 by 60 inches.

Large runners were certainly intended for home use within the large buildings of the Shaker community; a hall runner 80 feet long, for instance, was surely not made for an average farmhouse. Sometimes as many as four strips were matched together to fit the width of a room as well as the length, and since the rugs followed a regular, repeating design, they were indeed matched. This matching was in keeping with the Millennial Laws, where Shakers were told that "the carpets in one room should be as near alike as can consistently be provided."[12] Other rugs were made to fit specific areas. An "L"-shaped rug in the collection at the Shaker Museum at Old Chatham, for example, may at one time have followed the curve of a bed or stove in the middle of the room.

Since the rugs usually had a regular design, great quantities of particular fabrics were needed in the larger ones. These were not always *rags*; the cloth was probably bought and set aside for this purpose in some cases. Plate 5 shows a corner of a twelve-foot runner made with weft shots that alternate between wine-red velvet and indigo-blue-and-white worsted. Although this rug is unusually simple and does not conform to the characteristic diagonal effect, it is finished with the typical heavy binding on all sides. The velvet creates a luxurious effect on the highly polished wood floor of a Shaker retiring room.

The rich red is striking, but it is not atypical. The Shakers never set out to limit themselves to a drab environment, and in rugs their use of color seems to have been especially uninhibited. Blue and red were favorites, as always, but orange, green, brown, black, gold, rose, and purple were also common. Certain colors were not likely to be found in the rags of a Shaker community—orange, gold, or yellow, for example, were never used in clothing or bedding—but they appeared sometimes in the rugs. When they were used in rag rugs, it was most often through being incorporated into the multicolored, plied yarn wefts.

Andrews quotes an "inspiration" received by Sister Anna Dodgson in New Lebanon in 1841, in which Mother Lucy told her that "two colors are sufficient for one carpet." She went on to say, however, that one stripe should be made of "red and green, another of drab and grey, and another of butternut and grey," so she may in fact have been referring to the number of colors combined in any one *section* of the rug rather than to the carpet as a whole. She added that "the binding yarn may also be of two colors, and also the binding if necessary."[13] Whatever the inspiration, more than two colors were used together in a great many Shaker rag rugs.

As soon as aniline dyes were available, Shakers used them to color both the yarn and the cloth strips of their rugs and cushions; some pieces known to date from the 1860's have tones never achieved with vegetable colorings. Rugs made late in the nineteenth century from plied velvet strips rather than yarns were especially rich in bright golds, pinks, and purples. Unfortunately, many of the early aniline dyes were not very colorfast; many Shaker items have faded badly, and others may have changed beyond recognition. Of two identical rag rug strips found in the Hancock Shaker Village collection, one was apparently exposed constantly to light, while the other was shielded. The cotton warp on the protected piece is a rich purple; on the exposed piece, it has faded to a nondescript gray-brown. We cannot know in how many other cases rather dull colors were originally cheerful and bright.

The typical rag rugs described above—with a repeating design formed by a regular sequence of color, yarn, and cloth weft shots, and S and Z twist plying—were typically woven on two harnesses, with a cotton warp spaced about eight to ten threads per inch. The weft might consist of three or four rows of a blue wool rag strip, both preceded and followed (i.e. framed) by a row of red, yellow, brown, and white wool yarns plied together in an S-twist as one unit, alternating with a second unit similarly composed of rag strips and plied yarns of different colors. S-twist plied yarns might be found in unit A, and Z-twist plied yarns in unit B. There might be as many as seven or eight distinct units. Some rugs are woven as twills, on four harnesses. (Detailed analysis of several rugs is given in Appendix 4.)

Plied yarns were almost always wool. Rag strips were made of wool, cotton, and sometimes linen, from both woven and knit fabrics. Late in the nineteenth century, velvet strips were also used, at times plied together in the same way as the wool yarns, with either an S or a Z twist.

In many rugs there are *areas* of color. There might be three or four inches, for example, where white and off-white strips are laid end to end in a hit-or-miss fashion; the white area, however, is almost always a separate unit, found consistently wedged between a unit of plied yarns or two rows of another darker-colored rag. This device is an ingenious way of using up very short lengths of rag while maintaining a consistent design over many yards of carpeting.

In other cases there are approximate repeats; for example, a red

FIGURE 51. *This hand loom was made and used at Hancock. The rug that is on the loom has a textured effect that is achieved by puckering (pulling the weft strips up out of the warp) at irregular intervals.*

rag strip would be consistently used in a specific unit, but the same red might not appear twice. Here again, the lack of color uniformity was deliberate; the same unit would have approximate repeats throughout the rug, and the sense of unity and planning would not be lost.

About two thirds of the rag rugs I have examined are finished with some kind of border or binding. Braided borders vary in width from one third of an inch to four inches. They are often made, at least in part, of the same material as the weft; usually some of the yarns used in the plied rows, and sometimes the entire multicolored unit, are braided in. In the thicker braids, strands are sometimes made of long cloth strips rather than yarns. Braids are usually made of the normal three strands, but there are more elaborate examples with four, five, and even seven strands.

Woven borders also tend to be wide, usually between one and three inches. These are most frequently handwoven; the commercial bindings that appear on an occasional rug may have been added later. The handwoven bindings were made on narrow tape looms, though they could have been made on any sort of loom.

A large proportion of rectangular Shaker rag rugs are wider than 36 inches; some are as much as 60 inches, and many are about 40. They are an interesting contrast to the typical hit-and-miss rag rug, which in general is closer to 36 inches.

Some of the sisters at Sabbathday Lake are still weaving rugs—not true rag rugs, but very much in the same tradition as those described above. A weft-faced pattern is formed by colorful knitting yarn, which is woven over a cotton warp. The designs alternate areas of solid-color horizontal stripes with areas of diagonal patterns, formed by plied yarns. The pattern repeats in a regular sequence. Although they do not have the bulk of rag strips or heavy bindings (warp ends are knotted into fringe and the selvedge ends are left unembellished), they retain the feeling of the earlier rugs and are unmistakably Shaker.

Other Woven Rugs

There are a few examples of nineteenth-century woven rugs that were not made with rags or cloth strips. Since they do not conform to

FIGURE 52. *In this rug, rags are plied together in much the same way as yarns might be. The contrast of Z and S twist is especially noticeable at the corner. The four-strand cloth braid is attached to all four sides. (Hancock Shaker Village)*

any particular style, we can assume they were the work of individual sisters who were inspired to try some of their own ideas. Interestingly, characteristics of the rag rugs appear even in these atypical rugs. In one, a double-woven wool piece found in Hancock Shaker Village, the warp alternates between a deep green yarn and an olive-green/red plied yarn. The characteristic diagonal twist is used in a different plane, but it is still there. The selvedge edge is also finished and accentuated with a trimming of plied yarn—red, deep blue, light blue, and a deep green are twisted together.

Another rug at Hancock (Figure 54), dating from the twentieth century, does not appear at first glance to be Shaker-made at all; in some respects it is similar to Nova Scotia warp-faced "drugget" rugs.[14] But close examination shows the typical Shaker patterning. The rug

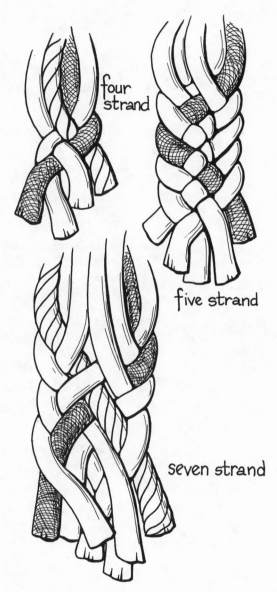

four
strand

five strand

seven strand

FIGURE 53.

FIGURE 54. *Detail of a warp-faced rug. At first glance this does not appear to be Shaker-made, but the carefully planned repeating pattern and internal symmetry are Shaker characteristics. The rug is analyzed in Appendix 3. (Hancock Shaker Village)*

is very large—10½ feet long and 57 inches wide now, and it was probably wider when it was made, since one side has been cut. The design comes from the placement of the warp colors (i.e. it is warp-faced), and these are the only yarns that show.* The piece was carefully planned. The design "reads" vertically from left to right (or right to left), with a bilaterally symmetrical repeat (1,2,3,4,3,2,1), and even within each section the colors are similarly sequenced (in section 1, A,B,C,D,C,B,A). Colors go through a gradation; for example, light green, medium green, and bright green flow from one another. Flamboyant colors and grand scale may be the most striking features of the rug, but the real secret of its success is much the same as in more sedate Shaker rugs: order, balance, and symmetry.

Braided Rugs

Shaker braided rugs were not very different from braided rugs made anywhere in the world, though even with these, some aspects were consistently and delightfully Shaker. The rugs were formed like any other braided rugs: long strips of cloth that had been sewn together, end to end, were braided into a three-strand braid and then sewn together into either an oval or a round shape.

Most Shaker braided rugs follow an aesthetically logical and pleasing color sequence similar to that of the woven rag rugs. Again, regular units were preferred to random or uneven placement of color, and in the braided pieces these were concentric color rings. Within the rings, as within a plied weft unit in the woven rugs, there was color mixing, often three different color strands, or two strands of one color and one of another.

Many rugs have a special emphasis on the outer rings, creating the effect of a border. For example, in one oval rug made in four sections, the inner three sections are made of braids of three colors, all fairly light. The outer section, only two rows deep, is of solid dark navy braid, forming a border that acts as a finishing statement, or frame. The border effect also emerges in other ways. One rug has a picot on the edge: the outer strand of the last braid is pulled out loosely at in-

*See Appendix 3 for an analysis of this rug.

tervals to form a scallop. In another case all the braids except the last are made of tightly packed worsted. The last row is of a thicker, more loosely woven handmade fabric which stands out strikingly from the rest.

All kinds of materials are found in the braids; these rugs used up as many rags as the woven ones. Wool is the most typical fabric, but cotton was also used extensively. There are occasional linen strands, and velvets were used in certain Victorian rugs. Some of the cottons in the late nineteenth-century rugs were from fabrics treated for wrinkle and moisture resistance and are still quite shiny.

In addition to braided rugs, there are many small braided mats still in existence. Made in the late nineteenth and early twentieth centuries, they were apparently to be used both as table mats—placed under lamps, vases, and the like—and as chair-seat cushions. They were popular fancy-goods sale items. Bright velvets were the most common materials—pink, rose, lavender, gold, forest green, royal blue, purple, yellow—but their dyes are among the worst victims of light of any of the Shaker textiles, and, sadly, the cheerful colors that gave them so much life have faded drearily.

Knitted and Crocheted Rugs

The Shakers made numerous round knitted and crocheted rugs which were very similar in feeling and design to the round braided rugs. For example, long rag strips were crocheted on large needles in a continuous circular shape. Different-colored rags were worked in concentric rings, often in alternating light and dark tones, giving a sense of radiating out from a central point.

A knitting technique which created a similar effect was used in both full-sized floor rugs and small chair-seat cushions. Yarn, rather than rags, was knitted in a tubular fashion, and long tubes were sewn together in a spiral. In the seat cushions short strips, often made of a single color, were attached to one another in a hit-and-miss color sequence—no concentric rings of color here (Figure 58).

In the collection of The Shaker Museum at Old Chatham there are several exceptional knitted rugs, probably made by the same sister late in the nineteenth century. All are circular, and all incorporate the two

FIGURE 55. *An unusual-shaped braided rug from Hancock Shaker Village.*

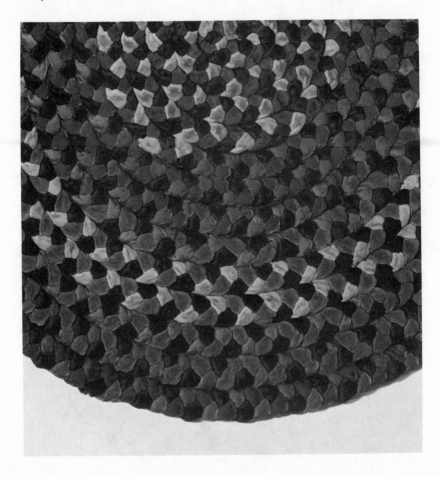

FIGURE 56. *Detail of a small mat, made entirely of velvet. The heavy signs of wear indicate that it was used as a chair seat cushion. The colors, badly faded, were originally bright and cheerful: pink, teale blue, black, and scarlet. (Hancock Shaker Village)*

FIGURE 57. *A crocheted rug from Canterbury, New Hampshire. Note the regular alternation of dark and light colors in the concentric rings.*

construction techniques described above. In the center, tubular knitted strips are sewn together in the spiral fashion. After the circular shape is well established by the tubular spiraling, strips of elaborately patterned flat knitting are sewn on in concentric rings. Like so many other Shaker rugs, they are completed with braided edging. (See Plate 9).

One rug of this type has particularly striking colors: the background is black, and the pattern colors are yellow, turquoise, and red, giving an almost Hopi Indian-like effect. Unfortunately the colors have faded, and while the pattern is still handsomely effective, the intensity of the rug is lost.

It is possible that the Shakers used knitted yarn in another type of rug, the raveled knit rug, a type of shag (below, page 126).

FIGURE 58. *A tubular knit cushion. The colors in these cushions were bright, and typically were placed haphazardly. (Shaker Museum at Old Chatham)*

Hooked and Hooked-Type Rugs

Some of the most delightful Shaker rugs were part of the American folk art tradition of the hooked rug. A hooked rug is made by drawing yarn or narrow cloth strips through a backing with a hook, creating a raised or pile surface on one side. Many authorities agree that this is a truly indigenous American style.[15] Other rugs (including many Shaker pieces) were similar in effect but not actually hooked. One type was the gathered or shirred rug. In this technique, strips of wool or cotton fabric were folded in half, sewn through with a running stitch, and pulled tight, creating shirred or ruffled "caterpillars" that were sewn onto a backing cloth.[16] (Unlike the world's peo-

FIGURE 59. *A circular knit rug with a braided center, from Canterbury. Concentric rings of color are characteristic of all Shaker round rugs.*

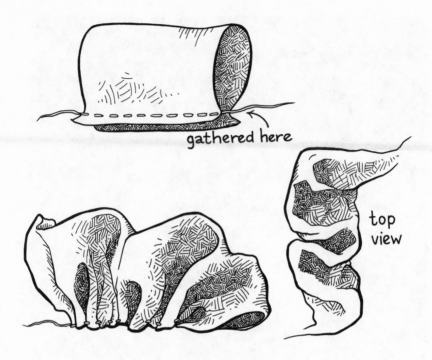

gathered here

top
view

FIGURE 60. *Shirring "caterpillars."*

ple who made rugs of this type, the Shakers sewed the unfinished edge to the backing rather than the folded edge. Depending on their placement in the design, the caterpillars might be tacked down in rows or gathered back and forth in an undulating row, which could turn with the contour of the design; or they might be wound into spirals, which were sewn together tightly, forming a design made up of many circles.

Another common Shaker product was the so-called dollar mat, or scaled rug. Circles about the size of a silver dollar were punched out of wool or cotton cloth several layers at a time, with a special cutting tool like a hole puncher or cookie cutter. The circles (dollars) were then sewn to a backing cloth, sometimes flat but usually folded in

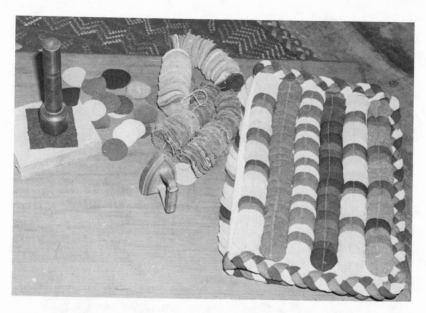

FIGURE 61. *"Dollar" display at the Shaker Museum in Old Chatham, New York. The dollar punch, or circle cutter, is on the left; cut dollars and dollars strung on a string are in the center; and a very simple small mat made by Sister Jennie Wells is on the right. A round knit rug is a companion to, but not the same as, the rug in color plate 9. This one uses yellow, turquoise, and red yarns against a background of black.*

fourths and tacked down either along the side or at the point of the pie-shaped edge. Extra-thick dollars were created by using several layers. Packed in very closely, the dollars gave a high-pile effect. The backing was always a sturdy material. Some Pleasant Hill rugs are actually sewn to old woven or braided rugs, others to plain linen, cotton, or burlap. Mattress ticking was used on some—a convenient choice, since the dollars could be sewn along the straight navy blue lines. Scaled rugs made in the world often used gradated sizes of circles (i.e. four or five circles together, those with the largest diameter at the bottom).[17] Shaker scaled rugs always use dollar-sized circles.

As with shirred rugs, the way the dollars were sewn down determined the final appearance of the rug. The design was enhanced by

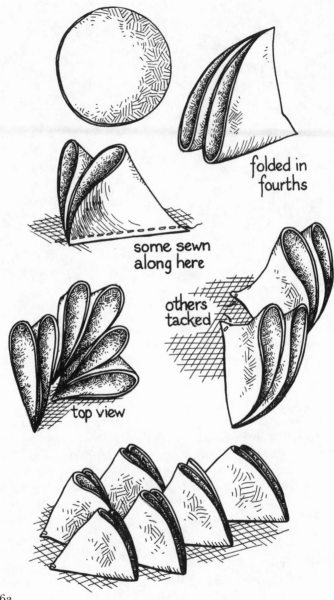

folded in
fourths

some sewn
along here

others
tacked

top view

FIGURE 62.

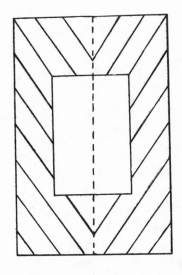

FIGURE 63. *Directional "dollar" placement.*

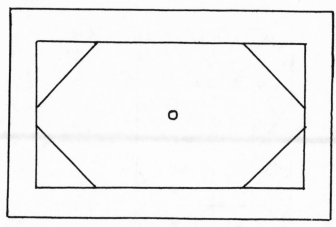

FIGURE 64. *Schematic design of Pleasant Hill rugs.*

the direction of the pieces. In one rug said to have been made in New Lebanon, for example, dollars are sewn in overlapping curves pointing toward the center (a design in blues) in bilaterally mirrored diagonals made of red and brown circles. In some of the Kentucky examples, the conscious use of dollar placement is even more explicit. In the recurring cross pattern, the circles point toward the center and outline the trapezoidal shape of the cross arm. Flowers are made of dollars placed in a circle around a central area, with the curve of each folded dollar leading out from the center like a petal. In contrast, the background circles are sewn on in straight rows.

One dollar mat having the circles sewn onto the backing as flat, overlapping pieces rather than folded is known to have been made in Watervliet by Sister Jennie Wells in 1902. The circles are machine-sewn in straight rows across the width of the mat, and there is a braid along the edge on all four sides. This rug, along with an original circle punch, is in the collection at the Shaker Museum at Old Chatham (Figure 61).

The great majority of shirred and dollar-mat rugs were made in the Kentucky community of Pleasant Hill; the style is so consistent, in fact, that we may reasonably assume that examples found in the northern communities were either made in Kentucky or directly inspired by rugs that were.

FIGURE 65. *Horses were a favorite subject for the Pleasant Hill Shakers, who lived among horse-breeding farms near Lexington, Kentucky. The use of borders within borders is well illustrated in this caterpillar rug. (Pleasant Hill)*

FIGURE 66. *The circle around this horse is not actually braided but is made to appear as if it were. The border is, however, a five-strand braid. (Pleasant Hill)*

Again, the sense of order and balance in these pieces is in keeping with the rest of Shaker life and work. All are rectangular mats, with an average size of three by five feet. Schematically, most of the designs work symmetrically in the four quadrants of the rectangle, with a clearly defined central point and a triangle in each of the four corners. In almost all examples, the design is contained in a rectangle considerably smaller than the size of the rug itself, and is framed by several borders. In one of the two famous "horse rugs," for example (Figure 65), the horse itself is in a rectangle defined by encircling scallops, with clearly defined triangles in its corners. The rectangle, in turn, is contained inside nine distinct border rows, eight of which are made of dollars folded in fourths (the horse itself is also made in this way). The last border row is a seven-strand braid of cloth strips. In the other horse rug, the horse is enclosed in an oval frame, which in turn is enclosed in a rectangle with rounded triangles in the corners, within the numerous borders.

Many of the rugs at Pleasant Hill combine several techniques. A rug with a design of concentric circles, for example (Figure 3), is made with shirred caterpillars in the central area, a scaled border, and a thick braided edge. (It is also sewn onto a braided rug.) It is common to use one technique in the main part of the rug and a second and possibly third technique in the border. In at least one rug a braid is used as an inside frame even within the central area. A few Pleasant Hill rugs also incorporate wool yarn loops and actual hooking.

Most of the rugs do not have pictorial images like the horses in Figures 65 and 66; Shaker discouragement of representational art precluded this. Some pieces have floral designs, but they are not clearly identified as particular flowers. Two examples have a Maltese cross as the central motif, and several others have geometric motifs—circles, triangles, or both. In one surprising rug the word GOOD is spelled out in folded dollars in the center of the inner rectangle. Small hearts are often sprinkled inside other shapes—ever-present reminders of the Shaker emphasis on love, both heavenly and earthly.

Many of these hooked-type rugs, as we have seen, have interesting backing fabrics. In several instances dollars or caterpillars are sewn to Shaker-made handwoven hit-and-miss rag rugs or braided rugs. In another the backing is a carefully patched arrangement of knitted,

FIGURE 67. *Bright reds and blues make the word "GOOD" seem to glow with an inner warmth. This is a dollar mat, with a braided edge. (Pleasant Hill)*

FIGURE 68. *Shirred caterpillars sewn to a backing cloth in geometric shapes make up this lighthearted design. Note the hearts that are worked into some of the triangles. (Pleasant Hill)*

woven, and printed pieces of cotton and wool. These backing details give us a clue to the way the sisters felt about their shirred and dollar mats: mundane braided and rag rugs or patchwork, also the products of their labor, were completely hidden and used solely to support the more fanciful rugs. Thrift may have dictated using heavily worn rugs as the basis for new ones, but some appear to be in fairly good condition. We may conclude that the hooked-type rugs were very special to the Shakers who made them.

None of these Pleasant Hill rugs is dated or signed, and it is difficult to date them definitively. Several clues point toward their time period, however. First, rugs whose design was applied to the surface (as in shirring) generally predate those whose design was actually brought through the backing material (as in hooking). This would date the hooked-type mats as early as 1840. Second, backing materials often offer clues to the age of a rug: linen backings predate burlap ones. In the Pleasant Hill rugs both are found, in addition to the unusual braided, woven, or patched ones described above. No definitive conclusions can be drawn except that, as noted, some of the rugs may be as old as 1840. The third key to their age is the nature of the dyes used in them. Most of these rugs are made with cloth that was dyed naturally rather than chemically, but we cannot be sure that older rags were not used even after chemical dyes were available. The rug designs are vaguely Victorian, but controlled design and border arrangement is characteristic of all Shaker work. Given all of these ambiguous factors, we can only speculate about the limits of the time period: 1840 to 1875.

Although the hooked-type shirred and scaled rugs were mostly indigenous to Kentucky, the Shakers in all areas made hooked rugs later in the century. Many photographs taken in the northern communities in the last two decades of the nineteenth century show hooked rugs on the floors. The designs are primarily floral and may have been taken or adapted from contemporary patterns. The definitive Shaker touch is usually added, however, with a thick braided border (see Figure 69).

Shaker sisters alive today remember making hooked rugs early in the twentieth century. They say the Shakers always made these rugs themselves and never bought them from the outside world. Hooked

FIGURE 69. *This photograph of the girls of the Church Family, Enfield, Connecticut, 1886, shows three hooked rugs edged by thick braids.*

rugs seem to have been made only for community use—not for sale. I know of only one extant Shaker hooked rug, which is in the collection of the Shaker Museum at Sabbathday Lake. It has a brightly colored floral-geometric design with an arrangement reminiscent of the Pleasant Hill rugs described above, and it is framed by a thick braid (Figure 70).

Shag Mats

In the late nineteenth and early twentieth centuries the Shaker sisters made thickly textured and piled shag mats. Some were plush mats made on a loom with a densely packed wool pile (see below, pages

FIGURE 70. *A hooked rug in the collection of the Shaker Museum at Sabbathday Lake. It was probably made about 1900. The layout of this rug is similar to the layout of the hooked-type Pleasant Hill rugs.*

140–142); others were thick shag mats made with cloth strips and possibly unraveled knit yarns.

The usual technique for making shag mats with cloth strips was to draw strips one half to one inch wide through a knitted or crocheted backing, probably as individual pieces 4 to 6 inches long, since the pile is 2 to 3 inches high and each piece was folded in half and knotted so as to form two pile ends. In one cheerful rug (Figure 71), the cloth strips are all from wool knits. The border is a deep pink surrounded on both sides by a khaki-beige, and the other colors, placed haphazardly in the central area, create an almost pointillistic effect in beige, blue, red, orange, and gold. In other rugs, multicolored cotton prints or deeply colored wools are used.

There are also shag mats made from raveled knit goods that may be Shaker products. These were made by cutting hand- or machine-knit woolens into strips and unraveling part of each strip to create a wavy, airy group of yarns, then sewing the still-intact part of the strips to a backing fabric. The unraveled section of the strip stood up from the backing and formed the shaggy pile. Some antique dealers claim that rugs of this type were made by Shakers living in Maine,[18] but I have not been able to authenticate this. Residents of Sabbathday Lake say they know nothing about them. New Hampshire Shakers, on the other hand, produced a great quantity of knitted material, and there is an orderly, bilaterally symmetrical placement of color and textured yarn in these rugs that has a Shaker flair. The most we can say is that possibly they were made by Shakers.

Covering Floors

Shaker rugs were not always placed on bare floors. Painted oil cloth was sometimes used as a floor covering in the first half of the nineteenth century, in both Shaker and non-Shaker dwellings. Later in the century the Shakers adopted patterned linoleum which, in addition to being decorative, was easily cleaned and therefore very practical. Since it covered the entire floor of a room, it also provided a certain degree of insulation. Many photographs taken at the turn of the twentieth century show area rugs sitting on top of patterned linoleum. In one, taken at Enfield, Connecticut, there is a linoleum floor covered

FIGURE 71. *The detail of this shag rug shows how different colored knit strips are used to form a design. (Hancock Shaker Village)*

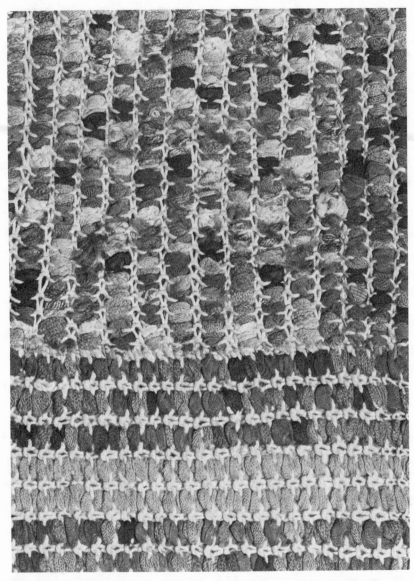

FIGURE 72. *This rear view of the mat in Figure 71 shows that the strips are drawn through a knit backing. (Hancock Shaker Village)*

FIGURE 73. *This photograph taken in New Lebanon illustrates some of the Victorian-influenced decoration in an early twentieth-century Shaker dwelling. Note the flowered wallpaper; two or three different patterns of linoleum (the central area with the scroll design is probably a purchased ingrain carpet); small hooked rug; plush stool cover; and decorative lambrequin, or shelf valence, at the upper right.*

by a rag rug covered by a small hooked mat. In another taken in New Lebanon, linoleum is covered by a (purchased) ingrain carpet, covered in turn by a hooked rug (Figure 73).

Chair Seat Tapes and Cushions

Tapes

Of all Shaker products, chairs are perhaps the best known. According to the *Centennial Catalogue of the Shakers' Chairs, Foot Benches, etc.*, Shakers were making chairs for their own use as early as 1776;[19] and by the 1860's Shaker-made chairs were very popular with the world's people all over the country.

Both rush and splint chair seats were used on Shaker chairs, but it is the cloth chair-seat tapes that have received the most attention. Woven chair seats were nothing new: splint, cane, and rush had been woven onto chair rails for many years. The idea of weaving cloth strips together to form a seat, however, quite possibly originated with the Shakers, and is in effect the forerunner of the folding lawn chair's webbed seat.

The tapes themselves were widely used in America in the eighteenth and nineteenth centuries for such items as garters, clothing ties like apron strings, carpet bindings, and straps.[20] There is no clear record of anyone using them for chair seats, however, before the Shakers began doing it—probably by the 1830's.

The taped chairs are extremely comfortable, as well as attractive and functional. Tape is carried over the wooden frame in what is essentially two layers, with a filling between them. The result is a firm, buoyant seat.

The majority of early Shaker tapes were made of wool, although some were made of linen or cotton and others combined fibers. A great deal of time went into their making, since approximately twenty to thirty yards were necessary for just one chair seat. Since tape was made for many purposes, it is difficult to know exactly what proportion was used for chairs, but it was probably quite high. Tape production was certainly a very important early Shaker activity. In the First Order in Watervliet, New York, the sisters wove 1,095 yards of tape in 1835; 3,166 yards in 1836; 855 yards in 1837; 1,270 yards in 1838; and 733 yards in 1839.[21] In the Girl's Order alone in the same community, 347 yards of "chair bottom binding" were woven in 1846.[22]

These figures may not be helpful in determining how much tape was used in any one year, however, for tape was also purchased in quantity from the outside world at least as early as the 1840's.[23] As usual, the Shakers produced what they could for themselves but were not afraid to use high-quality merchandise produced by others. By the 1860's, when chair-making had become an important industry, most chair seat tapes were commercially made, although a visitor to Hancock could still get handwoven "listing" as late as 1929.[24] By the 1860's the tapes were usually being made of cotton and tended to be of a single color rather than a complex color pattern.

The handwoven tapes do not seem to follow any one style. There

FIGURE 74. *Early handwoven tapes from Pleasant Hill. These tapes are not as carefully woven as most of the ones that are found in the Northeast. Note the uneven placement of tape at both the front and back of the chair.*

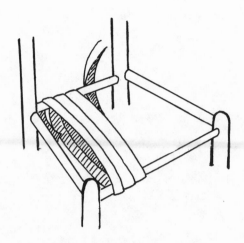

FIGURE 75.

are examples of warp-faced, weft-faced, and fifty-fifty weaves, and patterns vary a great deal. The one characteristic common to all is symmetry, or balance. A tape with a blue stripe on the left of the center always has a matching blue stripe on the right. The characteristic Shaker plying or twisting of colors, found so frequently in rag rugs and occasionally in other textiles, is also visible in some of the older tapes.

The vast majority of handwoven tapes were made on two-harness looms and follow the standard plain weave, or tabby, pattern in which the weft goes over and under alternate warp threads. There are also a substantial number made in a twill pattern. These must have been woven on four-harness looms, and since none of the remaining tape looms has any provision for more than two harnesses, they may have been woven on wider looms not made expressly for weaving tape. Twill patterns were at times rather fancy, with reverse twills and herringbone effects. The later, commercially woven tape was frequently woven in a twill pattern as well.

Tape was wound onto a chair seat, from a continuous roll, around a padding—cloth stuffed originally with sawdust or horsehair, more recently with foam rubber. It was then secured by a tack at one corner of the chair rails and wound around from top to bottom and back again for the width of the chair, forming the warp of the woven seat. Weft tape was brought through the warp, working a row first on the

FIGURE 76. *A view of the swiveling-chair clamp that turns the chair around constantly as it is taped. (Hancock Shaker Village)*

FIGURE 77. *Sister Sarah Collins, taping a chair seat in New Lebanon in the 1930's. Note how the tape is threaded through a wooden stick, which serves as a needle.*

top of the chair and then on the bottom. A special rotating clamp, in use at least by the mid-nineteenth century, turned the chair over and over, so that the taper could always be working on the top of the piece. The weft tape was threaded through a tapered metal or wood needle for ease in getting it through small spaces.

Most tapes were woven onto the chair in an over-and-under (tabby, or plain weave) pattern, but some follow a basketweave (over two, under two) pattern. Wefts floating over more than two warp tapes would not produce as firmly woven a seat, and the basketweave is the outside limit of variation in seat patterning. At the Shaker Museum at Old Chatham there are a few examples of chair seats woven in an unusual manner: a diamond shape was formed by using the basket-weave pattern on the outer edges of the seat and the tabby pattern on the inside. Very few seats were made in this way, and none of them uses the older handwoven tapes. Many chairs had contrasting colors, and often contrasting patterns, sometimes very striking, in the warp and weft tapes.

Chair Cushions

Despite the fact that tape-seated chairs were well made, practical, and comfortable, they did not conform to the ornate and heavily textured Victorian aesthetic of the nineteenth century. The Shakers were willing to cater to the demands of their market, however, and as part of their chair industry they began producing and selling plush chair-seat cushions as early as 1844.[25] No specific information is available about these early cushions, and I have seen none that can definitely be dated from that time; but we have a full range of information and pieces from the 1870's and 1880's.

The chair-seat cushions were made especially for Shaker chairs. A special chair, in fact, was designed for cushions: a round bar extending across the top of the back posts (Figure 81) fitted neatly into the top of the cushion as a supporting brace.

The standard seat cushion of about 1875 was a stuffed pillow, covered with a luxurious wool plush (pile). It was usually sold with a matching back cushion. The *Centennial Catalogue of the Shakers' Chairs*, written in New Lebanon in 1876, stated:

FIGURE 78. *Contrasting tapes woven on the chair in a tabby (plain weave) pattern. One set—the vertical, or warp tapes—is made with a plain stripe, while the other set— the horizontal, or weft tapes—is made with a reverse twill, forming a chevron. (Hancock Shaker Village)*

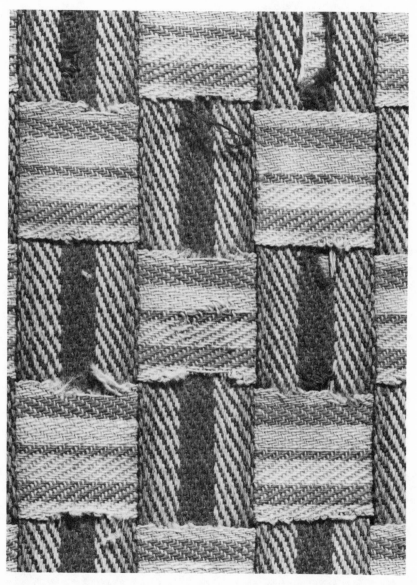

FIGURE 79. *Another chair seat made of wool tapes woven in twill patterns. Note the dark/light contrast.*

FIGURE 80. *Tapes woven onto the chair in a basketweave pattern. These tapes include irregular color blending—two or more threads are used as if they were one thread, and their different colors twist around one another as if they were plied. (Hancock Shaker Village)*

FIGURE 81.

The material with which we cushion our chairs is a specialty peculiarly our own. It is made of the best stock, and woven in hand looms with much labor, and forms a heavy and durable article, much more so than anything which we are acquainted with. We have all the most desirable and pretty colors represented in our cushions, and they can be all one color, or have a different colored border, or with different colored stripes running across the cushion.

This catalogue was prepared in conjunction with the Shaker booth at the Centennial Exposition in Philadelphia. In Figures 82 and 83 we can see the typical design—a striped seat and back rest (two colors in alternating rows) with a single contrasting color as a border on the sides and back of the seat. The "most desirable and pretty colors" usually meant red, blue, green, and bright purple (badly faded in most remaining cushions). A typical seat might have alternating rows of purple and blue or blue and red, with a green border.

Plush cushions were apparently not made by the Shakers themselves. An interesting description of plush weaving in New Lebanon (probably it was done no place else) indicates that European immigrants were hired to do this work. The description was written in 1873 by Canterbury Elder Henry Blinn, who was visiting other Shaker communities and kept a detailed journal of his experiences:

The plush for cushions is made in this same building. In one room we found two old men at work in hand looms, slowly weaving this peculiar cloth. Our guide informed us that they were not americans. He also informed us that this style of goods cannot be

FIGURE 82.

FIGURE 83. *Shaker chair shop, South Family, Mount Lebanon, about 1885. Note the plush-chair seat cushions and footstools and the different types of rugs. The contrast between the fashionably dressed customer and the Shaker sisters is also interesting.*

woven by power looms. It is beat up on wires that are grooved. They use only two wires, and when the second is secured in its place, they draw a knife across the first wire, in the groove, and then remove it beyond the one already in the loom. Every few minutes they must stop and cut out the wire which makes the plush. These men weave from three to four yards each per day, and are paid 50¢ a yard. One of the men informed me that they usually worked ten hours each day.[26]

The process Blinn describes is a basic tufting technique. In addition to the warp and weft, there is a third element on the loom—a supplementary weft—which is drawn up from the surface to create a pile. The pile (plush) in most Shaker chair cushions is about half an inch high, though it varies from a quarter-inch to an inch. The pile, or supplementary weft, is always wool, but the supporting warp and weft (which do not show) are cotton or linen.

There are also some cushions which look, on the surface, identical to those made on a loom but which are made on a crocheted or prepared cloth backing, such as a loosely woven monks-cloth-type cotton. The pile on these could have been drawn through with a needle or hook. They were probably made by the sisters, rather than by hired men, and perhaps at a later time. This plush material was fashioned into various shapes and sizes. Back cushions and seat cushions were available in eight sizes, and sets of both seat and back cushions were available in four sizes. They made matching foot or step benches and floor rugs too, as well as round stool covers with the same alternating color stripes surrounded by a solid border.

The plush seats were heavily stuffed, usually with horsehair or cotton batting, although one amazing piece in the Hancock Shaker Village collection is also padded with overlapping layers of folded cloth: various cotton fabrics, probably scraps, are sewn over one another like louvered blinds (Figure 84). A thick and resilient padding, probably used to supplement the stuffing, is created in this ingenious but simple fashion.

The cushions fit the chairs perfectly. A central piece is made to the exact size of the chair seat, whatever its dimensions, and—like the chair seat itself—is a trapezoid. The plush is sewn to a backing which forms an envelope for the stuffing. All sorts of fabrics were used for

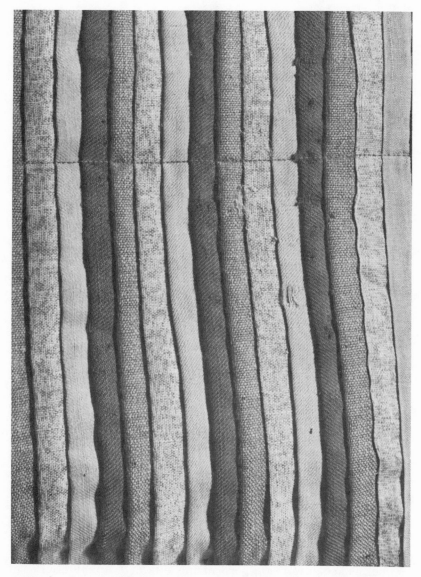

FIGURE 84. *An unusual lining detail of a plush-chair seat cushion. The line down the middle is a row of machine stitching. (Hancock Shaker Village)*

backings; they appear to be remnants, since some are dress or trouser material. One cushion in the New York State collection is lined with leather. Whether or not the sisters made the plush itself, it is probable that they sewed the seats together, and New Lebanon records of the 1860's indicate that the girls sewed cushion linings.[27] In many cushions the corners of the trapezoid were slightly rounded, since the cushion fits snugly between the posts of the four chair legs. The sides were made and sewn on separately: four oblong strips, usually of a contrasting color, were attached at the edges of the stuffed cushion, to fold down and hang like the dust ruffle of a bed. There is no stuffing behind them. In some cushions, ribbon ties are sewn on to these pieces, to be tied together around the chair leg; in others, the front plush pieces are sewn firmly together (or made in one piece), but a hole is left for the front legs, while the back pieces are tied around the back legs.

All chair-seat cushions were designed to fit over chair seats finished with rush, splint, or cloth tape, so that in a sense they were slipcovers. The chair was doubly versatile, since it could be used with or without the extra covering. Although most of the chair-seat cushions were made for sale to the outside world, the Victorian Shakers of the late nineteenth and early twentieth centuries were fond of them too; we see them in photographs taken of the Shakers at this time.

A few examples of other types of Shaker chair-seat cushions survive. At Hancock there is a stuffed cushion with the typical trapezoidal shape, but the fabric is knitted rather than woven or hooked into a pile. Several pieces of wool yarn are plied together and knitted straight across in a stockinette stitch, and the side flaps, or border—knitted in the same way—are a constrasting solid color. The New York State Museum collection has a cushion with a knitted seat, but this one has plush side flaps and is lined with a bright, cheerful cotton print. Judging from the print and the yarns involved, knitted cushions were probably made later than the all-plush ones, as were small, simpler chair-seat cushions. Both the coiled knit mat and the braided velvet mat, made to sit on top of a chair seat, were popular items with visitors to the Shaker stores.

The Shakers also made permanently attached, upholstered chair covers from solid-color plush or any other sort of fabric; as they said,

FIGURE 85. *The border of this knit cushion is blue; the center is blue, pink, and white (all of these colors are used together). The pink yarn is a fancy, textured bouclé, which probably means that the cushion was made in the twentieth century. (Hancock Shaker Village)*

"those who choose to do so can purchase the [chair] frames and have them covered to suit themselves."[28]

The Victorian penchant for thick stuffing, heavy fabric, and layer upon layer of cloth was well suited to Shaker chairs. The woven tapes could be covered by thickly stuffed and densely piled cushions or upholstery. A painting done in 1878, now on view at the Shaker Museum at Old Chatham, New York, shows how yet another layer of cloth was added in at least one case: an antimacassar (the doily-like crocheted piece placed over a chair back as protection from the popular Macassar hair oil) was placed on top of the plush backrest.

Chapter Five

Clothing and Personal Accessories

 The production, fashion, and upkeep of clothing was a major concern of the Shakers. Isaac Young, in his "A Concise View of the Church," stated:

> We may justly observe that this is a subject that absorbs a great part of our attention, time, and earnings. Our dress is a great expense to us, and much more than real necessity demands, owing to the taste and fancy of the people, about their dress.
>
> It is impossible to please the fancy, and conform to all the different opinions of color, form, etc. and yet maintain a due regard to uniformity and Economy.[1]

The history of Shaker costume may be seen as an attempt to find a balance among individual taste, communal uniformity, and frugality. Uniformity was an overall goal, but individual variation was always allowed. Styles changed from time to time with the changing availability of materials, new styles in the world, and the inventiveness of individual Shaker designers. By the late nineteenth century external influence was so great, and industrial production had made externally produced items so inexpensive, that much of the Shaker wardrobe was purchased ready made. The balance had shifted to greater individual variation, but Believers—being aware and proud of their unique situation—remained true in their dress, as in everything else, to their role as people who were set apart to create a heaven on earth.

Clothing in the Communal Environment

When the United Society was first "gathered in," there were no restrictions about dress, and Mother Ann Lee left no particular admoni-

tions or advice in that regard. In time, however, Shaker clothing
began to evolve a character of its own. As Elder Henry Blinn of
Canterbury wrote in his journal,

> When the societies were organized the Believers were not dis-
> tinguished by any peculiarities of their garments from the people
> who lived around them, but by retaining the form of dress then
> in use, as they did, they soon looked quite different from their
> neighbours, who tried to keep pace with the changing styles. Up
> to 1796 no uniformity of dress had been adopted and each group
> seems to have provided what seemed most to their advantage.[2]

When a certain degree of uniformity became a concern, the outlying
communities took their cues from the central bishopric at New Lebanon:

> The First Believers were very particular that all articles of wear-
> ing apparel . . . should correspond with the pattern accepted at
> New Lebanon. This was done for the sake of Union, one of the
> most important principles of their lives.[3]

When Mother Lucy Wright (of New Lebanon) visited Canterbury in
1806,

> She wore for the Sunday service a jacket or perhaps we would call
> it a smock of light striped cotton. The sleeves . . . extended below
> the elbows and it was longer than had been worn. . . . At once
> the Sisters adopted this style for their Sunday meeting costume.[4]

There were men and women in each community who were skilled
at tailoring and dressmaking. They originated variations in clothing
design and took them to the elders or eldresses for their opinion and
approval. If approved, a new design or style variation could be
adopted in the sewing rooms of the sisters' and tailors' shops. New
Lebanon Eldress Polly Ann Reed described such a situation in 1872:

> Sister Aurelia came to our shop with another new fashioned cap
> with wide forepart and crown set in. We thot it very nice for a sick
> person and for a corpse and we did not know but she was in-
> spired to get up something plain and easy for the colored sisters.
> Eldress P. will take one and some patterns with her.[5]

On another occasion she mentioned that the ministry "gave permission for the short dress to wear at dirty work and did not forbid large capes for everyday instead of neckerchiefs and talked of making a few plaits in our gown waists."[6] New Lebanon influence was not quite as strong in later years, and individual Believers in other communities came to initiate style changes also, seeking only the approval of their local ministry.

In addition to approving the actual styles, the ministry also made the broader decisions about the kind of clothing and clothing material that was considered appropriate. On February 28, 1835, for example, Eldress Ruth told the sisters in New Lebanon that "the girls need not have but one set of caps for summer and winter."[7] Similarly, Sister Anne Williams of the same community reported in her diary on October 2, 1839, that the "sisters . . . go to the elder sister's shop [and] are informed that gray surtouts are to be worn to meeting instead of drab."[8] Even the particular fiber mixture to be used was sometimes prescribed. Elder David Parker of Canterbury, for example, specified that worsted should be spun from 90 percent dark blue and 10 percent white (undyed) wool. This material became known as "Parker mixed."

The Shakers were concerned with uniformity in dress for several reasons. Most important, since they were striving to create a "heaven on earth," quality was considered important in all aspects of their daily lives. Centralized decision-making about materials and styles, they felt, would ensure uniformly high quality in the clothing of every Believer.

"Quality" material was well made, sturdy, and practical. An article written by the ministry at New Lebanon in the 1866 "Circular Concerning the Dress of Believers" outlined Shaker goals:

> to have quality that will wear, to have such colors of fabrics as
> are fast, and will not wash out or wear colorless and will not spot
> or stain. Also, such as will look well when worn, old, or soiled, and
> further, such as will be proper for a meeting suit or uniform
> when new and when old, soiled or worn, to wear out for service
> or fatigue dress.

Aesthetics was not stressed as such, but an aesthetic sensitivity in fact pervaded every aspect of Shaker life and work.

Another reason why uniformity was important to the Shakers is that they saw it as helpful in stabilizing and controlling their environment. Many despairing remarks were made about "temporalities" and "fluctuations" in style and temperament in the world;[9] for the Shakers there was an absolute standard which they could determine and remain loyal to.

Shaker life was hierarchical, and uniformity in dress also helped to identify the status of community members. Children, who had not signed the covenant and become full-fledged Believers, were always dressed differently from their elders. Young girls remained bareheaded until they reached the approximate age of 14, when they began to wear caps. Donning the cap was a rite of passage.

A woman who had grown up with the Shakers but later left to go out into the world described her coming of age (about 1832):

> my friend Joy and I were each 15 years of age when we were removed from the children's order and became young sisters. . . . A fresh palm leaf bonnet with a swiss muslin curtain and a brown worsted "meeting gown" made the summit of our bliss.[10]

Believers assigned to a specific job, such as a stint in the kitchen or laundry, were often given a kind of uniform to wear during that time, at least until the twentieth century. A "kitchen sister" in New Lebanon, for example, often wore a finely striped black and tan dress and a brown and white apron.[11]

Complete uniformity was by no means ever achieved. Communities far from New Lebanon geographically had come to develop their own stylistic variations by about 1830; thus neighboring communities in Maine or Ohio were likely to conform more closely to one another than to New Lebanon. Materials that were available in one part of the country were not necessarily available in another, and regional tastes and styles also varied. Individuals were usually able, furthermore, to adapt small details to their personal taste.

There were periodic attempts to increase uniformity and standardization, as in the 1866 article excerpted above (page 148). As time went on, however, and the Shakers came to rely more and more heavily on goods produced in the world and were increasingly subject to worldly influence, community and individual variation grew. By the twentieth century, Believers were able to choose their own colors and materials and to make decisions about their own clothing.

Uniformity or the lack of it, as we have been discussing it, refers for the most part to minor variations. From about 1795 until the beginning of the twentieth century, Shakers conformed to a distinct general style. Clothing changes were generally subtle and slow to come about, and a Shaker who went out into the world could easily be identified as a Shaker by his or her costume.

Shaker style had certain general characteristics. The sisters' dress style, established shortly after the turn of the nineteenth century, was a one-piece dress with a long and generally full skirt. The bodice was always completely covered by a white collar and a large neckerchief, or scarf, pinned so that a triangular point or points fell just below the waist. In the later years of the nineteenth and in the twentieth century, a separate shoulder cape or "bertha" replaced the kerchief.

Outsiders were often highly critical of this feature of Shaker dress. Marianne Finch, an Englishwoman who visited the Shakers in the 1850's, remarked that the bodice scarf was "certainly the most ingenious device ever contrived for concealing all personal advantage."[12] Another visitor stated that "the entire [Shaker sister's] costume seemed intended to make the whole body look like a tree-stem, without any curved lines."[13] These observers were correct, of course, in surmising that the Shakers were trying to play down the sexual attractiveness of their women; the beauty they were concerned with was on another plane. The observers were mistaken, however, in assuming that the kerchief was a device "contrived" by the Shakers. A similar kerchief was worn by rural women in the British Isles and northern Europe from the seventeenth century until about the turn of the nineteenth century. The Shakers simply did not abandon the style when other people did.

In all periods the sisters' hair was drawn straight back off the face and held up with hairpins. A white cap was worn at all times, and a straw, palm-leaf, or cloth bonnet was worn over this when they went out. The cap, too, was always remarked on by visitors; it was variously described as a "mob-cap," "a cap of clear muslin, fitting closely to the face, covering the head" (1841), "a plain cap of snowy whiteness" (1851), and a "would-be cap of transparent net" (1878).[14]

In reading visitors' comments about various aspects of Shaker costume, one should keep in mind the elaborate necklines, crinolines, and hairdos of the nineteenth century. Fashionable women of the time also were likely to wear silk dresses for special occasions, and the plain cotton and wool of the sisters' Sabbath clothes did not impress them. They often remarked, however, on the neatness and cleanliness of Shaker costume, and a certain distinction was awarded to it because of this characteristic. Descriptions of both dwelling houses and personal clothing abounded with phrases like "scrupulously clean," "neatly arranged," "spotless," and "distinguished-looking."[15]

The garments of Shaker brethren were not considered quite as odd as those of the sisters, but they were by no means fashionable. Shaker men wore the same articles of clothing as the men of the world—white shirt, vest, jacket, coat, and trousers or pantaloons—but their styles were old-fashioned and "peculiar." Generally, materials were plain but tailoring was intricate. They wore hats at almost all times: a type of top hat with a stiff crown and brim. Winter hats were made of felted wool or fur, and summer hats of straw or palm leaf.

By the end of the nineteenth century, the brethren were generally buying their clothing ready made, but this was not—and still is not—true for the sisters. Most women sewed their own clothing and were not dependent on family seamstresses, as the men were dependent on tailors.

Many people have the impression that the Shakers wore only dark and somber colors, but this also is not true. Though truly flamboyant yellows and oranges were not part of the Shaker costume, other rich and cheerful colors were allowed. The popular butternut was a glowing reddish brown, and a wide variety of rich blues were common. A visitor to a Shaker meeting in 1857, in fact, went home raving about the "brilliant ultramarine blue" of the sisters' shoes (see Plate 12).[16] Exquisite pink and rose shades were used in silk neckerchiefs, and maroons appeared in cloaks and quilted bonnets. Children were sometimes dressed in muted red colors that had been dyed in the same vats as the carpet binding.[17] Color regulation was primarily based on practicality, and the ministry was mainly concerned that the dyestuffs be available and dependable and that the dyed fabrics be colorfast and stain resistant.

All Believers had separate sets of clothing for everyday use and for Sabbath, and for summer and winter wear. There were also clothes for the transition seasons. Surprisingly, in fact, individual Shakers had a great deal of clothing—far more than their typical contemporaries. In the "Circular Concerning the Dress of Believers," the New Lebanon ministry remarked in 1866:

> It is believed that few people on earth, in proportion to their numbers, spend so much for dress, as do the Shakers; few who have so many suits, and such a variety of clothing on hand at once, belonging to the individual! Often times several changes to the season that are supernumary!

The following list of "sister's wearing apparel" deemed proper by a Hancock eldress in 1840 is quoted in its entirety because it is interesting to see how many clothes these "simple" people could have ("do" means "ditto"):

2 cloaks—gray and drab
2 habits—drab and butternut
1 overgown to milk in, etc.
1 or 2 worsted gowns—good
2 worsted gowns—poor
1 cotton and worsted do—good
2 cotton and worsted or cotton and wool [do] for common use
2 drugged [drugget] or woolen for everyday with an old one
    for washing, etc.
1 blue and white striped riding gown
2 light colored [do] striped
1 white for those that wear them and 1 light stripes
1 bengall or some other decent striped
2 common summer gowns with some old wash—do
1 flannel petticoat—good
2 flannel do—poor
1 worsted do to wear under a gown
1 to wear without a gown of some sort, for those who choose it.
    The skirt of an old gown does well.
1 cotton white or striped nice petticoat
2 cotton or linen for everyday
3 shimes [shimmies, or chemises] for summer—cotton or linen
3 shimes for winter—cotton or linen

2   flannel [do], 1 good, 1 poor—2 if you have them
3   or 4 silk neck handkerchiefs—good. Some common.
1   or 2 silk head handkerchiefs
8   white cotton or muslin neck handkerchiefs
6   light check do
6   blue and blue check do
1   some kind to wear on the head in common. The above are
       thought sufficient with some cotton and worsted.
2   nice aprons, worsted, cotton and worsted
1   good check [do] or striped
8   common for different kinds of work
2   or 3 white handkerchiefs
2   check do, good (or nice)
8   for everyday use
4   or 6 collars—good
8   poor and for common use
1   pair worsted stockings
2   pair woolen stockings—good
3–5   pair woolen—everyday
2   pair cotton
2   pair linen (for those that can't wear cotton)
5   pair cotton and linen for everyday
1–2   pair shoes, blue cloth, good
1   pair shoes—calf skin
2–4   pair butternut (with blue) [do] for everyday
1   pair thick leather shoes for washing
1   pair over socks, nice
1   pair over socks, every day
1   nice palm leaf bonnet
1   common with old for everyday
1   pair nice gloves
1   pair common
1   pair mittens [18]

Altogether, 130 items are mentioned. It is interesting to note that even in this list, written with the intention of assuring a certain degree of standardization, allowance is made for individual variation. "Those who choose" to wear a separate petticoat (skirt) are given the leeway to do so. White riding gowns are specified "for those that wear them," but are not made mandatory for everyone. Color is not specified at all for some of the articles—neck handkerchiefs, for example—and a certain degree of choice was presumably allowed for them. Some leeway is also allowed in acceptable material—cotton could be chosen over linen, or "some other decent" striped cloth could be substituted for bengall in a riding gown.

Tailoring and Clothing Production

In addition to choosing high quality materials for their clothing, the Shakers always emphasized good tailoring and good fit. From the very earliest days in New Lebanon, a tailoring shop was established, managed by David Slosson, who had been a tailor before he became a Shaker. He trained other New Lebanon brethren, and they in turn helped train tailors in other communities.[19]

Brother Slosson's shop made clothing for the men of the community and, at times, for men of the outside world. No tailors ever made clothing for the sisters, although female "tailoresses" did at times make clothes for the brethren.[20] In the eighteenth century the coats, vests, breeches, trousers, collars, hats, and so on that were produced by the tailor shop were primarily made from material the Believers wove themselves. Later on, as we have seen, much of the material and many of the garments were purchased from the outside world.

In 1825 the New Lebanon tailor shop was substantially reorganized, and greater standardization was stressed. In 1828 "A Short Treatise on the Processing of Cutting by the Square and Plumb Rule with some general observations on the business of tailoring" was written by a Shaker tailor, possibly from that shop, as a guide for other Shaker tailors.[21] This careful, well organized treatise gave detailed instructions for the best ways of cutting trousers, greatcoats, jackets, and surtouts (overcoats), and the author hoped that when other tailors were equipped with "scientific" instructions, their work would be uniformly excellent.

Other similar treatises followed. An anonymous New Lebanon tailor recorded the measurements of individual Believers in the year

FIGURE 86. *Tailoring equipment from Hancock Shaker Village. Top to bottom: tailor's shears, compass, and curved ruler. The curve was to accommodate measurement of a (curving) shoulder.*

1838 and left precise instructions for "drafting pantaloons," jackets, and so forth, for these individuals, for the use of his successors at New Lebanon and his counterparts in other Shaker communities.

In 1849, a tailor named Hervey L. Eades of Union Village, Ohio, determined to prove that tailoring was a science that anyone could learn with the proper instruction, wrote the "Tailor's System for Cutting Shaker's Garments." Referring to himself in the third person, he described his own beginnings:

> His first efforts in the art of tailoring were in the year 1836, without a teacher. . . . He was recommended . . . to take some scientific work published on the subject for a short season, which would lead into the principles of the article [of clothing] . . .

Eades divided the body into a series of angles, planes, and proportions, as the illustration indicates, and he gave instructions for coordinating them all in the proper relationship. Paper patterns were included. His system was flexible, and he even gave such special guidelines as the proper way to fit a "corpulent person." Judging from his references to the ministry and ministerial approval, we can surmise that Eades wrote this treatise for tailors in other Shaker communities. Reference is also made to the fact that patterns were sent from Union Village to New Lebanon.

"Systems" and treatises were also written by Shaker seamstresses. One, probably from New Lebanon, created the "Dressmaker's Magick Scale," a system of pattern relationships similar to Eades's but focusing on the sister's gown rather than the brother's jacket. Written as a series of lessons, with "practice for beginners" and methods for substituting individual measurements, the book gave separate instructions for drafting each part of a Shaker gown: front, back, sleeves, waist, and so on.

Tailoring and dressmaking instructions were also exchanged in person. Shaker journals are full of references like New Lebanon sister Sally Bushnell's diary note that "Frederick Wicker [was] in our P.M. meeting; he is teaching the different families about cutting clothes for the Brethren" (May 3, 1857).

Efficiency was stressed in all aspects of tailoring and sewing. According to Dana Goodrich, an eldress at Hancock, Mother Ann was

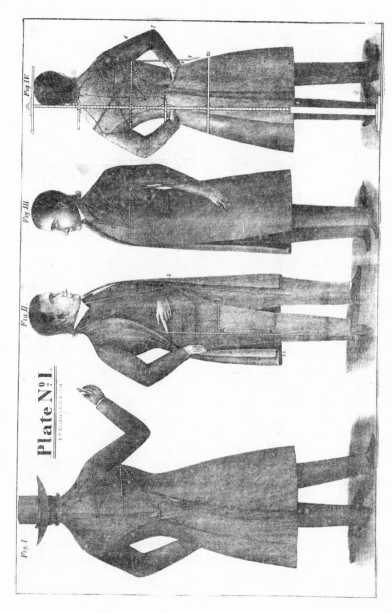

FIGURE 87. *A diagram from the "Tailor's System for Cutting Shaker's Garments" by Hervey Eades from Union Village, Ohio.*

specific about the most efficient way to mend clothes: "She taught us
to mend them in season, and not let them go 'till it would take double
the time, cloth, and thread to repair them."²² The 1866 New Lebanon
circular on uniformity in Shaker clothing called efficiency of this kind
a way of "saving anxiety." The diaries of the sisters who worked in the
sewing room speak often of mending. "I have worked at the shop this
week altering and mending gowns" is a typical entry, written by Harvard sister Mary Babbitt on June 2, 1854.

Material from clothing that was no longer serviceable or fashionable was often cut up and reused. "I commenced to work over my
linen mantilla made at Canterbury into an overgown by putting on a
cape and putting in sleeves," wrote New Lebanon Eldress Polly Ann
Reed on June 12, 1873. The preceding April she had written that they
"spent the week in making . . . over silk handkerchiefs." In 1892 an
anonymous New Lebanon sister wrote:

> I attempted to repair my worsted gown. . . . The cloth cannot be
> less than 70 years old, at least some parts of it, the cloth having
> been made for Mother Lucy. . . . [The] dress was inherited from
> Molly Bennet.²³

The Shakers were also willing to use unfashionable clothing or material from the outside world. On February 19, 1872, Polly Ann Reed
noted that she "went to [a] shawl factory in Troy and got shawls which
were out of fashion." These shawls—80 in all—were sold to the Believers at a substantial discount.

Despite the attempt to make the tailor and dressmaking shops efficient, uniform, and "scientific," the daily routine was always varied.
Work was not mechanized. Believers were always willing to help one
another out, and sisters often exchanged sewing jobs. Mary Babbitt,
speaking in the third person, wrote in her diary that "M. finished off
her gown and cut one for the Elder Sister (Debage) and worked on
it in exchange for her helping on the carpet" (April 2, 1860). Polly
Ann Reed mentioned that she "cut out a couple of drab delain gowns"
and that another sister took them "after the breadths were sewed together and the facing on and plaited them for us" (April 1872). The
sisters' journals also contain references to working on clothing for the
brethren.

FIGURE 88. *This small (about two-inch square) patch on a handwoven silk neckerchief is indicative of Shaker mending. The underside of the patch is shown. (Hancock Shaker Village)*

Although they were not concerned with high-fashion styles, flattering lines, or frivolous adornment, the Shakers remained sensitive to good design and fine detail. Clothing was so well fashioned that Believers could take pride in a well-turned coat or the stylistic detail on a sleeve. The following description of one of the first standardized items of clothing—a brother's Sabbath coat—gives an idea of the kind of tailoring detail that the Shakers might be proud of:

> That which was adopted as a uniform for Sabbaths for the adult males, was a blue, fulled-cloth coat, with a cape, coming up to the neck, and lying down flat to the shoulders.
>
> Cuffs about six inches long, to the sleeves, with pockets at the waist, and large flaps, covering the pocket holes, the upper edge of which set on the line of the waist, which line was about to the hollow of the back.
>
> The front edge of the coat was nearly strait, with six or eight buttons, and very long button holes, perhaps three inches long. Some of the button holes were wôrked with a double stitch, called "false button hole," with no holes cut through the cloth. Also a portion of double stitch was often worked on at the inner end for ornament.
>
> On the back side of the coat, at the lower extremity of each side seam, was a large double fold or plait, on the forebody side, taking about three inches of cloth and folded twice, making about one inch wide and one inch on the back to correspond. At the waist of the back was a large "square stitching," three or four inches long, and about one fourth as wide, and a button at the head of each fold and also one at the bottom. Length of the coat, a little below the knee.[24]

The sleeve seen in Figure 89 illustrates the kind of subtle detail the Shakers delighted in. It is the bottom of a close-fitting, full-length sleeve, with no cuff, on a simple brown and white striped linen gown, probably made about 1870. At what is probably the selvedge of the fabric, a decorative element is achieved by working a group of seven textured stripes into the weft (each stripe made with four or five thicknesses of weft thread instead of just one). The textured stripes are on the bias, placed about the middle of the forearm, and are emphasized by another wedge of fabric, also having border stripes, added at the

FIGURE 89. *The sleeve on this linen dress illustrates the kind of subtle tailoring detail that the Shakers used in their clothing. (Hancock Shaker Village)*

FIGURE 90. *This collar (stock) is covered with red- and black-striped silk on the outside and is lined with blue cotton decorated with white dots. (Hancock Shaker Village)*

bottom of the sleeve. Similar stripe treatment was used near the neck of the dress, an area that was completely covered with a collar and a large kerchief.

There are many other details in Shaker clothing, not obvious to the casual observer, which the Believer himself was well aware of. The linings of the sisters' dresses, for example, were often made with cheerfully patterned cotton cloth. The brethren's neck covering, or "stock," was of a stiff material about three inches wide covered with cloth. In the late nineteenth century, stocks were often made from special colored or patterned silk materials, with as many as three different patterns in a single stock.

Sisters' Clothing

Dresses and Bodice Coverings

The clothing of the early Shakers, as we have seen, was no different from the clothing of their contemporaries: it was only as styles changed that the Shakers, who retained their original fashions, began to look old-fashioned and "peculiar."

In the late eighteenth century, rural women in the northeastern part of America generally wore a work outfit consisting of a "short-gown" (a long-sleeved jacket-like bodice covering which typically fastened in front, was gathered at the waist, and extended to about hip length) and a petticoat—not an undergarment but a full, gathered skirt. The shortgown was covered by a square neckerchief folded in half to form a triangle and draped over the shoulders, and the petticoat was protected by a long apron.[25] A white cap and a bonnet completed the costume.

The first "uniform dress" of the Shaker sisters, according to Isaac Young ("A Concise View of the Church"), was an outfit of just this type. It was the standardized type of cloth, the color, and the exact cut of the garments that made them uniform, rather than any unusual style. In the summer the New Lebanon Sabbath outfit included a worsted petticoat, first black and later blue, which was worn with a "light colored striped short gown made of linen which the sisters had

FIGURE 91. *A linen shortgown made and used by the Pennsylvania Germans. The style and material is probably similar to the shortgown worn by the Shaker sisters in the eighteenth century. (Schwenkfelder Museum)*

spun and woven themselves." The gown had sleeves that extended to just below the elbow, with stripes which "went roundwise of the arm."

> Over the gown in front was a [blue and white] checked Apron, two breadths wide (about 1½ yard wide) cut hollowing at the top, and nicely gathered, to about two feet in breadth and the top, with a white binding, an inch wide, and white tape strings that were brot round before, and tied in a double bow.

After about 1800 the same type of gown and apron was made of cotton.[26]

For a short while, the sisters wore "black silk shoulder handkerchiefs" over the bodice of the dress. These were replaced by "fine white lawn [cotton] or linen [handkerchiefs which were] neatly spread and pinned over the shoulders."[27]

The sisters' outfits for regular days was very similar. They wore "petticoats, the same as on Sabbaths, excepting [of] a plainer quality, and striped linen short gowns." Instead of the plain white neckerchief, they wore "blue and white checked handkerchiefs with a conspicuous blue border."[28]

Everyday dress in the winter consisted of a woolen drugget petticoat and a drugget shortgown. The color was not specified, but Young said the gown had a "bias at the waist behind . . . , a long waist down to the hips, and a skirt eight or ten inches long."[29]

On Sabbath days, or "for nice use," "some wore a kind of plaited gown, coming a little below the knees, and some wore long gowns." The long gown was usually made of butternut colored worsted cloth,

> [with the] waist fitted snug to the back and hips. Under the gown they wore stays, laced tight around the body, which kept the gown in good shape. The waist of the gown ran down the back in the center, two or three inches wide, to a point. The sleeves came just below the elbow, and had plaited cuffs, fitted to the bend of the arm. The gowns were open before, and had two box plaits in the skirt behind, and from them single plaits, about half an inch apart, and laid towards the hips, and there met the plaits from before.
>
> With these gowns they wore blue and white check Aprons similar to those for summer dress. And blue cotton handkerchiefs, with two or three white borders, about ⅜ of an inch wide, and about ½ an inch apart.[30]

When kerchiefs were worn, the border design outlined the triangular shape, with the apex falling just below the waist. When the sisters were working, they often pinned this point of the kerchief up, out of their way (Figures 8, 12, and 93).

Henry Blinn, an elder at Canterbury, also wrote extensively about the clothing the Believers wore over the years. His description of the early outfit of the sisters in his community was essentially the same as Young's, but he referred to a worsted dress that may have been of one piece: the "hemline on the bottom of the skirt was about four inches from the floor," and the skirt "opened some eight or ten inches to the front to make the dress easy to put on."[31]

This early costume must have given the effect of today's "layered look." The full petticoat skirt was covered by the hip-length (or longer) skirt of the shortgown, which had a fitted waistline. The apron was generally tied beneath the skirt, or peplum, of the shortgown, although sometimes above it; in either case, it covered the front of the petticoat. On the top half of the body, the gown was covered by the large neckerchief.

Shortly after 1800 the clothing of both the sisters and the brethren underwent radical changes. Young tells us:

> About the year 1806, foreign muslin was introduced, after which the sisters never made much cloth [for clothing of this kind.] In the year 1810 the sisters began to wear white cotton or linen collars, buttoned on the neck in front, with a cape attached, and spreading out on the shoulders, and over this the common shoulder handkerchief. Before this, the neck was bare, so far as the handkerchief did not cover it. Girls have worn these collars, without any handkerchief over them.[32]

Blinn's journal also records that the sisters adopted a collar in this period, but he sets the date a little earlier:

> Mother Lucy Wright sent the first collar to Canterbury in 1801 that was made for the Sisters and the same year a company of Sisters, visitors here from New Lebanon, wore them while at this place. Previously the Sisters had worn what was called a "tucker." The tucker was a narrow collar of fine white cloth attached to the chemise which was worn under the dress.
>
> The collars were put on before the neckerchief was put into place. Like everything else they changed general shape and size over the years. At first it had a turnover and fastened with a removable collar button.

In 1811 the general contour of the outfit was changed: dresses became longer and narrower. According to Young,

> Long gowns were adopted altogether for summer and winter dress. They were made short waisted behind. The hind breadth

was plaited, or gathered, and the side breadths were slanted, and to the front side was attached an apron, of the same cloth. With this they left wearing separate aprons, for meeting dress.[33]

Blinn describes the narrower dresses in a little more detail, although he does not say clearly what year the style was adopted in Canterbury. It is possible that not all the details in his description apply to the dresses worn in New Lebanon or other communities, of course, but the styles were essentially similar.

[The dresses] were made with short waists, about two or three inches below the armscye [armhole] and the skirts very narrow. The cloth from which they were made was woven twenty eight inches wide. One breadth was used for the back and one for the front or apron with gores set in at the sides, thirteen inches at the top and twenty seven at the bottom for a medium sized person. The front or so-called apron of the dress was plaited into a binding having two single plaits each side of the center box plait, the side plaits about an inch and a half apart.

The "so-called apron" was a feature of the sisters' dresses throughout the nineteenth century and even into the twentieth. It was a stylistic or aesthetic device and had none of the practical advantages of a detachable apron—it could not be washed separately, for one thing. We have no information about why the vestigial apron was adopted or why it remained popular for so long, though it might have become psychologically necessary because, like the kerchief, it was an integral part of the Shaker outfit. Separate protective aprons were still worn for messy work even after this style was adopted.

Blinn continues his description of the dresses made in the first quarter of the nineteenth century:

A little later, worsted dresses had four box plaits in the back, and each had a one and one fourth surface. The gore plait was made to face these being 1½ inches distant. Cotton dresses were gathered in the back and ironed into single plaits, 2 or 3 on a side. They seem to have returned again to blue and white stripes for the whole dress this time for we are told that the stripes passed horizontally around the sleeves but lengthwise on the skirt. The sleeves were about half length as before stated. Waists gradually lengthened as time passed until they measured some four or five inches from the armscye.

Long sleeves were introduced in 1827, Blinn tells us, on both summer and winter dresses, and have generally remained the style until the present day.

The style of the gowns remained essentially the same through the first half of the century; colors and materials, however, did vary. An 1838 observer remarked that the sisters' winter dress was wine-colored alpaca, drugget, or worsted, and that the summer dress was white muslin or "very light striped."[34] Young mentions that after 1835 the sisters "under 40 or 50 years of age [wore] white cotton gowns on sabbaths in summer; and the older ones wore a variety of light colored striped."[35] The older sisters may have been more inclined to stay with the tradition that they had known.

An all-white Sabbath costume was adopted even earlier in some communities; as a color representing purity, white was symbolically fitted to Sabbath use. In Union Village the sisters appeared in meeting on June 10, 1827, with white dresses, and one Believer remarked that they "looked like a crowd of saints."[36] Many observers at Shaker meetings also remarked on the white outfit, though their comments were not invariably flattering. Seth Chandler, describing the Shakers of either New Lebanon or Hancock in 1850, wrote that the females were "in frocks or robes of snowy whiteness,"[37] but to another visitor they looked "like a gaggle of geese."[38]

In 1855 the New Lebanon ministry gave the sisters permission to alter their dress style, allowing four or five additional pleats on each side of the skirt, "where they were formerly smooth." Young says the style was adopted by "some who choose it";[39] apparently not every sister took to it immediately. Blinn noted that the skirts were made much wider in 1856, so it must have taken about a year for the new style to travel from New Lebanon to Canterbury. The waists were also lengthened at this time "until they became some 5½ inches from the armscye." Sister Myra Greene, "who at the time of the Civil War was a grown woman," told Blinn that the sisters wore what they called "war dresses" at that time; apparently it was difficult to get dyestuffs, and color choices were therefore limited. Sister Myra said the war dresses were made from a cloth of black and white thread—probably

FIGURE 92. *Shaker dress made in the last quarter of the nineteenth century. Note the five plaits (pleats) on each side of the central "apron"; the long, cuffless sleeve; the patterned collar trim; the bodice pocket; and the horizontal pleats on the arms and the skirt hem. (Hancock Shaker Village)*

FIGURE 93. *Two sisters in Enfield, Connecticut, in the last quarter of the nineteenth century. White collars are visible under their bodice kerchiefs. Note that the tip of the kerchief on the sister at left (Miriam Offord) is pinned up above the waist. This was often done while a sister was working. The sister at right is unidentified.*

the black was actually the dark indigo blue of "Parker mixed" cloth, which appeared to be a mottled gray.

For a time in the 1860's, the Canterbury sisters wore jackets and skirts, much as they had in the eighteenth century, instead of full dresses.[40] This was a short-lived style, and may not have been adopted at all in other communities.

Neckerchiefs were always worn with the regular waisted dress. Before 1840 they were typically the dark blue cotton with white border stripes mentioned by Blinn, or dark drab-color silk. Dove-colored kerchiefs were "worn at funerals and on Christmas."[41] White kerchiefs became the norm after about 1840—muslin for everyday, and silk for Sabbath.[42] Many kerchiefs were colorful, however, and judging from the excellent condition of those which remain today, they must have been highly prized. They were of brightly colored silk woven in the southwestern communities, most notably South Union, Kentucky: pink, rose, orange, purple, and shades of blue. Believers from the South sometimes gave them to the northern sisters as special gifts. They were also sold; David Parker traveled to South Union in the 1850's and bought a number of them for the sisters at Canterbury.[43]

A great many recipes for dyeing silk appear in Shaker receipt books, with "scarlet," orange, "slate color," "blood red," and yellow particularly specified for this use; and at least some of these colors must have been intended for kerchiefs.

The Sabbathday Lake collection has two examples of full-sized silk kerchiefs (about 25 inches square), originally white, that had been tie-dyed. First, small regularly spaced squares were tied off tightly while the silk was dyed red. The silk was then bound in additional places and put in a blue dyebath. When the bindings were removed, the squares that were tied off in both dyebaths remained white, and the squares that were tied off in the second, blue dyebath remained red. The body of the kerchief, subjected to both red and blue dyebaths, became purple (Figure 94). The design in both kerchiefs, carefully planned and controlled, is exactly the same. They were probably dyed and used in Alfred in the nineteenth century, and are possibly only two from a number of similar scarves.

Neckerchiefs were fastened in front, at about breastbone level, with a straight pin. This practice was developed not by the Shakers but by the people of the world; straight pins were generally in vogue for fastening women's garments in the late eighteenth century, and women who were too isolated or impoverished to get them sometimes substituted thorns of the prickly ash tree.[44] The Shaker shortgown, and later the long gown or one-piece dress, were also fastened in this way.

About 1875, the neckerchief began to be replaced by a half cape, or bertha. These were worn in the world as early as the 1840's, in a number of different styles but all covering the shoulders and fastening in front. Those worn by the Shakers were almost semicircular in shape (Figures 95, 96) and were often made of the same material as the dress, though by the end of the century silk was the most popular material for them. Often they had an attached, stand-up collar, thus eliminating the need for a separate collar. The straight pin was aban-

1

2

3

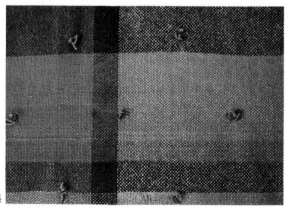

4

PLATE 1. *These cloth swatches show that even when the Shakers used a standard color stripe, subtle variations were frequently found. (Hancock Shaker Village)*

PLATE 2. *The interior of a needle case made early in the nineteenth century. The colorful prints were also popular in the world at this time. (Hancock Shaker Village)*

PLATE 3. *Corner detail of a handwoven blanket. This simple twill-check design was typical of Shaker weaving. The colors in the blanket were dyed with indigo and madder. (Hancock Shaker Village)*

PLATE 4. *Areas of gradated color are evident in this detail of a tufted coverlet made in Canterbury in 1880. (Hancock Shaker Village)*

PLATE 5. *Corner detail of a long runner made in alternating stripes of wine-red velvet and blue and white worsted cloth. (Hancock Shaker Village)*

PLATE 6. *Detail of a rag rug made entirely of plied-cloth strips. (Hancock Shaker Village)*

PLATE 7. *Detail of a rag rug made of alternating strips of wool rags with plied-wool and cotton yarns. Note how both S and Z twists are used. (Hancock Shaker Village)*

5

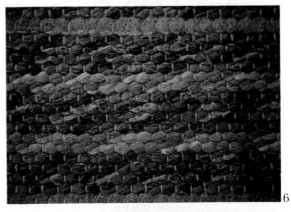

6

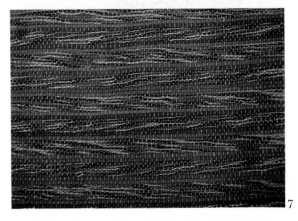

7

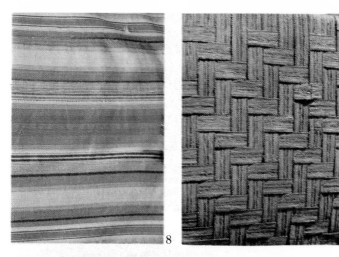

8   10

9

PLATE 8. *Detail of a large, warp-faced rug with a well planned complex design of gradated colors. The unit visible in this photograph is only a part of the whole design. The warp sequence is analyzed in Appendix* 2. *(Hancock Shaker Village)*

PLATE 9. *Detail of a round knit rug in the collection of the Shaker Museum at Old Chatham, New York. Note the central area, knit in a tubular fashion; the flat, patterned rings around it; and the two rows of braided border.*

PLATE 10. *View of a chair seat covered with colorful, handwoven tape of wool or linen. Some of the colors are plied together, creating a diagonal effect in the finished tape. (Hancock Shaker Village)*

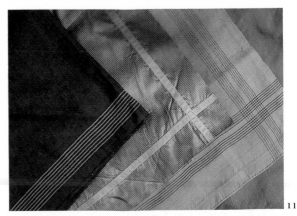

13

11

PLATE 11. *Details of silk kerchiefs woven in Kentucky or Ohio. Note the fine weaving, rich colors, and subtle blended shades. (Hancock Shaker Village)*

PLATE 12. *This sister's shoe is covered with a bright "ultramarine" blue-cotton cloth. Note the shaped high heel. (Hancock Shaker Village)*

PLATE 13. *Interior of a sewing box covered with poplar cloth. The rich pink color of the satin lining is typical of these Victorian boxes. A hand-carved spool of silk thread, a strawberry emery, and a poplar-cloth needle folder are included inside. The white-kid edging is clearly visible. (Hancock Shaker Village)*

PLATE 14. *Detail of a crazy quilt made early in the twentieth century. The bright, cheerful colors and the pink binding are unusual for quilts of this type. (Hancock Shaker Village)*

12

14

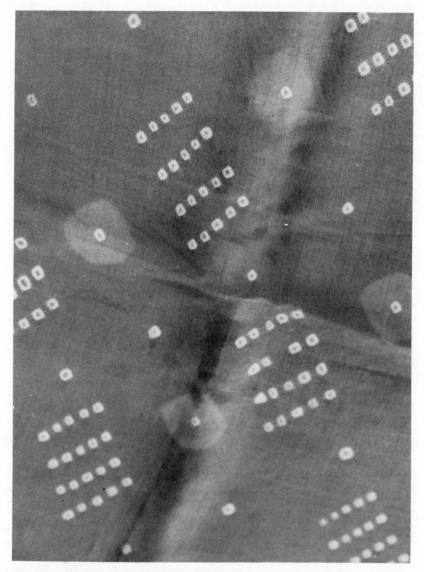

FIGURE 94. *Detail of tie-dyed silk kerchief in the collection at Sabbathday Lake, Maine. The white squares were formed by the first binding of the cloth, and the larger red squares were formed by the second binding.*

FIGURE 95. *Bertha-trimming details are well illustrated in this photograph from Canterbury, New Hampshire. Note also the large number of pleats in the skirts, the net caps, and the straw bonnets with silk capes.*

doned in favor of a row of buttons which ran the length of the front opening.

One reason the bertha was adopted may have been that outerwear had begun to change. Closely fitted cloaks were becoming more popular among Believers—and kerchiefs wrinkled badly when they were covered by a cloak. The bertha was thicker and fuller bodied, and it was constructed from flat pieces of cloth, rather than folded on a bias, so that it could keep its shape well even when covered.

The main reason that Shaker sisters began to wear berthas, however, was probably a desire to be a little more fashionable; the outmoded triangular neckerchiefs had been worn for a full hundred years. A bertha covered the bodice in essentially the same way as a neckerchief and was more in keeping with the styles and sensibilities of the day. Most berthas had some kind of trimming—usually lace or rickrack of some kind—which followed the contour of the bottom hem, often with a second row added near the neckline. The trimming carried on the same visual function as the border on the scarf: it drew the eye downward, to just below the waist.

The sisters presumably made their own berthas, whereas they had not usually made their own kerchiefs. Standards for absolute uniformity had relaxed considerably by this time, and berthas varied quite a bit, in general reflecting much more individual taste than the neckerchiefs. Regional variations were also a factor. Berthas made in and near the New Lebanon bishopric often had rounded necklines, while those made in New Hampshire and Maine had a more V-shaped neck. Victorian influence is seen in the extensive use of velvets, fringe, and ruffles.

The bertha did not completely replace the neckerchief overnight; a great many photographs taken between 1875 and 1890 show both being worn. Again, individual comfort and preference were the determining factors (Figures 12, 105).

By the time the bertha had taken hold, the skirt of the sister's dress was changing once again. More and more cloth was added. Blinn says:

> In the '80's and '90's and in fact until about 1915 ten yards in the skirt was not unusual in order that there might be enough cloth to make the pleats of about 1″ in surface width. To make the skirt set properly a crinoline or very full skirt was worn beneath it.

FIGURE 96. *A silk bertha from the late nineteenth century. The lace trimming at the top, middle, and bottom is a sign of late Victorian taste. (Hancock Shaker Village)*

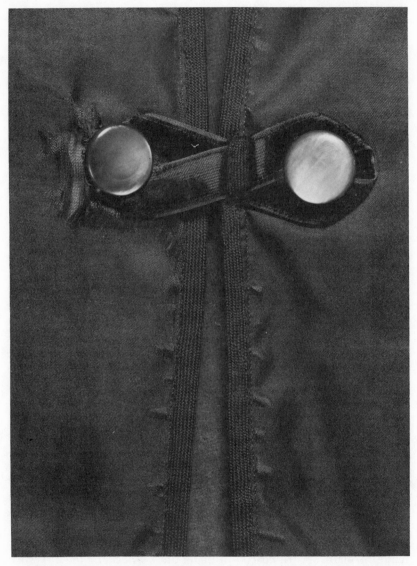

FIGURE 97. *The frog-button fastening on this silk bertha is a velvet ribbon shaped into a figure eight. Similar closing details were found on cloaks of the 1870's and 1880's. (Hancock Shaker Village)*

Then the first World War came and cloth became expensive and hard to get.

Most of these full skirts also had one or two extra horizontal pleats about five inches from the bottom hem, and a wool braid trimming that was sewn to the inside of the hem. In some, cotton or wool lined the bottom few inches. These details added body and weight so that the skirt was fuller and stood out better around the ankles. The braid trimming, being closest to the floor, was able to protect and prolong the life of the skirt, for it, rather than the skirt itself, collected dust and was exposed to wear. It could be removed easily and cleaned separately, or replaced entirely (Figures 73, 92).

In the 1890's the sisters in some communities wore fashionable blouses that were probably made in the world. Judging from photographs taken at this period, these were not uniform in style, color, or material. They were worn with a long skirt, and no kerchief or bertha covered them. Contemporary hairstyles were sometimes also adopted during this period (Figure 98). For the most part, however, the Shakers retained their unique clothing, and one-piece dresses remained the basic style through the twentieth century. They became more individualized. After World War I, a gored or gathered skirt was adopted, replacing the formal box pleats, and it was shortened to mid-calf length. Sleeves usually remained long, but they sometimes became fuller and had cuffs or ruffles. Sleeves were lined with colorful materials that matched the lining in the neck and hem. Whereas earlier dresses had no fastenings other than straight pins at the neckline (to attach the front panels of the bodice) and the apron (to attach it to the bodice), twentieth-century dresses had full-length zippers.

In addition to their gowns, the sisters wore various sorts of workdresses. "Milking gowns" were probably plain cotton or linen overdresses or smocks; they were intended to protect other clothing and thus had no detailed tailoring. Generally, workdresses made in the second half of the nineteenth century were also smocks, which were fastened in front by a long row of buttons running from the neck to the bottom hem. Round-necked and collarless, they were typically made of plain or striped cotton material. No neckerchief was worn with them.

Present-day Shaker women wear a modified version of the tradi-

FIGURE 98. *A photograph taken in the New Lebanon sewing room in the* 1890's, *showing sisters wearing fashionable blouses and skirts.*

tional dress, though individual styles vary a good deal. Typically made in one piece and having long sleeves, the dress has a hemline falling somewhere below the knee, depending on individual taste. A bertha-shaped flap of material on the bodice is often attached as an integral part of the dress, and lace neckline trimming is even more pronounced than in the older berthas. The sisters use any fabric that suits them. Bright flowery prints are not uncommon.

Caps and Bonnets

The sisters wore white caps at all times from the earliest days of their society, when a white cap was an essential part of the costume of all women, both Shaker and non-Shaker. In the eighteenth century the caps were made of fine lawn or of linen which the sisters had prepared. According to Isaac Young,

> They were formed by plaiting and gathering, so as to fit to the head behind, being strait before, with a border about an inch wide, with open work, so as not to obstruct the sight sidewise.
> There was a wide hem behind, in which was inserted tape-strings, that were brot up over the head, and down again, and tied behind. The cap was also secured to the fillet by a pin.
> Also there were tape strings at the lower part before, that might be tied under the chin.[45]

Unfortunately, no caps known to have been made in this early period have been identified, so it is hard for us to picture them.

About 1806 imported muslin replaced homemade linen for the caps, but the style remained the same until 1819, when, according to Young,

> the crowns were larger and cut in the form of a half circle. On the circling side was a wide hem, in which was inserted a tape string (as in the former caps) by which to draw up the cap. The foreside of the caps, was a straight piece, about three inches wide, and fifteen or sixteen inches long, on one side of which was set a border of leno, or open work, as on the former caps, and the other side was set to the straight side of the crown, without any gathering.
> These caps were ironed out flat and smooth, and then drawn or gathered up by the tape, to fit the head, as aforesaid.[46]

In 1838 the caps were described as "white muslin and bordered with lace, not crimped, but smooth and starched stiff."[47]

During the Victorian period caps underwent further modification. In 1872 Eldress Polly Ann Reed's journal mentions "the latest fashion lace caps . . . with only one thread in the forepiece and no strings" and "new grenadine caps with round ears." When the new style was approved, the sisters made a great many caps at once so that they could all be in style; they "had a bee at the ironing room to starch, iron and draw up the sisters new grenadine caps."⁴⁸ By 1878 net caps had been adopted in the same community. Elizabeth Reclus, a visitor to the New Lebanon Shakers at that time, described a "would-be cap of transparent net stretched on a wire frame."⁴⁹ Blinn describes a cap which he says replaced the muslin cap "as years progressed into the twentieth century." He claims that a "bunch of tin covered with black broadcloth" attached to the "comb" served to keep the cap rigid and away from the face. In fact, most Shaker sisters today wear net caps set off from the face (Figure 102). Twentieth-century caps have many individual styling details, probably added as finishing touches.

When the sisters went out, they wore hats or bonnets over their white caps.

> From the gathering of the Church till 1805, females wore for going abroad, what was called a *chip hat* of braided straw. It was covered inside and out with black silk, the crown was about an inch high, or deep, with a band of silk, of the same width, and lain in fine plaits cross wise the band.
>
> Silk strings of riban were sewed to the crown about central, and brought down over the brim, and tied behind the neck. The brim was six or seven inches wide.
>
> After [1805] the *Dress up*, as it was called (meaning the nicest outside headdress) changed from chip hats, to plain simple Bonnets, much similar to those worn by Quakers, but deeper or longer, projecting more forward of the face. These were made of paste-boards nicely covered with silk, of lightish color. The crown was all made of cloth, fitted to the shape of the head, by plaiting, and set to the forward part. This kind of bonnet had no capes to them.⁵⁰

Blinn describes similar bonnets worn at Canterbury. Under them, the sisters wore white cotton hoods, "starched quite stiff and ironed so that they might help keep the cap unharmed," with attached capes. The hoods were abandoned, but capes "were attached to the bonnets for common use as early as 1810. These were made of a cheaper article, as cotton or cambric. . . . In 1825 capes two inches deep were attached to the silk bonnets. The plaits were made smaller and the number increased."

Palm-leaf bonnets replaced pasteboard-and-silk bonnets between 1827 and 1830. Palm leaves, imported from Cuba by the bale, were split, sized, and dampened, then threaded individually through a wooden needle and woven into rectangular pieces ("chips"). The chips were varnished on one side and lined with fine cloth on the other. (The earliest bonnets were not covered with cloth.) Each chip was cut into two pieces; one half became the main piece—the part that curved around the top of the head—and the other became the semi-circular back piece. The bonnet was shaped over a mold, and supporting wires, concealed by a braided straw trimming, were sewn around the front edge and the back seam. Usually, a cape was attached to the bottom.[51] Bonnets of 1838 were described as made in a "cylindrical, ungula [hoof-like] shape, lined with white silk, and furnished with a veil of white lace."[52]

In Canterbury in 1859 the sisters made their bonnets by setting in crowns without pleats and attaching silk capes about six inches long running around both sides and covering the ears. Later on, the capes were shorter and narrower. For some time, according to Blinn, palm-leaf bonnets, which were worn both for "dress up and Every Day," were looked upon as quite a novelty.

The Civil War interrupted trade with Cuba, and palm leaf became difficult to obtain. Rye or oat straw replaced it as the materials from which chip cloths were woven, and bonnets were made in essentially the same way with the straw cloth.

In the later part of the nineteenth century, straw bonnets of a very rich appearance, obviously made for special occasions, were again sometimes covered with silk or a transparent material, such as lace net. Also, using silk and silk brocade, velvet, and cotton treated for water repellency, the sisters made quilted cloth bonnets for winter wear. They usually did the quilting on a sewing machine, and attached capes and wide silk chin ties to the finished bonnets.

Many Shaker sisters still wear bonnets when they go out (Figure 102). No straw bonnets have been made since the 1940's, however, and the sisters take great care of those which are still wearable. The need to get in and out of cars and the risk of hitting the bonnets against low metal car doors has proven treacherous to the fragile straw.

FIGURE 99. *Straw bonnet covered on both the inside and the outside with blue silk. Note that in this later style the bonnet cape stops short of the front of the bonnet, at about ear level. (Hancock Shaker Village)*

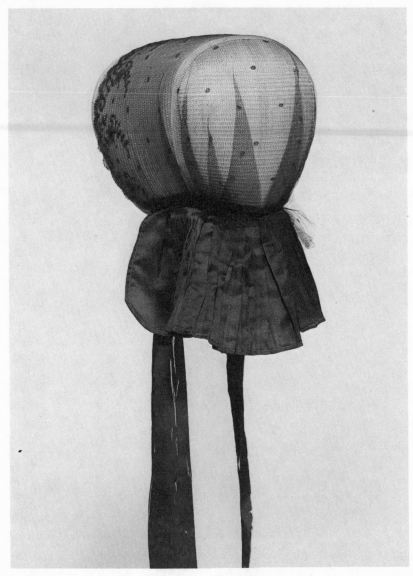

FIGURE 100. *Straw bonnet covered with black-lace net and lined with light-colored silk. Late nineteenth or early twentieth century. (Hancock Shaker Village)*

Shoes and Stockings

Sisters wore stockings they knitted themselves, from the first gathering of the Church until the twentieth century (Figure 40). They were usually hand knit, of cotton, linen, or wool, but were partly machine-made after machines became available. Generally, they were no different from those made in the world, except that the Shakers never incorporated fancy patterns in their knitting, as people in the world often did. Shaker stockings were well designed and highly respected, and one sister—Ada Cummings of Sabbathday Lake—was well known for her design of a superbly fitting gusset, or heel detail, around the turn of the century.[53] Later in the twentieth century, the sisters often bought stockings from the outside world, particularly after they began to wear shorter dresses, and sheerer stockings were in demand. Nowadays, most of them wear nylon stockings.

Farm women in the world usually went barefoot in the summer, but it seems that the Shaker sisters wore shoes. These were pumps, with thin soles and low heels. In the early years, however, high heels were fashionable; they were 1½ to 2 inches high, made of leather-covered wood, and were tapered from "the width of the shoe to about ¾" diameter at the wearing surface. The bearing of the heel was also made to be about 1½" forward from the end of the foot."[54]

The upper part was cloth for winter shoes and leather for summer shoes. Up until about 1810 they had brass buckles, which were replaced by laces. Most shoes were "formed on straight lasts, the toes of which were carried to a . . . sharp point," according to Blinn. Because of this, a shoe could be worn on either foot. "The shoes were sewed and a white band was placed around the edge. Some of the best-made shoes [from Canterbury] had 18 stitches to the inch with yellow silk." Until about the middle of the nineteenth century, each community had its own cobbler, who made up a permanent last for each adult Shaker. In later years Believers bought their shoes ready made from the outside world.

For winter in the first half of the nineteenth century, the sisters wore a type of "gaiter," or oversock—a sort of legging that covered the top of the foot and was held in place by a stirrup-like strap that fitted over the sole of the shoe. Many gaiters worn in the world were leather or fabric, but Shaker records refer to knitted gaiters.[55] Galoshes, which were made of leather or heavy cloth, or of rubber after 1845, were also worn by rural people in America—probably including the Shaker sisters. It is unlikely that the sisters wore pattens (a kind of clog made of metal and wood worn by rural New Englanders in mud season)[56] or the leather boots used by the brethren, but Young refers to "leather shoes to wash in, etc." and "overshoes for going abroad."[57]

In the late nineteenth and early twentieth centuries the sisters knitted and crocheted numerous slippers, "booties," and "footsocks" for sale to the outside world, and it is reasonable to assume that they also saved some for their own use. They must have used some kind of slipper at earlier periods as well, but no specific descriptions are available.

Underwear and Outerwear

Very little is known about the sisters' undergarments, for this was a subject the Shakers did not discuss. We do know, however, that "shimmies," or chemises (plain, full-length white slips) were worn at all times. In the early period, these sometimes had high necks that were visible over the shortgown;[58] later on, they had a simple round neckline and were often sleeveless. Chemises probably also served as nightwear.

The stays that Isaac Young mentioned (page 164, above) were not worn after 1811. It is unclear whether any other type of corsetry was used at any other time, but we can surmise it was not: the sisters did not have to mold their bodies to fit the latest fashions.

"Drawers," or underpants, were not commonly worn by women until the middle of the nineteenth century, and we can assume that this was as true for the Shaker sisters as for the women of the outside world. The first drawers were made of white cotton or linen and were long (about knee length) and loose. In the later part of the nineteenth century, long underwear was probably worn in the winter by the sisters as well as the brethren, although only men's long underwear has come to light.

The sisters also made warm gloves and mittens. Wool, cotton, linen, and silk were commonly used, and special fiber combinations such as raccoon fur and silk were also worked into gloves. Cotton wristlets (knitted tubes that slipped over the wrist and were worn when coat sleeves were short, at least in the world) were worn in some periods, as were mitts (fingerless gloves) (Figure 41). Mitts, usually made of silk, kid, or lace, were generally part of a dressy summer outfit in the world. Many Shaker mitts are of natural-color silk.

Shawls were worn indoors for extra warmth at least by the second half of the nineteenth century. Shawls and "mantillas" are mentioned in Shaker records by 1872.[59] The sisters both knitted and crocheted shawls, and no one style seems to have predominated. They also bought them from the world. Cashmere shawls were popular, both with the world's people and with the Shakers. Sweaters were also made in many of the northern communities.

We have only a little specific information about the outer garments the sisters wore before the second half of the nineteenth century. Young says that in the early years of the sect the sisters had "cloaks with hoods to turn up over the head . . . [and] a kind of riding hood, or over garment, quilted with cotton batting, thick and warm to ride in, in cold weather."[60] These same garments may have remained standard for many years: an 1838 visitor described "drab capuchins" (hooded cloaks) and "deep blue riding-cloaks" as winter garments.[61] In the world, short, tight jackets called spencers and three-quarter jackets called pelisses were worn in addition to cloaks, but it is unlikely that the Shaker sisters wore them. By the 1870's they wore cloaks made of wool broadcloth and partially or completely lined with silk or wrinkle-resistant material. These were hoodless, and three-quarter length, and they could be said to resemble overgrown berthas: they had upright velvet collars, figure-eight (frog) button fastenings (Figure 97), and decorative trim around the open armholes. Cloaks of this type were very popular with women of the world, and large numbers of them were sold in Shaker stores.

The best known Shaker cloak was the "Dorothy" cloak, designed about 1890 by Eldress Dorothy Durgin of Canterbury. It was a full-length cloak, without arm slits; open in front, it had a large shoulder cape and a heavily gathered attached hood. Long, wide, decorative silk ribbons tied under the chin; the front opening and hood were silk lined, and there were interior pockets in the silk lining.

The sisters wore dusters—so called because in the early days of open automobiles they protected the clothing from dust stirred up on

FIGURE 101. *Hancock Sister Anna Delchaff posing in a "Dorothy" cloak. The broad ties were made with fine silk ribbon that matched the silk in the hood lining.*

FIGURE 102. *Eldress Emma King and Sister (later Eldress) Gertrude Soule are shown standing in front of the meeting house in Hancock in 1963. Note their mid-calf length print dresses and their coats.*

unpaved roads by passing cars. Like cloaks, they had wide, almost cape-like collars and front openings, and were usually made of plain linen cloth.

At present, the sisters wear regular commercial coats of their own choosing (Figure 102).

Brethren's Clothing

Brethren's Outfits

The typical outfit for men in rural America in the late eighteenth century consisted of a white shirt covered by a waistcoat or vest (also called a jacket), a long coat (closer to a present-day jacket), knee breeches, and long stockings. Breeches began to be replaced by long trousers in this period, but there were many years when both breeches and trousers were fashionable. "Frocks," similar to the artist's smocks of today, were worn as work clothes.

The first Sabbath "uniform" that the Shaker brethren adopted, according to Isaac Young, was true to this fashion. It consisted of a white shirt, a blue waistcoat, a long blue wool coat, breeches, and long stockings. The waist of the vest (waistcoat) "came a little below the small of the back behind, and the waist line pitching quite a level before. The skirts, below the waist line, 7 to 9 inches long. Ten or twelve buttons on in front; and large pocket flaps set to the waist line."[62] The white shirt was collarless; it had rather full sleeves that were kept in place with blue worsted strings tied around the arm just above the elbow and fastened in a double bow knot.[63]

Breeches were either black or blue, and they extended to just below the knee, where they were fastened by a buckle. Three or four decorative buttons were placed at the outside of the knee. Long stockings were worn under the breeches and were held in place by a woven tape garter; these garters were worn by men in the world and presumably also by Shaker men. Besides being the Sabbath costume, breeches were worn when the Shakers went "journeying" outside the community.[64]

For everyday use in the late eighteenth century, the brethren wore long trousers made of a thick woolen cloth for winter wear and "mostly brown tow cloth" for summer. Everyday coats and vests were essentially the same as those worn on the Sabbath, but they were "made of grey, or other inferior colors."[65]

Dress styles changed as radically for the brethren in the early part of the nineteenth century as they did for the sisters. Breeches were almost completely replaced by long trousers, or pantaloons, about 1805. In the winter these were made of a thick, fulled wool or of worsted, usually brown or deep blue. Summer Sabbath trousers were blue and white checked linen or cotton, and summer everyday trousers were still of coarse tow cloth.[66]

Although they varied in length, breeches and early trousers were styled in essentially the same way. They were fitted at the waist with laces put through bound eyelets on each side of a gusset at the center back, and they had a double fall with two sets of buttons in the front. The buttons, of bone or wood, were covered with the same fabric used for the breeches or trousers. The legs of early trousers were cut very narrow and had no cuff. Blinn described them as "very difficult to get over boots." Later, they were cut more loosely.

Suspenders, or braces, were introduced in the world around 1787, but the Shakers did not wear them until about 1812.[67] Trouser waistlines had to be raised to accommodate them; the medium height of the new waistbands, according to Blinn, "was about 2 inches above the line level with the small of the back, whereas they had been cut an inch or two below before." The laces at the back of the trousers were eliminated when suspenders came in. The brethren may not have worn suspenders at all times—possibly only when a coat covered the shirt sleeves. James Silk, an Englishman visiting a Sabbath meeting in 1841, commented that "there were neither straps to keep [the trousers] down, nor braces to suspend them upward."[68]

The colors of the fabrics used in the trousers varied, although the styles remained basically the same. From 1811 to 1820, Young tells us, they were dyed with nutgalls,* and in 1820 vertical blue and white

---

*Galls are swollen areas of plant tissue, usually caused by a sort of parasite or fungus. I am not sure if nuts themselves formed galls, or if the galls formed on a nut-bearing tree.

stripes were adopted[69] (1816 in Canterbury, according to Blinn), and an 1838 visitor spoke of "reddish-brown or claret pantaloons" for winter.[70] By the 1840's, a plain dark shade had become standard.

The colors used in other articles of clothing were also changed. In New Lebanon about 1806, "blue for coats and jackets . . . began to fall into disuse . . . it being very costly and hard to work, and grey mixed color was adopted as the uniform."[71] About 1810 drab (a khaki-beige-brown) became the norm. Tailoring details were also changed at this time:

> The double folds of the skirts [of the vests] was set aside, and a single fold or plait adopted. The fore edges were cut more rounding, and slanted back at the bottom, three or four inches.
>
> The capes of coats and jackets, instead of being cut with two scallops, at the lower edge, leaving a point in the middle, were cut with a true curve on the lower edge, parallel with the top, or upper edge. . . . [They] were cut shorter in front . . . and the skirts were not so long, the medium length being about 7–7½″ for adults, proportioned to the person's height.
>
> To the neck of the coat a collar was added, about 1½″ wide, setting up perpendicular, or round-neck, and over this a cape, setting up with the collar, and spreading out a little on the shoulders.
>
> Also the buttons and buttonholes on the coat, were entirely omitted, and two or three pair of hooks and eyes put on instead.[72]

Blinn points out that coats (equivalent to our suit jackets) were not often worn. They were seldom used "for passing from the dwelling to the church" for Sunday meeting, and only shirts and vests were worn during the service itself. The coats were often omitted completely in the summer. In Canterbury they were a blue or a "light iron grey" color rather than drab, and they had ten 1½ inch wooden buttons, covered with worsted cloth.[73] (The buttons were made in the Village. Other early Shaker buttons were made from bone or horn, or from polished brass or pewter: Figure 103).

The cloth that went into vests varied a great deal over the years. Between 1810 and 1822 there was no standard summer vest; then in 1822 blue cotton and butternut worsted, waled cloth were adopted, only to be replaced in 1828 by plain cloth. Drab vests were worn for

FIGURE 103. *A large bone (probably the leg of a cow) with two circular buttons cut out of it. (Pleasant Hill)*

Sabbath, and blue vests were worn for other days. A "home-made, fine-wail worsted," adopted about 1836, was "superceeded by a still nicer variety of foreign cloth, a delicate fine-wail, light colored blue introduced in the year 1854. Blue became so popular by the 1850's that many of the former drab jackets are colored over, with pursley [purslain] blue."[74]

The men always wore some kind of neckpiece—in the eighteenth century a stock, or cravat (a stiff three-inch band that fastened at the back of the neck). The original costume called for a white stock on the Sabbath and a blue one for other days. In 1810 the New Lebanon brethren began wearing fine white neckcloths or "handker-

FIGURE 104. *Rose-colored silk neckerchief from South Union, Kentucky. The name "Wm. Booker" is written in the lining. On New Year's day, 1833, each brother in South Union was presented with a collar of this type.*

FIGURE 105. *Group portrait of the Shakers at New Lebanon. Note the different types of dresses that the sisters are wearing, the prints in the clothing of the little girls, the brethren's coats and straw hats, and the frock-type shirt that the brother at the right is wearing.*

chiefs," what we would call bandanas, tied in front, under a separate collar. These were made of cotton, linen, or silk, in "various colors."[75] The style came to Canterbury two years later.[76]

In the last quarter of the nineteenth century, the brethren gradually stopped dressing in a specifically Shaker style. The vest they wore was the same "as cut for the people not of the Society," and the coat was cut "like the frock coat of the world." By 1893 most of the brethren's garments were "bought ready made."[77] Colors also conformed to those popular in the world, and by 1884 Believers were "often seen in a suit of steel mix or dark blue."[78]

Even in this later period, however, brethren's shirts seem to have been made by the sisters rather than purchased; in fact, one of the New Lebanon sisters' industries was the production of men's shirts.[79] Turn-of-the-century shirts in Canterbury were

> made with a starched bosom and those who prefer have them button on the back. The collars are of the same patterns as worn by the world, and may be of paper or linen as best suits the pleasure of the wearer. Long and starched cuffs are attached to the shirts or the cuffs may be bought. . . . Studs of varied patterns are used to fasten the bought linen cuffs.[80]

The brethren's work clothes consisted of a pair of rough trousers (tow, until about the mid-nineteenth century) and frocks, or smock-like tops. "At some work," according to Young, "leather aprons [were also] worn, to defend outer clothes."[81] Shaker frocks were basically similar to those worn in the world at the time of the gathering of the Church—long, open shirts with side seams slit at the bottom and an opening at the neck to facilitate slipping them on over the head—except that the Shaker ones had a yoke across the shoulders and rather full gathered material below it. The original frocks, like the sisters' shortgowns, had cuffless sleeves which came to about the middle of the forearm; full-length sleeves came in only later. The basic style was adapted to specific needs—mechanics, for example, wore open frocks that did not have to be put on over the head. Winter frocks were made of "oilnut colored cloth" in Canterbury[82] or gray "full cloth" (that is, wool) in New Lebanon.[83] Summer frocks were usually plain undyed tow or linen. Dressier frocks were also worn, by both Shakers and people of the world, sometimes in place of white shirts.*

Underwear and Outerwear

People's reluctance to discuss or even mention undergarments has hampered research into the brethren's clothing as well as that of the sisters. Shaker records do mention drawers; presumably these were

---

*"There have been other kinds for nicer use; as drab worsted, drab drugget, drab cotton, and also butternut, or reddish worsted, or cotton and worsted open frocks for meeting, visiting, etc."[84]

FIGURE 106. *A Shaker brother in his work outfit. His cotton frock has a yoke at chest level and has gathered, full sleeves.*

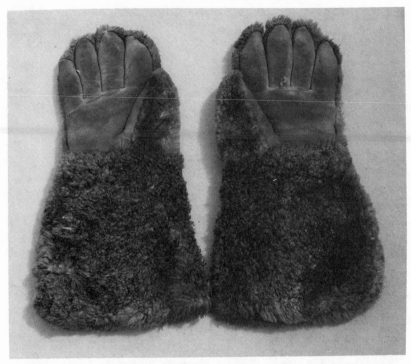

FIGURE 107. *Brethren's warm sheepskin gloves, from Hancock Shaker Village. There is also a sheepskin lining.*

knee-length (or shorter) boxer-like undershorts of white linen or cotton. Long underwear, worn in winter for extra insulation, was made of wool or heavy cotton, and some pieces in the New York State Museum collection have decorative trimming, such as a longitudinal side stripe. One pair, probably dating from the late nineteenth century, is bright red. Long nightshirts—loose shifts with set-in sleeves— have also been found, one of red flannel and another of starched white linen.

When the weather demanded it, the brethren wore surtouts over their jackets—close-fitting, double-breasted coats. From about 1813 to 1847 they were usually a drab color (although an occasional one was gray); "but the feelings of many were so unfavorable to drab that by about 1847 drab surtouts were abandoned, as to making any more

new ones, and dark grey only was adopted."[85] Those made in the latter part of the nineteenth century were not very different: according
to Blinn, they were double breasted and had two pleats (tails) in the
back fastened with decorative buttons. They tended to have large
cuffs and square-cut collars. In the world this kind of garment was
called a greatcoat. Greatcoats were warm, woolen overcoats, worn
primarily while traveling, which fitted over all the other clothes (coats
included). The ones worn by the Quakers in Pennsylvania had a collar and a cape over the shoulders, and wide cuffs.[86] The Shakers also
refer to greatcoats, though it is not clear whether the term was used
interchangeably with surtout or whether the Shaker greatcoat and
surtout were in fact different garments.

For general protection the brethren wore knitted wool mittens, and
occasionally gloves. An extraordinary pair of men's mittens at Sabbathday Lake was knitted with a thick, uncut pile on the outside and
a red flower worked on a white background in the pile. It is the only
pair of Shaker mittens of its kind, but according to a journal written
in 1803 by Ruth Henshaw (a non-Shaker), this was the "new mode of
knitting mittens."[87]

For heavy outdoor work in winter, the brethren had warm, heavy
gloves and mittens, often of sheepskin or fur and sometimes with an
additional lining for extra warmth (Figure 107).

Hats

Charles Daubenny, an Englishman visiting the United States in 1843,
observed that the brethren's "hair was allowed to grow behind and
was combed straight, so that it hung over their back and shoulders"
(Figures 105 and 106).[88] Hats were worn over this long hair; Shaker men, like all men in early America, considered a hat an essential
garment.

Hat making was a complex craft, and hatmakers, to learn it, usually
had to serve many years as apprentices. In 1810 a hatmaker in one of
the 842 commercial "hatteries" in the United States could make about
two hats a day.[89] According to one reporter, "experienced hatters
were among those who accepted the faith of the Believers, and the
manufacture of fur and wool hats began with the beginning of the

Community. These were made not only for New Lebanon, but for Believers in other States and for persons not of the Society."[90] The Shaker-made hats were essentially the same as those made in the outside world. The first hats were always black, with three- or four-inch round crowns and brims five or six inches wide. As time went by, the crowns grew higher and the brims narrower. Gray wool hats were introduced in 1803. "The rims of some of these hats were held in place by one or two sets of cords on each side of the crown, attached to the edge of the rim."[91]

Felted hats, made in all communities, were the most popular in the first part of the nineteenth century. But not all hats were available in all communities. The brethren at Union Village, for example, did not have fur hats until 1837,[92] though an account book of 1813 from South Union mentioned rabbit hats, fur hats (probably made from beaver, raccoon, or fox fur or even colt's hair), "castor" hats (felted beaver fur), and "naped" hats (probably wool felt—"napped"). Blinn in 1838 described hats at Canterbury:

> Most of them were very heavy and extremely hard for the head. The best [winter hats] were made of fur and colored a beautiful light drab and were sold [to the outside world] for $6.00 each. The wool hats were of multiplied shades, but filled with shellac till the rim and crown was as hard as a board. The fur hats had a silk cord while the wool ones had a cotton cord.

Casual summer hats were made of the same braided straw as the trim on the sister's bonnets. In Canterbury they were trimmed with a band of narrow white cotton tape. Other hat bands were of leather, silk, or braided palm leaf. Soft hats, introduced in 1860, had by 1885 generally replaced stiff hats. By this time most hats were bought outside and "worn as purchased."[93] Other kinds of hats may have been worn at various times: the collection at Pleasant Hill, Kentucky, for example, has a close-fitting black silk skull cap.

Shoes and Stockings

Once breeches were discarded about 1805, the brethren had no further need for long stockings. New Lebanon records of items given to

Believers when they left their community for the outside world mention footwear; for example, William Bates, Jr., was given eleven pairs of "footings" in 1850.[94] Footings were always listed separately from stockings, here and in the records of Shaker spinning mills. They may have been short stockings or socks, or they may have been the part of the stocking that fits over the foot. There are also references to *re-footing* stockings. Whatever they were, footings were always white or gray.

In many ways the brethren's shoes were like the sisters'. Shoe straps and buckles were used until 1812, when they were replaced by leather laces. Straight lasts were used for many years. Most of the brethren's shoes were made of leather, but cloth shoes were occasionally used for meeting. Because the men did much more outside work than the women, they also wore high, sturdy leather boots, most of which were a lace-up style. French author J. Milbert noted in 1817 that the brethren wore "yellow-topped boots."[95]

Accessories

Handkerchiefs, like neckerchiefs, were a standard part of rural costume in the eighteenth century. The Shakers used them well into the nineteenth:

> Of these . . . *napkins*, as they are sometimes called, the males and females have always used alike, a great variety: being about from 18 to 24 inches square; of linen or cotton; checked, with copperas [gray] and white, or blue and white, various sized checks, with borders; or sometimes all white, except blue borders, of different kinds or sizes; or all white, with no borders.[96]

Other handkerchiefs were green and white check, solid blue, and beige.

White handkerchiefs were worn over the arm during Sunday meeting. In 1841 James Silk observed, "on the left arm each female had a white napkin, neatly folded and hanging over the arm."[97] The brethren did the same (Figure 108). The reason for this custom is not clear; perhaps it had symbolic, spiritual significance. It is also possible that they were used to "mop the brow after strenuous dancing."[98]

SHAKERS near LEBANON state of N YORK.
their mode of Worship.   *Drawn from Life*

FIGURE 108. *An engraving made by a nineteenth-century visitor to a Shaker meeting.*

Children's Clothing

Clothing for the children who grew up with the Shakers has not been well or consistently documented. In general the styles were similar to, though not exact copies of, adult styles; the materials and colors set them apart.

Little girls wore long dresses like the sisters. These were covered by the standard neckerchief through the first part of the nineteenth century and by a full-length pinafore or a shorter, bertha-like garment later (Figures 8, 109). Often all girls in a single family or community wore dresses of the same material—frequently stripes, plaids, or prints rather than plain colors in the late nineteenth and in the twentieth century. Young girls went bareheaded until they were about ten years old, when they were given hair nets. They began to wear caps when they were "graduated" from the children's order at about age fourteen and took on the responsibilities of an adult sister. Even when they did not wear caps or hair nets, however, their hair was pulled straight back from their faces in a severe style, usually a bun at the nape of the neck (Figure 69).

Boys generally wore long trousers and loose-fitting pull-over frocks like those worn by the brethren, and on Sabbath days they wore vests and jackets of a different color and material from the brethren's. In 1828, for example, adult vests were of cotton and wool, but boy's vests were entirely cotton. Boys were bareheaded in summer, and in winter they wore wool knit caps which, according to an anonymous observer in 1832, were "surmounted by a woolen pompom." [99] In the late nineteenth century boys wore dark double-breasted jackets with brass buttons, and soft caps with visors in the front (Figure 109). It is not clear whether the Shakers made or bought these outfits.

Coats and cloaks were made in small sizes for children. Usually they were like the cloaks of the elders, though an observer in 1832 remarked that the "girls wore long drab cloaks with hoods drawn over their heads." [100]

After Death

The Millennial Laws of 1821 specified the kind of garments that Shakers were to be buried in:

> A corpse should be dressed in a shirt and a winding sheet, a handkerchief, and a muffler if necessary—and for a female add thereto a cap and collar. [101]

The Shakers' love of fine clothing and clothing detail, and the fact that it could take on spiritual significance, is indicated by a vision of "heavenly costume" promised to Believers in the "City of Peace" (Hancock) by the spirits of Mother Ann and Father William. The vision, "concerning the robes and dresses that are prepared for all such as go up to the Feast of the Lord," was received by a member of the

FIGURE 109. *Children in Canterbury, New Hampshire, 1880's. The girls are wearing long dresses with either pinafores or aprons and berthas. The older girls are wearing hairnets. The boys are wearing dark, double-breasted jackets and caps.*

ministry, and was recorded on New Year's Day, 1842. Typical Shaker garments and accessories would take on spiritual qualities in heaven:

> [For the brethren there would be] a pair of beautiful fine Trousers, as white as snow; these resemble a garment of purity, with many shining stars thereon. The buttons of a sky blue color and the appearance of them like glass. A jacket of a sky blue color also, with gold buttons thereon; and on these are wrought in fine needlework, many elegant and pretty flowers of different colors.
>
> A fine white silk handkerchief, bordered with gold, to tie about the neck; this resembles a band of Holy Love; and Heavenly union. O then let these heavenly graces shine.

The beautiful jacket resembles a garment of meekness, and sincerity, peace and goodwill.

A coat of heavenly brightness, of twelve different colors, which cannot be compared to any natural beauties, for no mortal eye hath ever seen the glory of my holiness; saith Eternal Wisdom.

A pair of heavenly shoes, perfectly white . . . These are a preparation of peace and a mark of humility, and that ye may walk softly before your God are ye shod with these.

A fine fur hat, of a silver color, which is to shine upon your heads, even as your holy faith in your Mother's work, doth cause you to shine.

For both Brethren, and Sisters, is a white pocket handkerchief of fine linen, these are tokens of honesty, simplicity, love, peace, and purity. Upon these are printed each one's names, and under this, is a *seal* of approbation and love, in the form of a little star.

. . . Now the Sister's garments are these. . . .

A gown of heavenly brightness, even like that of the Brethren's coats which have twelve very beautiful colors and do shine exceedingly, these are the emblems of holiness, virtue, and purity. A pair of Silver colored Shoes, resembling true innocence, and are for way marks to guide your feet in your Mother's lovely path.

A fine muslin cap with beautiful trimmings, also a pretty Color and handkerchief for the neck.

On these are many stars and Diamonds, and your names are also written thereon. These are garments of meekness, simplicity, freedom, gospel love, and heavenly Union towards each other.

A Bonnet of silver color, trimmed with white ribbons, also a pair of blue silk gloves. These denote holy faith, and true honesty, and cheerful cross bearing.[102]

Chapter Six
Fancywork

 It is ironic that although Shaker history extends over more than 200 years, the popular conception of their life and products is limited to the period just before the Civil War. The Shaker environment changed over the years. Although purposely isolated and guided by spiritual ideals, Believers were never unaware of what was going on around them, and they were always subject to external influence. New converts brought contemporary tastes and attitudes to the community throughout Shaker history.

As a result of the general bias toward "early Shaker," the subject of Victorian and post-Victorian Shaker products and design has not received the attention it deserves. The small sale items that the northeastern community sisters worked on late in the nineteenth century and in the twentieth have not been studied in any detail.

The Millennial Laws specifically prohibited the Shakers from making "fancy articles of any kind, or articles which are superfluously furnished, trimmed or ornamented."[1] By the post-Civil War period, however, the Believers not only were making trimmed and ornamented articles, but were even referring to them as fancy goods, and to their stores as fancy goods stores.

"Fancywork" is a Victorian term. As the industrial revolution got thoroughly under way in this country, bringing with it a population shift to urban areas and an expanding middle class, more and more women found themselves with an increased amount of leisure time. The phenomenon of the ladies' instruction manual began to emerge. Books with titles like *The American Woman's Home, or Principles of Domestic Science* and such periodicals as *Godey's Ladies Book* offered advice on a multitude of subjects—etiquette, fashion, children, marriage. One of the more influential innovations of these publications was universally available sewing and needlework patterns, with step-by-step instructions. Small, decorative, "fanciful" items for adorning the home or person were suddenly the rage. Mundane materials like linen and cotton were shunned in fabor of rich, sumptuous velvets and silks. Fussy details were admired. The general idea was to display as much fancy handwork as possible.

The Shakers' work took on some of these characteristics. Believers loved fine materials, and they turned to velvets, silks, and satins for many of their projects. The Victorian penchant for miniaturization was evident in their tiny baskets, sewing emeries stuffed in acorn caps, and the like. Decorative ribbons, bows, fringes, and embroidery—which never would have been tolerated earlier—appeared on Shaker clothing. Crocheting, a Victorian passion, began to supplement plain knitting, and crocheted furniture covers (doilies, antimacassars, "tidies"), clothing (hats, booties), facecloths, washcloths, and toys appeared in great number.

The Shaker insistence on practicality was, however, not lost. While their counterparts in the world were busy making items just for show —perhaps on a bric-a-brac shelf or under a high glass dome—the Shakers never made anything that could not be put to actual use. Embroidery served only as an embellishment on something functional. Rich materials were worked into everyday items—chair seat cushions, rugs. The Shakers were not drawn to such Victorian passions as draping windows with many yards of dust-catching, light-blocking velvet.

Shaker workmanship, in fancy items as in everything else, was superb. General Victorian taste sometimes led to a greater concern for frills or surface adornment than for good design and construction, but the Shakers avoided that pitfall. The Victorians were collectors: the autograph album and the photograph album, for example, were originally Victorian phenomena. Late nineteenth-century taste tended strongly to memorabilia, clutter, and tangible evidence of abundant friends, relatives, and possessions. The Shaker concept of sharing as a central spiritual and temporal principle precluded development in this direction. They were able to draw on the finer decorative aspects of Victorian life without succumbing to its excesses.

It is interesting that Shaker fancywork was often a little behind current fashions. Instructions for making penwipers first appeared in *Godey's Lady's Book* and *Peterson's Magazine* early in the 1860's, but the

Shakers did not begin to make them until late in the century; nor did they make crazy quilts until after the turn of the century, though they were introduced in the world by the 1880's. It was as though a style or fashion had to be firmly embedded in the general consciousness before the Shakers picked it up, and in fact by the time some fancy items appeared in Shaker stores, their appeal may have been primarily nostalgic.

Shaker fancywork was done primarily by women for women. As the number of Shaker men declined and agriculturally related activities became less lucrative, the sisters' sale items became an increasingly important source of income in the northeastern communities. The villages in Kentucky and Ohio retained their agricultural character as long as they were open, however, and fancy goods were never significant sale items for them. Improved rail and other transportation systems meant that Shaker villages were not too difficult to reach on special excursions, and there was increased traffic at Shaker stores; the fancy-goods store at New Lebanon, in fact, became a "must" visit for vacationers at the nearby fashionable health spa in Lebanon Springs. The Shakers also brought their sale items to country fairs and resort areas, and at times sold them through quality retail stores.

The items sold in these stores were geared to the lady of the house. Although there were occasional products made for men (for example, knitted neckties), most of the sale goods were for women and children, or for household use. That fancy goods were a phenomenon of the domestic realm may be one reason why they have thus far eluded close examination.

The last quarter of the nineteenth century witnessed a transition to women's industries. Brother John Vance of Alfred remarked in his journal in 1876:

> It is a noted fact that all manufactures of wooden ware was dropped two years ago. The tan yard was permitted to run down. The Garden Seed and Herb business were destroyed in consequence of the great competition of extensive establishments in the West who flooded our State with Seeds.
>
> The Sisters Fancy work consisting of a variety of Ladies work caskets, pin and needle cushions, Feather Fans and Dusters is the only brand of manufacture in the Society.

FIGURE 110. *Sisters in a Shaker store. On the right is a jar of peacock feathers, sold as ornaments for hats. A shag rug with a braided border is under this jar. Feather dusters hang from the ceiling, and many poplar and basket items are visible on and behind the counter.*

The store catalogues and sales records that appeared early in the twentieth century give a feeling for the business dealings of the Shaker fancy-goods stores, which were at the height of their popularity from about 1895 to 1920. Alice Braisted of Enfield, Connecticut, kept excellent sales records. Enfield was in a period of serious decline early in the twentieth century, but even though only a small number of sisters there were producing fancy goods, a large number were sold. The list below includes most of the items mentioned in Alice Braisted's 1909–10 record. It is representative of the items in every Shaker store, although it should be understood that each community had its own special wares and Enfield was unusual in its dearth of poplar goods at this time. The variety and range of sale goods, however, is typical. Nontextile items—outside the realm of this book—are included to give a true sense of what the fancy-goods stores offered.

shoe string handbag
ironing holder
kittie penwiper
dolly raffia hat
water lily penwipe
handkerchief case
eyeglass cleaner
embroidery set—
    scissors, emery and
    needle
macrame cord mat
round table mat
folding work basket
fascinator
hairpin receiver
doll bonnet
horse ring
ball
tamoshanter
raffia parasol
pasteboard pinwheel
face cloths
dolly sack
dolly komona
square tourist pin
    cushion
crocheted belt
crocheted neck-tie
wool duster
package walnuts and
    butternuts
one serving of chicken
rose jelly
quart of milk
bottle of Helolene

peppermint and
    wintergreen
small butter plate
ginger jar
pint of dandeline wine
elderberry wine
fudge
blackberry wine
electric comb
trundle bedstead
Shaker chairs
candlestick set
coat hangers
shell cushion
home made rug
needle book
pewter plate
old decanter bottle
large blanket birds eye
    weave
linen face cloth
cotton face cloth
fancy thread doily round
silkiton doily
string pinballs
fancy D.M.C. [thread]
    mat
maple leaf penwiper
dolly hammocks
cheese cloth duster
baby carriage robes
child's slumber socks
pair flannelette night
    shoes
second-hand bonnet

long hat pincushion
baby's bib
toy cat
scissors case
pair thumbless mittens
  [D.M.C.]
small palm leaf basket
  fancy
cross stitch teapot
  holder
pair golf stockings
pair shovel and tongs
canvas doll hat
knit reins
crochet reins
puff chair back
small iron kettle

large work apron
cakes of wax
trinket tray
basket tomato cushion
old fashioned butter
  crock
small brown bottle
small stand with drawer
dressing sack Ladies
dried sweet corn
child's sweater
pair ladies shoes
velvet pillow top
child's kimona wool
pair gentleman's mittens
doll in crocheted cloths
package of popcorn

A picture emerges of an almost casual approach to what items might be offered for sale. Sisters apparently made single items as the spirit moved them and put one or two out on display; a match scratcher, for example, appears in the records only once in five years, and it was most likely the only one on the shelves. A "puff chair back" (probably made with small gathered circles—puffs—of cloth, in the style of the puff quilt) must have been made as a way of using up fabric scraps.

Certain items were standard inventory, but each one might differ. Aprons came in many sizes and sometimes were even fashioned from old kerchiefs. Mats, one of the most typical Enfield items, were rectangular, oval, or round; were knitted, crocheted, or macramed; and were made with everything from heavy cord to fancy D.M.C. thread (silk or polished cotton).

The Enfield sisters were also willing to sell their own household items as second-hand goods. One ginger jar, one small butter plate, one candlestick set, and "one small stand with drawer" were obviously taken from the Shaker dwelling house. There was an overabundance of furniture and household accessories after the community population declined drastically. (The community was so debilitated, in fact,

No. 502.   Interior of Shaker Store, North Family, Mt. Lebanon, N. Y.

FIGURE 111. *This postcard was available for sale in Shaker communities around the turn of the century. It shows the "Interior of Shaker store, North Family, Mount Lebanon, New York." Similar postcards can be seen in the corner on the far right. Wool dusters are hanging from the ceiling, and straw bonnets are hanging on a vertical stand in the center of the picture.*

that it was disbanded in 1917.) The situation was similar in other Shaker villages. Several of the longer-lived communities sold household goods during the depression years of the 1930's as a way of raising badly needed cash. "One serving of chicken," which sold for 15 cents in 1909, was surely offered on the spur of the moment to a hungry visitor, while one quart of milk, two loaves of bread, and one bunch of asparagus (listed in 1911) must also have been taken from the family larder.

Sale products, as we have seen, were all household oriented. Brushes, shoe bags, aprons, doilies, teapot holders, and doll accessories had appeal for the woman of the house. Most of the inventory fitted the category of "notions." Small, inexpensive objects like watch or handkerchief cases or candied nuts would appeal to the impulse buyer, and the casual visitor probably never went away empty-handed.

FIGURE 112. *Shaker store, New Lebanon, late nineteenth century. Many items are visible in this photograph: wool dusters, hanging from the ceiling; spool holders; hexagonal knit washcloths; "dressed" dolls; postcards; balls of wax; miniature baskets, on the table; bottles that presumably contain wine; stuffed animals and miscellaneous crockery, on the shelves; and crocheted items, on the back wall. Note also that the Victorian influence is evident in the patterned wallpaper and linoleum.*

Such items could serve as souvenirs and mementos as well as small gifts. The Enfield store sold more postcards than anything else: in 1911 about 600 with a printed design and 800 with photographs. These were, of course, among the cheapest items in the store and were still something of a novelty. Presumably a card from a Shaker village would have been a curiosity, and a very special thing to receive in the mail; and judging from the number of them bought at a time by some visitors, they must have been popular as unusual gifts.

Around this same time Alfred, Maine, was a thriving community with many more sisters and more formalized industries than Enfield, Connecticut. The 1908 catalogue of the Alfred fancy-goods store, with its long list of regularly available (standard) stock, provides an interesting contrast to the Enfield record. We must remember, too, that the Shakers were always careful to point out in their catalogues that many items available for sale were not listed, and there was always the odd crocheted toy, "dolly" accessory, or bunch of asparagus in addition to the regular stock.

The main portion of the Alfred sale items were poplar cloth boxes or cases of some kind—unquestionably the heart of the fancy-goods inventory produced in Maine, New Hampshire, and New York. These poplar cloth items are listed in the Alfred catalogue:

> veil box (oblong)
> handkerchief box (square, three sizes)
> jewel cases (small square box, ladies' compartmentalized semicircular case, and gentlemen's rectangular case)
> plain satin-lined oblong boxes (3 sizes)
> plain octagonal box
> plain hexagonal box
> work boxes (sewing boxes with accessories: round (tubular) boxes in 3 sizes; octagonal boxes in 5 sizes, and bell shaped boxes)
> bifoid
> quadrifoid
> work caskets (4 types)
> reticule
> ladies cuff and collar holder
> razor box
> stud box
> ribbon holder
> tray
> jewel tray

Other items in the catalogue are:

> hat brush
> toilet cushions (6 types)
> pincushion
> tomato cushion
> emery balls
> needlebooks
> wax balls
> ladies sweaters
> knit knee warmers

babies leggings
bed socks
knit laundry bags
double-headed cloth doll (one face white, one face black)
walnuts in maple sugar
orange peel in sugar
sweet flag (Calamus root) in sugar

A catalogue from Canterbury, New Hampshire (undated, but probably about 1920), lists the following poplar items:

plain satin lined boxes
sewing baskets
handkerchief boxes
jewelry boxes
card trays
crochet boxes

Knitted items include:

sweaters
jacket sweaters
sponge cloths
sponge cloth bags
slumber socks

Other items from this catalogue are:

haircloth brushes
tomato cushions
dolls in Shaker costume
wool dusters
emeries
eyeglass brighteners
   (chamois cloth)
handkerchief cases
watch cases
toothbrush cases
teapot holders
potholders
laundry bags

pin flats
penwipers
sewing chains
scissors point protectors
waxes
twine balls
shoe bags
spool stands
toys (cats, dogs, mice,
    and rats)

"Products of Dilligence and Intelligence," a New Lebanon catalogue from the early years of the twentieth century, includes many of
the same poplar boxes (oblong, octagonal, square, for handkerchiefs
and jewels), oval and oblong carriers, spool stands, needlebooks, penwipes, and emeries. Additional items include Shaker dolls, shopping
bags, book marks, knitted table mats, yarn mops, and doll sunbonnets.
(For a discussion of the manufacture of poplar cloth and items made
with the cloth, see below, pages 216–223.)

Catalogue descriptions of cloaks advertised in the twentieth century
are an excellent indication of the extent to which the Shakers catered
to their market; they would not compromise their high quality, but
they tried to please their customers. A New Lebanon advertisement
for the Dorothy cape (see above, page 185) claimed that it was "made
in all popular shades of broadcloth, for auto, street or ocean travel, or
in pastel shades for evening wear." It was a "serviceable and unique
wrap" and came in "Harvard red," "Dartmouth green," "Navy blue,"
grey, black, and white.[2] During World War I, poplar cloth boxes
sometimes included small American flags—a sample of how the Shakers kept abreast of contemporary happenings.

The Shakers had good business heads. In addition to issuing catalogues describing their products in terms that potential customers
liked to hear, they took their products to places where customers were
likely to be. Every community seems to have sent a delegation of Believers to local state and county fairs. Booths were erected and stocked
with items from the store shelves at home. In the Enfield sales record
there are entries like "Took in from fair at Stafford Springs $46.74."
Canterbury sisters sold some of their products through such high-

quality retail stores as Jordan Marsh in Boston: Eldress Bertha Lindsay recalls that knitted and crocheted items like doilies, shawls, children's sweaters, baby jackets, and booties were sold there early in the
twentieth century.[3] Boston newspaper clippings and photographs
show that at times several sisters made the trip into the city to deliver
items and simultaneously enjoy an excursion.[4] Trustees of Maine
communities made seasonal trips to local resort areas with supplies of
sale items. Publicity would be distributed throughout the resort town,
and the Shakers would set up their display in the lobby of a fine hotel.
A Poland Springs (Sabbathday Lake) account book lists receipts from
visits to the coastal towns of Swampscott (Massachusetts), Cape Elizabeth, Old Orchard Beach, Scarboro, Bar Harbor, Squirrel Island, and
Sam-O-Set (all in Maine), and the inland resort area of Rangeley
Lakes. These trips began late in the nineteenth century and continued
until about the time of World War I.

The Shaker sisters developed numerous personal friendships with
their regular customers. Correspondence about products had a personal tone, and visitors reported that they felt they were treated with
special attention.[5] Customers also felt confident that they could return
their purchases if there was anything wrong with them or if a much-
used item needed refurbishing. A Sabbathday Lake account book
from about 1910 lists in the receipts many *relined* carriers (lined,
wooden boxes)—carriers that had proved useful, sturdy, and pleasing
enough to warrant bringing them back to be restored.

In addition to quality in workmanship, the Shakers always insisted
on quality in materials; their products were sought after because,
among other reasons, only the best went into them. The Shakers
shopped around for their materials, even if it meant importing them
from other countries. Much of the excellent wool broadcloth that
went into making the cloaks, for example, came from France, and
wool for the famous twentieth-century Canterbury stockings was imported from Australia. The dolls that were meticulously dressed in
Shaker costume were brought from Germany. Sisters would stop
making an item when they could no longer get the raw material they
needed for it. Although capes are occasionally made on special order
even today, cape production was severely hampered in the 1930's
when the right kind of broadcloth could no longer be found. Blanket
combings, bought as mill by-products, had been used to stuff pin-

cushions and toilet cushions, and no satisfactory substitute was ever found after these became unavailable. Poplar box linings became impossible to make properly when true (silk) satin was replaced by synthetics.[6]

At the present time, the Shaker sisters still make a number of sale items. There are shops at both the Canterbury and Sabbathday Lake communities, and some of their products are available at the Shaker Museum at Old Chatham, New York. Aprons and crocheted items predominate, but twine balls, tomato cushions, woven rugs, pillows, and the like can still be purchased. Poplar work is no longer sold, and the Believers are keeping what is left of their furniture as "antiques" for themselves. As in the early part of the century, post cards and other souvenir items are most popular with the casual visitor to the store. The production of fancy items is still an important activity, but it is no longer a major source of income for the few women in the two remaining villages.

Poplar Cloth and Poplar Items

We have discussed the processing and preparation of narrow poplar strips. These were made into small baskets, and served at times as the supporting "fiber" in bonnets, mostly those made for children or dolls. Occasionally they were made into other small items such as whiskbroom holders and coaster-size mats. Most often, however, they were woven into poplar cloth, a flexible, almost fragile fabric used for numerous articles, as noted above (page 45).

The sisters usually did the weaving on special looms used for straw and poplar work. The looms had a weaving width of 20 to 25 inches, with two harnesses and an overhead beater. The warp was always a fine white cotton thread—in one description, a Number 30 cotton sewing thread was specified.[7] The thread was wound onto the loom from a spool rack, between nine and thirteen threads to the inch. Long warps were generally used; according to a journal reference from April 2, 1878, Sabbathday Lake, "The sisters christen their new Loom for weaving the Popple [poplar] Webbing for sale work by putting on a web of one hundred yards warp."[8]

The sisters softened the poplar in water to make it flexible, some-

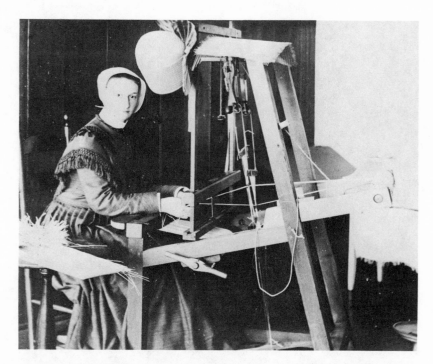

FIGURE 113. *Canterbury Sister Bertha Mansfield weaving poplar cloth. Note the finished poplar cloth sheet sitting on top of the loom.*

times keeping it in a damp cloth as they worked. This must have been an enjoyable task; the damp poplar had a very pleasant aroma. The strips were drawn through the cotton warp, one at a time. Two methods seem to have been used. In the first, the strip was threaded through a large, flat wooden "needle," which was then "thrown" between the warp threads in much the same way as a weaving shuttle, and drawn out at the far end, leaving the poplar strip in place. In the second method, described by Sister Elsie McCool of Sabbathday Lake, special tongs, outfitted with sandpaper on the end to catch and control the poplar strands, were drawn through the warp.[9] There was a right and a wrong side to each strip, so that by either method the weaver had to be careful to insert it right side up, and also to make sure it lay perfectly flat. It was an exacting job, and had to be done slowly.

FIGURE 114. *Detail of poplar cloth made in Sabbathday Lake, Maine. The dark-colored stripes are sweet grass. This pattern is analyzed in Appendix IV. (Hancock Shaker Village)*

Most poplar cloth also incorporated other materials in the weft. This was usually the same fine white thread that constituted the warp, added for strength and variety of pattern. Oat straw, carefully chosen and processed for its decorative qualities, was sometimes worked in; with its golden-colored, almost polished appearance, it was a fine complement to the white matte finish of the poplar.

In the 1890's Sister Ada Cummings of Sabbathday Lake experimented with other variations in poplar cloth. She introduced sweet grass, both natural and dyed, and occasionally dyed strips of poplar as well. The products made with these extra colors and textures did not sell as well as the plain poplar cloth, "for many [people] seemed to associate the sweet grass with Indian crafts rather than traditional Shaker work." [10]

Poplar cloth patterns are handsome. The sisters chose subtle, carefully planned designs that highlighted the inherent qualities of the materials. A unit of four or five rows of poplar strips might combine in a repeated pattern with a unit of alternate rows of poplar and fine thread: even though the thread was effectively hidden by the much thicker wood, that unit would have a totally different appearance from the all-wood unit (Figure 115). When sweet grass or oat straw was incorporated in the design, it was always used at regularly repeating intervals and in harmonious proportion to the poplar (Figure 114). The cotton warp was often threaded on the loom in an uneven (but regular) spacing, and part of the success of many poplar cloth designs lay in this feature.

At least in the twentieth century, poplar cloth was generally woven in rolls about ten yards long. The finished rolls were cut from the loom and taken to the ironing room, where white paper was glued to the back to add strength and prevent raveling. "Sad" (cool) irons were used to help dry the glue. The paper backing was sometimes covered once again with a fine white cotton cloth. The firmer the backing, the easier it was to perform the next step: cutting the cloth to the sizes and shapes needed for specific projects. This could be done with scissors, but it was more efficient to use a machine that resembled a paper cutter.

Fancy boxes covered with poplar cloth were made in a myriad shapes and sizes. The simplest were squares and rectangles. Handkerchief boxes ranged from 4½ to 6 inches square; a veil box was 10

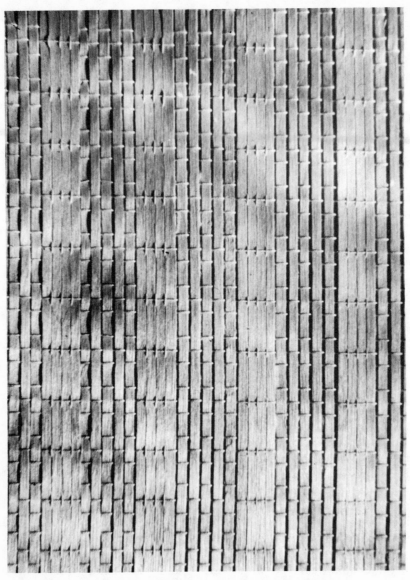

FIGURE 115. *Detail of poplar-cloth covering on a sewing box. This is analyzed in Appendix IV. (Hancock Shaker Village)*

by 6 inches; and plain satin-lined boxes came in two sizes, 6 by 2 inches and 9 by 2½ inches. Round (tube-shaped) work boxes ranged from 5 by 2½ inches to 8 by 3½ inches. There were also ladies' cuff and collar holders, shaped like long, folded-over clutch purses; semicircular, compartmentalized jewelry cases; bell-shaped work boxes; and octagonal and hexagonal boxes in many sizes. Most complex of all were "bifoid" and "quatrefoid" boxes, with two and four semicircular bulges respectively, each with its own lid and opening independently (Figure 117), and "work caskets," which were large boxes outfitted with smaller boxes and pockets on the lid or sides (Figure 117).

Most boxes, whatever their shape, were made in essentially the same way. The poplar cloth was cut to the exact size needed and glued to cardboard pieces of the same size. Colored satin, lined with a wadding material, was stitched by machine to the top of the side pieces and then folded over and carried to the inside of the box. A separate satin-covered piece of cardboard was fitted into the bottom. Brass escutcheon pins tacked the sides of the box to a precut base of basswood, pine, or poplar (Figure 116). White kid imported from France was cut into thin strips (skivers) and glued over corner seams, serving both as a practical "cover-up" and an aesthetically pleasing trimming. The underside of the box was covered with a piece of cardboard, sometimes decorated with glued-on fancy paper or wallpaper. By the beginning of the twentieth century, this part of the box was stamped with a trademark designating it as a Shaker product from a specific community.

Sewing boxes, work boxes, and work cases came with a number of accessories, all tied in with ribbon. Two adjacent holes were punched through all layers of poplar cloth, cardboard, and lining. A satin ribbon was folded in half and drawn through the holes, holding the accessory inside, and the two ends were tied in a bow on the outside. "Fully furnished" sewing boxes were equipped with a pincushion, an emery for sharpening needles, a piece of molded beeswax (used to stiffen thread so that it would not break), and a needle folder. Some of the fanciest boxes had a large number of bows, many of them purely decorative. Some boxes for holding handkerchiefs, jewelry, and so forth were covered with bows purely for decoration. Leftover pieces of poplar cloth were made into small items like needle folders and pincushions (Figure 123). A strip of poplar cloth only one inch wide,

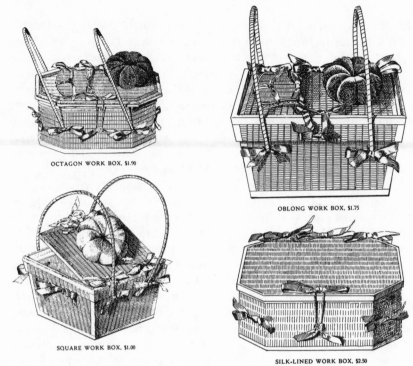

OCTAGON WORK BOX, $1.90

OBLONG WORK BOX, $1.75

SQUARE WORK BOX, $1.00

SILK-LINED WORK BOX, $2.50

FIGURE 116. *Illustrations from the catalogue "Products of Dilligence and Intelligence."*

for example, could be glued to a strip of cardboard wrapped around a "tomato" pincushion. Shakers in the Maine communities sometimes made unbacked poplar cloth into placemats.

The production of poplar cloth dwindled in the 1940's, when the supply of poplar began to run out on Shaker land. Canterbury underwent the further setback of having its poplar-cutting machine stolen in 1957. Sisters at Sabbathday Lake continued to make sewing boxes in the 1950's, substituting what they called "tapestry cloth" (highly textured commercial cloth or wallpaper) for poplar cloth (see Figure 120).

Poplar cloth and poplar boxes are remarkable for the amount of work that went into them. From the painstaking preparation of the poplar to the careful finishing details of a box, an enormous amount of time and energy was involved. The Shakers are well known for

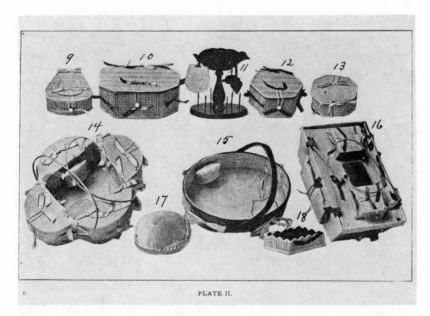

PLATE II.

FIGURE 117. *This page from a 1908 catalogue from Alfred, Maine, shows various elaborate poplar boxes. Clockwise from the upper left: 9, scallop shaped box; 10, octagonal box; 11, spool stand with poplar cloth needle folder; 12, hexagonal box; 13, hexagonal box; 16, work casket; 18, pin tray; 15, oval carrier; 17, toilet cushion; 14, quatrefoil.*

their invention of labor-saving devices, but here is an excellent example of an industry in which speed and efficiency were not prime values. The very nature of the Believers' unpressured communal life style enabled them to evolve and perfect this unique industry.

Sewing Accessories

Sewing accessories were an essential part of the inventory of all Shaker fancy-goods stores. The accessories that came in "fully furnished" sewing and work boxes were also available separately.

Pincushions were almost always the standard "tomato" shape, covered with a variety of fine materials but most typically with satin, brocaded satin, or velvet. They were tightly stuffed with wool blanket

FIGURE 118. *Canterbury sisters Bertha Lindsay and Lillian Phelps constructing poplar boxes. The sisters are nailing the side pieces to precut octagonal bases. Completed boxes are on the shelf at the rear.*

combings bought by the sisters from local mills. Many of the pincushions sold individually were fitted into a base; straw basket cushions, with the pincushion sitting in a woven basket, for example, were popular in some communities. Poplar cloth, tapestry cloth, or fancy cardboard edged with white kid was another type of base.

Pin trays, or pin flats, were oblong or round uncovered trays of poplar cloth or handpainted tin. A chestnut burr pin ball and a chestnut burr chain are also mentioned in store records.[11] Chestnut burrs were probably glued or sewn together and used in the same way as a pincushion made of fabric.

Sewing emeries, used to keep needles sharp and rustfree, were made in great quantities. The most typical ones were the size and shape of a strawberry, covered with tightly woven wool in the beginning and with satin in the twentieth century. The emery was formed

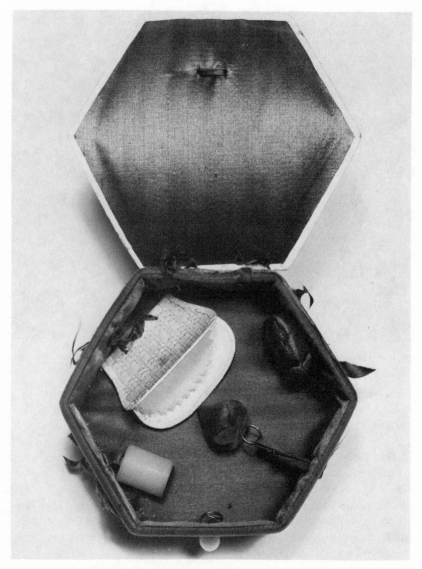

FIGURE 119. *Interior of a poplar cloth sewing box. Accessories are (left to right): cylindrical cake of beeswax; poplar-cloth-covered needle book; pincushion; and strawberry emery. (Hancock Shaker Village)*

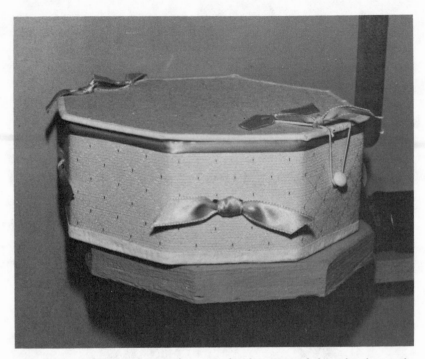

FIGURE 120. *An octagonal sewing box covered with "tapestry cloth" rather than poplar cloth. (Canterbury)*

by sewing the fabric into a conical shape, putting it into a specially carved wooden mold, and filling it with emery powder, a finely-ground crystallized mineral. A "hull," usually cut from a piece of felt, was sewn with a loop-handled "stem" at the top. On some especially elaborate strawberry emeries, little seeds were embroidered or painted on. Daisy-shaped emeries were popular in later years. Emery powder was stuffed into a circular felt pouch, which served as the center of the daisy. The petals were felt of a contrasting color, and ribbons were tied on for decorative stems. Novelty emeries were also made by stuffing emery-filled pouches into such tiny natural containers as acorn caps, walnut shells, and sea shells.

Molded cakes of beeswax were sold individually, each wrapped in paper to keep it clean and fresh. Beeswax was especially important in the days before mercerized cotton sewing thread. The seamstress ran the thread across the wax to give it a light coating, which strengthened it and kept it from twisting into knots.

Needle cases—sold in great numbers—were made with several pieces of wool flannel or felt stitched together like a book, with covers of felt, leather, poplar cloth, or fabric-covered cardboard. The scallop was the most common shape, but rectangles and novelty shapes were also sold. A Canterbury sister made a needle folder in the shape of a Shaker bonnet (Figure 124), and Sister Christine Greenwood of Sabbathday Lake made a hat-shaped one: a circular needlebook was the base, made by stitching together two round cloth-covered pieces of cardboard with felt circles between them; and the top was a pincushion covered with the same fabric.

Spool stands, used for holding spools of sewing thread, were another popular item (Figure 126). These were one of the few fancy items made by the brethren. The stand itself was hand turned, as were the fine individual spools sometimes sold with it. Many spool holders had round velvet-covered pincushions on top and other furnishings (emery, beeswax, needlebook) tied to them with ribbon.

Sewing cases came in many shapes and sizes.* The boxes, as we have seen, were usually covered with poplar cloth. "Furnished" carriers, as noted, oval or rectangular, were lined wooden boxes with wooden handles; made by the brethren, they were lined and furnished by the sisters. Workbags (cloth sewing bags) had a round, firm bottom, shaped by either cardboard or an embroidery hoop. The fabric was gathered into a drawstring at the top, or, in another design, a tall drawstring bag rose out of a scallop-shaped needle case. Some elaborate sewing cases were used by the sisters themselves. The one belonging to Sister Mary Dabon—who lived in Watervliet, Hancock, or New Lebanon—was a tin box covered with padded maroon leather and decorated on the outside with a large silk bow and metal clasp; inside was a matching leather-covered needle folder and scissors scabbard, pincushion, sausage-shaped thimble holder, pouches for holding small spools of thread, and a case for an ivory crochet hook. Fancy

*One, in the shape of a Shaker bonnet, is described and pictured in complete detail in Appendix 4.

FIGURE 121. *A daisy emery from Hancock Shaker Village. The emery powder is in the pouch that makes up the center of the daisy.*

FIGURE 122. *A scallop-shaped, wool-covered needle folder. (Sabbathday Lake)*

boxes of this type may have been used later than the turn-of-the-century poplar cloth cases and may possibly have been sold in Shaker stores.

Sewing chains, also mentioned in store records, were long yarn chains, probably crocheted, with various sewing aids like scissors attached to the ends. They could be draped around the neck like a shawl, to keep the sewing aids within easy reach.

Other sewing accessories were button boxes (no information about them is available, but they were probably cloth- or poplar-covered boxes); darning sets (probably a wooden darning egg and a needle); embroidery sets (including scissors, needle cases, and emeries); knitting-needle and scissors scabbards; and thimble and tape-measure cases. The latter was a novelty item in the shape of a hat, with space for a rolled tape measure in the crown.

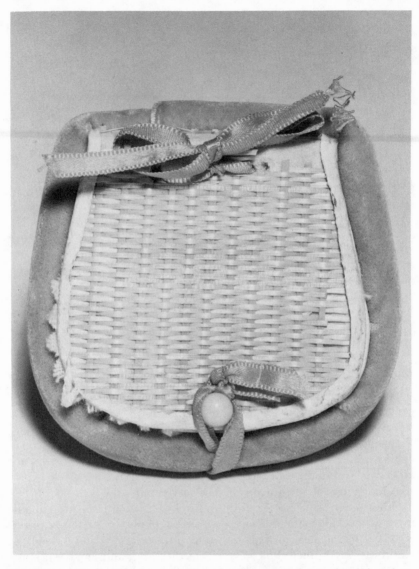

FIGURE 123. *Needle folder covered with poplar cloth, trimmed with white kid, and mounted on pink velvet. Small folders like this provided a use for small pieces of poplar cloth. (Hancock Shaker Village)*

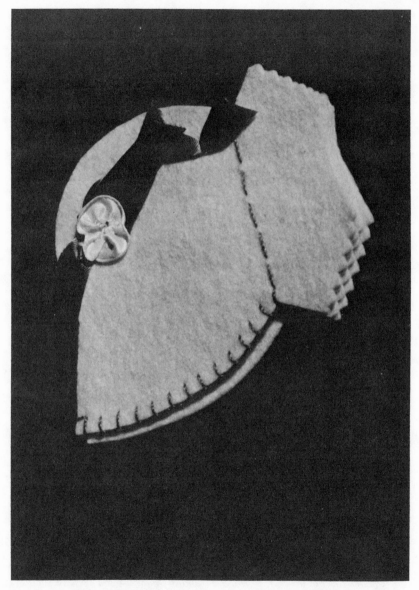

FIGURE 124. *A felt needle folder in the shape of a Shaker bonnet. (Sabbathday Lake)*

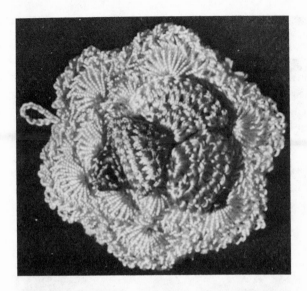

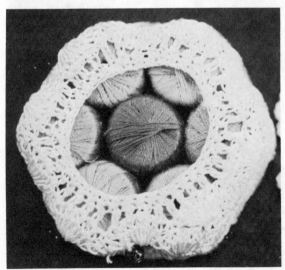

FIGURE 125. *A crocheted cotton spool case with seven spools. Bottom, the body of the case. Top, the cover of the case, embellished with three colored roses. The case is a pumpkin-orange color. (Hancock Shaker Village)*

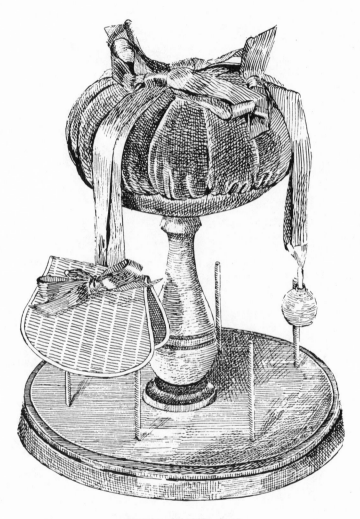

SPOOL STAND, $1.75

FIGURES 126–128. *Illustrations from the catalogue "Products of Dilligence and Intelligence."*

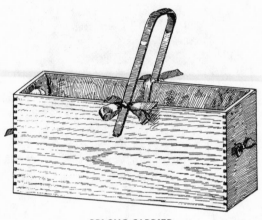

OBLONG CARRIER

* See Price List

WOOL DUSTER, 40c.

11

FIGURE 127

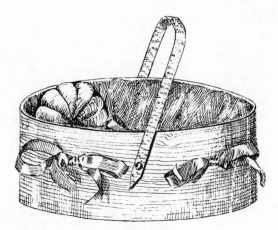

† See Price List

OVAL CARRIER

WORK BAG, $1.00

12

FIGURE 128

FIGURE 129. *A fancy sewing case. The main body is a leather covered tin cylinder with a hinged lid. The many pockets and lining are made from striped silk, and there are leather insets. This case is from Pleasant Hill, but similar cases were made and used in other communities.*

FIGURE 130. *This scissors scabbard is made of cardboard covered with an embossed wallpaper-like material. It is edged with purple silk. (Hancock Shaker Village)*

Household Accessories

As we have seen, household accessories were an important part of the inventory of the fancy goods stores. Items were made for every part of the house.

Pillows and cushions were made for many different purposes and came in all sizes. There were chair seat cushions; bureau cushions (large cushions with a straw base, which held hat pins); toilet cushions (presumably to go on a dressing table); and balsam-stuffed pillows, which were popular because of their fresh aroma.

Mops and dusters were made in the broom shop. Mopheads were of cotton string, brightly colored wool yarn loops, or spun tow linen. The feathers in feather dusters were usually turkey feathers; wool dusters were made from unspun wool dyed a bright shade and decorated with a colorful bow (Figures 111 and 112). Duster mitts—rectangular, knitted bags with long yarn pile—were worn over the hand and operated by simply running the hand along the dusty surface. A cheesecloth duster, mentioned in the Enfield store records, was presumably also a mitt.

Brushes—hat brushes, hearth brushes, and clothes brushes—were another popular sale item. They were made of "raveled horsehair cloth" glued and nailed to a wooden handle (Figure 131).

Different kinds of "holders" were made for various household uses. Potholders were knitted, crocheted, or made of padded cloth. One popular cloth design looked like a chicken when folded and a heart when open. There were teapot holders (tea cozies) and iron holders (for hot irons); the latter sometimes had long wool pile like the duster mitts or shag rugs.

Penwipers, or penwipes, were popular fancy items in the Victorian age. A penwiper was a piece of absorbent cloth for wiping excess ink from fountain pens. The cloth was often worked into an elaborate holder or case, however, and made as a novelty item. The Shakers made fancy penwipers well into the twentieth century. "Dolly" penwipers were small (3 inches high) bisque doll figures dressed in voluminous pleated skirts, which were the absorbent material (Figure 133). The sisters made other penwipers in the shape of water lilies, chickens, "kitties," maple leaves, and mittens. The simplest ones were small pieces of undecorated chamois cloth.

FIGURE 131.

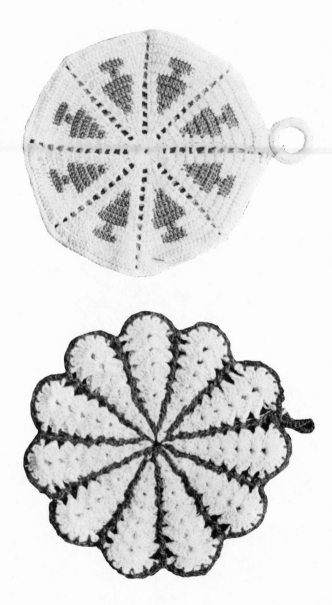

FIGURE 132. *Crocheted cotton potholders, early twentieth century. Both are at Hancock Shaker Village.*

FIGURE 133. *A "dolly" penwipe. The voluminous folds of the skirt were used to absorb the ink from fountain pens. Actual height: 4 inches. (Sabbathday Lake)*

FIGURE 134. *Embroidery on a linen table scarf. This kind of decoration was found on bureau and table scarves that were made for sale in the twentieth century. (Pleasant Hill)*

Items for the linen closet included decorated hand towels, face towels, and handkerchiefs; face cloths and wash cloths; bureau scarves; table covers (crocheted) and tablecloths (embroidered); an occasional blanket; and table mats. The Shakers sometimes applied hand trimming or decoration to commercial linen products; plain white face and bath towels, for example, would be bought in large quantities at wholesale prices, and young girls would crochet lace edging around them in cotton thread. One towel style had a 1½-inch crocheted rose sewn on about 2-inches above the edge in the corner. Martha Hulings, who lived at the South Family in New Lebanon, remembers a time when girls made large numbers of these roses—as many as one hundred in one day.[12] Towels were also trimmed with embroidery. The initials "BV," for "Believers' Visitor," were embroidered on a towel bought at Hancock in 1929.[13]

The standard design for knitted face cloths was a circle made up of triangular wedges, and for washcloths a checkerboard-type combination of knit and purl stitch; but variations were not uncommon. Table mats were knitted, crocheted, or woven of cloth or palm leaf. Knitted afghans were also popular. Antimacassars were usually crocheted. Interestingly, the Shakers not only sold these to the world but also used them, even though it is unlikely that they used the Macassar hair oil from which antimacassars were designed to protect upholstery. Tidies—small, doily-like cloths placed on the arms of upholstered chairs and under vases and lamps on tables and bureaus—were generally crocheted. Like antimacassars, they kept the furniture neat and clean. Both sponge cloths and sponge-cloth bags were sold. Sponge cloths, made of absorbent, heavily-textured knitted cloth, were used in the bath. No information is available about the bags. Another item was an expandable shopping bag, similar to French net shopping bags, made with cotton in a looping (knotless netting) technique.

Shaker stores stocked an occasional doorstop. One interesting stop, now in the collection at Hancock Shaker Village, is a sand-filled bottle with a sock and dressed like a Shaker sister (Figure 136). Other household items were bookmarks made of handpainted cardboard, match scratchers, twine balls, wire carpet beaters, embroidered luggage straps, napkin rings (one kind was covered with beads), bead baskets, rugs, and floor mats.

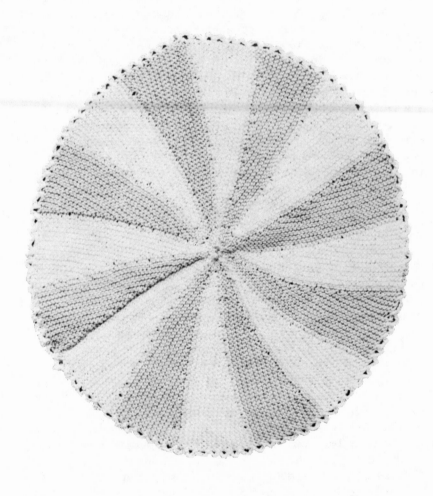

FIGURE 135. *Round knit face cloth. The colors are blue and white. (Hancock Shaker Village)*

FIGURE 136. *Novelty doorstop from Hancock Shaker Village. The base of the doll is a bottle filled with sand. The head is made from an old sock.*

Personal Accessories

Many of the personal accessories sold in fancy goods stores were the poplar items described above—handkerchief boxes, jewelry boxes, veil boxes, and cuff and collar holders. Others were jewel trays (uncovered oval trays with scalloped, kid-trimmed edging); long, narrow razor boxes; ribbon holders (semicircular boxes with a slit for feeding out ribbon); semicircular boxes for shirt studs; and pendant boxes. Hairpin holders (also called hairpin receivers) were small trays intended for the dressing table. Bags of lavender bath salts and lavender sachets were popular. A "string of sachet shells" was mentioned in one record.[14] Bath mitts were also mentioned, with no further details. Laundry bags and shoe bags were also sold. Toothbrush cases and watch cases were made out of wood, at least some of the time. "Handbags" may have been net bags similar to shopping bags, and "reticules" were purse-like containers, made sometimes of poplar cloth and sometimes of other materials, notably leather.

Eyeglass wipers—simple pieces of chamois cloth—were frequently sold. Hat boxes and hat plumes (usually peacock feathers) were featured and must have been popular with the fashionable women of the world, who wore elaborate hats. Fans were sometimes also made of feathers: in the late nineteenth century, there are references to plucking turkey feathers for this purpose.[15] Other fans were made of palm leaf and paper.

Clothing

The sisters made a great variety of clothing articles to be sold. Most were knitted or crocheted, but some things were hand and machine sewed or embroidered.

Aprons were a staple item—both work aprons and fancy "dress" aprons. Sometimes Shaker-made silk scarves were made over into fancy aprons.

Cloaks (capes) were among the most important clothing items. The same cloaks the Shakers made for themselves were offered to the world, and they had such an excellent reputation for quality and attractiveness that a brisk business was established by the 1890's. So highly were these cloaks regarded, in fact, that Mrs. Grover Cleveland ordered one of dove gray for her husband's Presidential inauguration in 1892. According to legend, the sisters discovered that the cloak they had prepared for her was flawed, whereupon they immediately set about making another—a perfect one.

Most cloaks were made on special order. On request, the Shakers provided potential customers with sample swatches of cloth; the selected material would then be sent back to the Shakers with the appropriate neck, shoulder, and length measurements. Customers, if they wished, could supply their own material. In a broadside from West Pittsfield (Hancock), Massachusetts, Sister Sophia Helfrich wrote that "for the information of the parties wishing to furnish the material for their cloaks made by us" four yards of 56-inch cloth, and 30 inches of silk for the hood, would be necessary. "A perfect fitting garment [could] not be made from narrow goods." "Ladies of medium height," she went on to say, "require 11 yards of silk of ordinary width "for a completely lined cloak."

Most cloaks were made in the popular "Dorothy" style. Sometimes referred to as an opera cloak, this was generally advertised as a dressy outer garment. A 1910 Sabbathday Lake catalogue described it:

> Enveloping the whole person it falls in graceful folds to the hem of the dress, having a silk-lined hood for use in storms. These cloaks are made in many shades of the finest domestic and imported broadcloth. The latter is generally selected when one wishes a cloak lined throughout with silk.
>
> All inner edges are prettily pinked, including the border of the pocket on each side of the garment.

The pocket referred to here was usually made of silk that matched the hood lining. The same silk was used as an interfacing along the length of the front opening in some cloaks.

Cloaks were made for sale in the stores until the 1940's. After World War II, production stopped except for special orders; even today, Sabbathday Lake sisters turn out an occasional cloak on request. Despite great demand, there is no commercially available pattern for Shaker cloaks of any kind. The design is still treasured and carefully guarded by the Shakers and Shaker-affiliated organizations.

Shaker-style bonnets were also popular in the fancy goods store. Al-

FIGURE 137. *Sisters, at the turn of the century, preparing Dorothy-style cloaks, New Lebanon. Note the bolts of broadcloth at the right.*

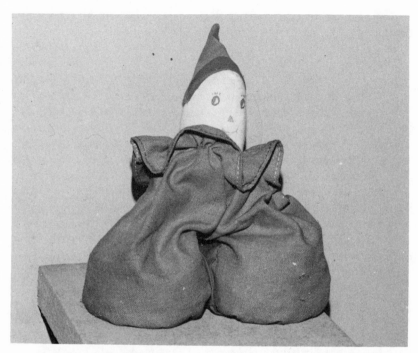

FIGURE 138. *This clown exemplifies the kind of toy that was made for children in the twentieth century. (Chatham)*

though this type of bonnet was no longer fashionable for women of the world, it was no doubt accepted as a novel sort of head covering. Straw bonnets trimmed with large bows and chin ties of gaily printed cotton were sold in the twentieth century. These were made solely for sale; the sisters did not wear them. Sunbonnets made entirely of cloth were also featured in the twentieth century.

Most of the bonnets sold in the twentieth century were actually miniature-sized, for dolls. The sisters dressed china and cloth dolls in complete Shaker costume—underwear, dress, cap, bonnet, cloak, and shoes—and these were favorites of the buying public. "Dolly bonnets" were also sold separately.

Hoods were made for ladies and for children. Both velvet and woolen hoods were available in a variety of colors. Knitted hats and "fascinators" (knitted or crocheted head coverings with long ties that came down over the ears and tied under the chin) were also sold.

Shoes, booties, slippers, and slumber socks were all mentioned in catalogues and store records. The three latter articles were either knitted or crocheted, but shoes were sometimes made of kid and stitched together on a sewing machine.

Baby bibs, baby jackets, belts, neckties, shawls, wool knee warmers, gloves, mittens, and wristlets were all handknitted or crocheted and sold in the Shaker stores. The wristlets were tubular wrist protectors and warmers. In the 1890's special gloves were made of raccoon fur and silk in New Lebanon.

Stockings, knitted by machine but finished by hand, were important in the northernmost communities. "Golf stockings" were popular by 1920, but no detailed description of them is available. Sweaters were also knitted by machine and by hand. "Jacket sweaters" were the most expensive ($4.70 to $7.50, depending on the size, in 1920), and there was an extra charge for either an additional pocket or an "auto collar."

A "ladies' dressing sack" (defined by Webster as a "loose jacket worn while dressing or lounging") was listed in the Enfield record. This kind of garment would probably not have been worn by the Shakers. "Mysteries," also mentioned in store records, remain mysterious to-day; I have not been able to discover what they were.

Toys and Children's Items

Small-size clothing was made for children, and special baby items were part of the standard fancy goods inventory. In addition, a large number of playthings were stocked in every store.

"Children's whips" were presumably toy horsewhips. There were also toy horse reins—continuous yarn chains made on knitting spools. Pinwheels made of pasteboard were sold from time to time, and beanbags and stuffed animals were very popular. The latter were made from cloth scraps or crocheted from cotton thread; pigs, rabbits, dogs, cats, mice, and rats were all made around 1920.

Much attention was given to dolls and doll accessories. Dolls were dressed in miniature Shaker clothing, accurate to the last detail; and a great number of doll bonnets were sold. Doll clothes that were not

FIGURE 139. *A doll dressed in Shaker costume. The doll is complete with three layers of underclothing, a dress treated for wrinkle resistance, a hooded broadcloth cape, a cap, and a miniature straw bonnet. (Hancock Shaker Village)*

related to Shaker outfits were also available, among them "dolly kimonos," raffia and canvas hats, tam-o-shanters, robes, jackets, shoes, and "togues" (togalike robes).

Stocking dolls, made from men's stockings, sold well in New Lebanon. A two-headed doll was made in Alfred: one side of its cloth head had a black face, the other side had a white face.

Doll hammocks and "dolly sacks" were also specified in store journals.

Edibles and Apothecary Items

Brief mention should be made of the prepackaged edible and apothecary items sold in twentieth-century Shaker stores. The following foods were available at various times: apple figs, butternuts and walnuts, candied flag root (also called sweet flag, or calumus root, and preserved in sugar), candied orange peel, mixed nuts, walnuts in maple sugar, peppermint and wintergreen drops, fudge, dried corn, chewing gum, jellies and jams (rose jelly was especially popular), pickles, and wine (grape, elderberry, blackberry, and dandelion). Hamamelis (extract of witch hazel), rose water, peach water, and soap were also sold regularly.

Appendixes

Appendix I
Location of Shaker Communities

LOCATION OF
THE
SHAKER COMMUNITIES

LEGEND

1 Alfred (1793–1931)
2 Canterbury
   (1792–present)
3 Enfield, Conn.
   (1792–1917)
4 Enfield, N.H. (1793–1918)
5 Groveland (1836–1892)
6 Hancock (1790–1960)
7 Harvard (1791–1919)
8 Mt. Lebanon (1789–1947)
9 North Union (1826–1889)
10 Pleasant Hill (1814–1910)

11 Sabbathday Lake
   (1794–present)
12 Shirley (1793–1909)
13 South Union (1811–1922)
14 Tyringham (1792–1875)
15 Union Village
   (1812–1910)
16 Watervliet, N.Y.
   (1787–1938)
17 Watervliet, Ohio
   (1813–1900)
18 West Union (1810–1827)
19 Whitewater (1824–1907)

Appendix II

Government and Organization of the Hancock Community and Church Family

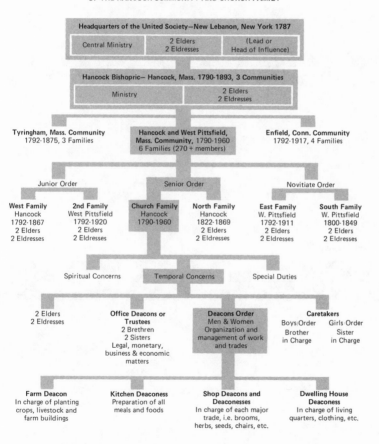

GOVERNMENT AND ORGANIZATION
OF THE HANCOCK COMMUNITY AND CHURCH FAMILY

Headquarters of the United Society—New Lebanon, New York 1787

| Central Ministry | 2 Elders 2 Eldresses | (Lead or Head of Influence) |

Hancock Bishopric— Hancock, Mass. 1790-1893, 3 Communities

| Ministry | 2 Elders 2 Eldresses |

Tyringham, Mass. Community
1792-1875, 3 Families

Hancock and West Pittsfield,
Mass. Community, 1790-1960
6 Families (270 + members)

Enfield, Conn. Community
1792-1917, 4 Families

Junior Order

Senior Order

Novitiate Order

| West Family Hancock 1792-1867 2 Elders 2 Eldresses | 2nd Family West Pittsfield 1792-1920 2 Elders 2 Eldresses | Church Family Hancock 1790-1960 | North Family Hancock 1822-1869 2 Elders 2 Eldresses | East Family W. Pittsfield 1792-1911 2 Elders 2 Eldresses | South Family W. Pittsfield 1800-1849 2 Elders 2 Eldresses |

Spiritual Concerns

Temporal Concerns

Special Duties

2 Elders
2 Eldresses

Office Deacons or
Trustees
2 Brethren
2 Sisters
Legal, monetary,
business & economic
matters

Deacons Order
Men & Women
Organization and
management of work
and trades

Caretakers
Boys Order   Girls Order
Brother   Sister
in Charge   in Charge

Farm Deacon
In charge of planting
crops, livestock and
farm buildings

Kitchen Deaconess
Preparation of all
meals and foods

Shop Deacons and
Deaconesses
In charge of each major
trade, i.e. brooms,
herbs, seeds, chairs, etc.

Dwelling House
Deaconess
In charge of living
quarters, clothing, etc.

Appendix III
Weaving Patterns

Modern Interpretation of
Original Shaker Weaving Drafts

The following three drafts were found in a form similar to the one illustrated in Figure 25, above, p. 56.

SQUARE DIAPER

PRUSSIAN DIAPER

SMALL HUCKABACK

TIE UP

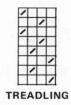

TREADLING

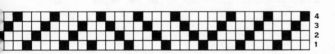

TREADLING

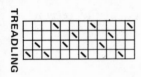

TIE UP

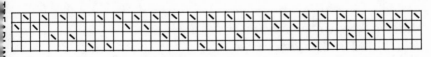

TIE UP

Partial Draft of the Dogwood Pattern

The pattern below has been drafted by the staff at Shakertown at Pleasant Hill, Kentucky, from original Shaker weaving found there. Pleasant Hill does not wish to have the entire Dogwood pattern published, but this is a useful sample.

DOGWOOD

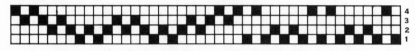

Order of Drawing in Palm Leaf for Weaving Diamond Fans

The "drawing-in" sequence shown below appeared in the receipt books of several Shaker communities. Presumably, the weave would have been a straight twill.

1234/1234/3214/321/234/1234/1234/3214/321

Analysis of Selected Woven Rag Rugs

All of the following rag rugs are in the Hancock Shaker Village collection. Many items have faded badly; the early aniline dyes were not always colorfast. The colors listed in Appendix 3 refer to the original colors, sometimes visible only in areas where light has not touched them.

1. Museum accession number: 62-165.
    Length: 17 feet 4 inches.
    Width: 3 feet 9 inches.
    Sett: 11 ends per inch.
    Warp: indigo dyed cotton.
    Finishing: braid and binding.

Weft sequence:

Unit A: 2 rows black woolen cloth strips.

Unit B: 1 row white cotton cloth plied with light blue cloth, Z twist.

Repeat Unit A.

Repeat Unit B.

Repeat Unit A.

Unit C: 1 row white cotton cloth plied with 6 strands madder dyed red wool yarn, Z twist.

Unit D: 2 rows blue woolen cloth strips.

Unit E: 2 rows of same plied yarns as Unit C (white and red) *overdyed* in indigo, making a light blue and deep red; S twist.

Repeat Unit D.

Repeat Unit E.

Repeat Unit D.

Repeat Unit C.

Repeat entire sequence.

The rug is finished on the selvedge ends with a braid made of yarn: 2 strands of red plied with gold and black, and one strand of red plied with white and black. It is finished on the open side with a handwoven binding having a natural linen warp, and weft stripes of red wool, indigo blue wool, linen, and blue cotton.

2. Museum accession number: 70-21.x.

Length: 38 inches.

Width: 30 inches.

Sett: 6 ends per inch.

Warp: beige cotton.

Finishing: binding surrounded by braid.

Weft sequence:

Unit A: 3 rows plied strips—e.g. green and blue, blue and brown. Primarily wool cloth, but some cotton is included. Not an exact repeat.

Unit B: 2 rows red cloth plied with light blue, olive green, and white yarns.

Repeat Unit A.

Unit C: 4 rows plied wool yarn—green, red, white, light blue.

Unit D: 3 rows plied cloth strips—brown and white plied with yellow-green.

Unit E: 1 row white cloth (2 strips plied together).

Repeat Unit D.

Repeat Unit C.

Repeat Unit A.

Repeat entire sequence.

The rug is finished on 4 sides with a twill-woven striped tape of pink, lilac, and white. The binding is surrounded by a 3-strand braid of purple, brown (originally green?), and grey cloth, about 3 inches thick.

3.   Museum accession number: 73-245.14.

Length: 48 inches.

Width: 41 inches.

Sett: 17 ends per inch.

Warp: light blue cotton.

Finishing: binding on 4 sides.

Weft sequence:

Unit A: 1 row red wool cloth.

Unit B: 1 row olive green wool cloth.

Unit C: 5 rows plied yarn in red, white, and blue; S twist.

Repeat Unit B.

Repeat Unit A.

Unit D: 5 rows plied yarn in red, white, green, and blue; Z twist.

Repeat Unit A.

Unit E: 1 row blue wool cloth.

Repeat Unit C.

Repeat Unit E.

Repeat Unit A.

Repeat Unit D.

Repeat entire sequence.

The rug was originally finished on all four sides with a narrow blue binding, probably handwoven. This is now visible only in a few frayed threads. At a later time, an olive green binding, a 1¼-inch-wide machine woven twill, was sewn over it.

4. Museum accession number: 63-318.
    Length: 18 feet 8 inches.
    Width: 46 inches.
    Sett: 11 ends per inch.
    Warp: white cotton.
    Finishing: selvedge ends, none; open ends, self-hem.

    Weft sequence (all cloth strips; no yarns):
    Unit A: 2 rows purple wool.
    Unit B: 2 rows light blue (aqua) cotton.
    Unit C: 3 rows rose red and white cotton print.
    Unit D: 2 rows yellow cotton.
    Repeat Unit A.
    Repeat Unit C.
    Repeat Unit B.
    Unit E: 2 rows thick gray wool.
    Unit F: 1 row yellow cotton.
    Unit G: 10 rows dark green, gray, and black (short strips, forming an area of color).
    Repeat Unit F.
    Repeat Unit E.
    Repeat Unit B.
    Repeat Unit C.
    Repeat Unit A.
    Repeat Unit D.
    Repeat Unit C.
    Repeat Unit B.

5. Museum accession number: 63-318.
    Length: 18 feet 8 inches.
    Width: 46 inches.
    Sett: 12 ends per inch.

Warp: cotton, in the following color pattern: 1 baby blue, 5 beige, 1 baby blue, 1 beige.
Finishing: braid.

Weft sequence:
    Unit A: 1 row light blue wool cloth strip.
    Unit B: 2 rows plied yarns—white, black, and orange.
    Unit C: 1 row black wool cloth strip.
    Unit D: 2 rows plied yarns—red, green, black.
    Unit E: 1 row white (or light beige) wool cloth strip.
    Repeat entire sequence.

The rug is finished on 4 sides with a 4-strand braid of yarns that appear in the weft: orange, red, green, and black.

Warp-faced Multicolored Striped Rug

Museum accession number: 63-337 A & B.
Width: 57 inches (pieced together; 1 piece is 40 inches wide).
Length: 10½ feet.
Warp: wool (color sequence listed below).
Weft: tan cotton (does not show).
Pattern: tabby, warp-faced.

Warp color sequence:

Unit A:	7 black.
10 inches wide	8 each, alternating orange and black (creates horizontal lines).
	7 pink.
	2 white.
	4 pink.
	2 white.
	4 brown.
	2 white.
	2 gold.
	6 brown.
	8 red.
	6 brown.

2 gold.

2 white.

6 light green.

5 medium green.

7 bright green.

5 light orange.

10 blue-green.

> Repeat in reverse order, starting with bright orange and ending with black.

Unit B:
7 inches wide

2 medium brown.

13 light brown.

37 beige.

13 light brown.

27 medium brown.

8 black.

Unit C:
3½ inches wide

22 purple plied with gray.

8 blue.

2 white.

4 blue.

4 purple.

2 white.

2 gold.

6 black.

6 green.

6 black.

2 gold.

2 white.

4 purple.

1 white.

Unit D:
8½ inches wide

9 pink.

15 medium red.

26 deep red.

27 sienna.

13 light sienna.

27 sienna.

26 deep red.

15 medium red.

9 pink.

Repeat Unit C in reverse order (starting with white, ending with purple plied with gray).

Repeat Unit B in reverse order (starting with black, ending with medium brown).

Repeat Unit A.

Analysis of Selected Chair-Seat Tapes

The following tapes are found in Hancock Shaker Village. Exact dates are not available, but they were all probably made in the first half of the nineteenth century.

1. Tape width: 1¼ inches. Total number of warp ends: 48.
    Warp: cotton (sequence of colors listed below).
    Weft: green wool; indigo overdyed on yellow.
    Pattern: tabby, 50/50 weave.

Warp color sequence:
    Unit A: 4 beige.
    Unit B: 1 brown.
             1 white.
             1 brown.
             1 white.
             1 brown.
             1 white.
             1 brown.
             1 white.
    Unit A: 4 beige.
    Unit C: 1 blue.
             1 white.
             1 blue.
             1 white.
             1 blue.
             1 white.
             1 blue.
             1 white.

(midpoint)
Repeat in reverse order:
Unit C, starting with white and ending with blue.
Unit A.
Unit B, starting with white and ending with brown.
Unit A.

2. Tape width: 1 inch.
    Total number of warp ends: 40.
    Warp: cotton (sequence of colors listed below).
    Weft: dark indigo blue wool.
    Pattern: tabby, nearly warp-faced (some weft shows).

Warp color sequence:
    Unit A: 1 dark red.
             1 light brown.
             1 dark red.
             1 light brown.
             1 dark red.
             1 light brown.
             1 dark red.
             1 light brown.
    Unit B: 2 medium blue.
    Unit C: 1 white.
             1 brown.
             1 white.
             1 brown.
             1 white.
             1 dark red.
             2 white.
             2 blue.
(midpoint)
Repeat, in reverse order:
Unit C, starting with 2 blue and ending with white.
Unit B.
Unit A, starting with light brown and ending with dark red.

3. Tape width: 1 inch.
   Total number of warp ends: 34.
   Warp: wool (color sequence listed below).
   Weft: blue wool.
   Pattern: twill, basically warp-faced.

   Warp color sequence:
     8 blue.
     3 white.
     4 green.
     4 red.
     4 green.
     3 white.
     8 blue.

4. Tape width: 1 inch.
   Total number of warp ends: 32.
   Warp: wool (color sequence listed below).
   Weft: indigo blue wool.
   Pattern: tabby, warp-faced.

   Warp color sequence:
     4 deep blue (indigo).
     2 white.
     2 deep blue.
     2 red.
     2 blue.
     2 red.
     4 blue.
     2 red.
     2 blue.
     2 red.
     2 blue.
     2 white.
     4 blue.

5.   Tape width: ¾ inch.
     Total number of warp ends: 35.
     Warp: linen and wool.
     Weft: light blue wool.
     Pattern: tabby, warp-faced.

    Unit A: 2 natural color linen.
    Unit B: 15 strands red and white wool (two threads used as
            one, but not actually plied).
    Unit C: 1 thick green wool.
    Unit B: 15 strands, as above.
    Unit A: 2 natural color linen.

Note: Tapes number 4 and 5 are used as the warp (4) and weft (5)
     of the same chair seat. (Museum accession number 63-181).

Appendix IV.

Recipes and Instructions

These recipes have been specially selected because of the insights they provide about Shaker life. Recipes that are particularly relevant to the types of textiles the Shakers worked with (carpets, bonnet capes, palm leaf, etc.) or to the large size of the communities have been included. The recipes appear here as they do in the original recipe books, and no attempt has been made to update them or reduce them to a scale that would be practical for the home dyer of today.

1. *New Lebanon Manner of Washing With Sal Soda.*
   The Brother rises early and gets a scalded pot of sal soda suds, one spoonful to the pailfull, puts the sheets and pillow cases in lets them stand 1 hour with frequent stirring, etc. Order: . . . collars, sheets, sisters clothes. Then browns, then sister's checks, then stockings and footings.
   > Source: Journal of Irena Bates
   > Unidentified Community

2. *To Make Oil Cloth.*
   1 pint wheat flour and 1 quart water, 2 teaspoons Alum and scald but not boil. Add 1 gallon soft soap and ½ pint boiled oil with some kind of paint, about 2 TBs. Spread with a brush on the cloth you intend to paint and smooth with hot flat irons until it is dry. Then it is fit to spread paint upon which should be mix[ed] with boiled oil without spirit.
   > Source: Journal of Irena Bates
   > Unidentified Community

3. *Painting Cloth for Table Coverings, Carpetings, etc.*
Apply rye paste with a little glue in it. Then paint the pasted
side with a base coat. Take the color you wish, mix with vin-
egar, mix with oil for painting, and brush on. Before it dries,
spread putty all over. Cover with varnish.
Source: Receipt book of Rosetta
Hendrickson
Unidentified Community
1837

5. *To Dress Silk Hankerchiefs.*
Take 1 ounce Irish moss, and soak it in warm water. Strain,
and use it to size the silk. Stretch on a damp cloth, and use a
hot iron. Swish the thread.
Source: Receipt Book
Second Family, Tyringham

6. *To Gloss and Stiffen Silk.*
2 ounces gum arabic, 1 ounce isinglass, dissolved in alcohol.
Put this in water, enter silk, drain, and iron.
Source: Church Family Recipes
Unidentified Community

7. *For Varnishing Straw.*
Dissolve in a tin canister, well steeped, 6 oz. Isinglass in
1 pint of the best alcohol. The canister should be kept near a
warm stove while dissolving the Isinglass, occasionally shaking
it up well. Let stand 24 hours.
Source: Receipt Book
Hancock

8. *For Bleaching Palm Leaf.*
Wash your palm leaf well with bar soap and a little sal soda,
just enough to make a decent lather. Then steep your palm
leaf for four hours in the . . . liquor. To two gallons of warm
water—add 8 oz. of Oxalic acid then drain it, and bleach while
wet about three hours.
Source: Receipt Book
Hancock

9.   *To Color Purslain Blue on Wool.*
Take one bushel purslain to one pound of logwood. Boil each separately, then strain and add them together which is sufficient for 11 pounds of wool. Prepare the wool in alum water, as you would to color red; then steep the wool an hour or more—not quite boil. It should be turned over occasionally.
Dip it off into hot suds, let it remain until it is cool enough to handle, and then it is finished.

> Source: Mary Ann Gill's Receipt Book
> Canterbury
> 1857

10.   *To Color Green on Woolen.*

5 oz. oil of vitriol	20	(the same
1 oz. indigo	4	proportions
2 oz. cream of tartar	8	can be applied
8 oz. alum	32	to any number
32 oz. fustic	128	of pounds)

> Source: Mary Ann Gill's Receipt Book
> Canterbury

11.   *[To Color] Butternut on Cotton Cloth.*
Boil cloth 3 hours in pure soft water. Fill your copper ½ full of bark, sink it to the bottom and begin to dip the cloth as soon as your bark begins to yield its strength. Run an hour and spread smooth in the sun for the sun turns and sets the colour. You may colour any quantity by taking out the bark when the strength is out and adding more. Rinse in pure soft water as all alkalis tarnish the color. The cloth should not be wrung at all.

> Source: Journal of Irena Bates
> Unidentified Community

12.   *Rule for Coloring Bonnet Capes with Hemlock.*
Use ground hemlock prepared for tanning leather. Have dye warm—let it steam—boil, let it out, fix it in suds.

> Source: Journal of C. Chaffin
> Canterbury

13. *For Red Expressly for Carpets.*
For one pound of woolen take 3 oz. alum, 1 oz. cream of
tartar, 1 lb. Nicaragua. Prepare the liquor in a brass or copper
kettle. Take a pail of water to a lb. of woolen, put in the tartar
and alum, bring to a boil; put in the woolen and boil an hour
and a half; take it out, dry, and rinse and empty away the
liquor; put into the kettle two pails of water to each lb. of yarn
and the Nicaragua in a bag. Boil an hour and a half, take out
the bag, put in the woolen, boil about an hour, gently stirring
it occasionally; it is then to be rinsed and dried. If you wish a
scarlet red, add a little fustic to the Nicaragua.
Source: Receipt Book
New Lebanon

14. *Method of Setting Up a Woad Vat Capable of Holding 40 Barrels.*
Put in 600 pounds of English woad on 300 of French woad,
1 bushel of bran, 5 pounds of madder, 20 pounds of indigo
and 5 quarts of lime. Rake up all together then cover it up for
12 hours. Open and add 5 quarts of lime then 3 or 5 quarts of
lime every two hours till you get in 4 quarts to every 100
pounds of woad. . . . Put in a pattern of wool and let it stay in
half an hour, and if it comes out a good grass green and after
the period of 4 minutes turns to a bright blue your vat is in
good order. But if the green holds on longer it needs more
time. Keep your liquor 130° hot and put in as much indigo
every day as you take out. The rule for a full blue is 16 pounds
of wool to one of indigo. Your vat will need about 2 quarts of
lime, 1 of madder, 2 oz. of bran per day.
　　If your vat gets too much lime the dye will look like lye and
smell like lime. Then you must put in a bag of bran. Let it stay
3 or 4 hours and ferment it.
　　For a full blue dip three times.
　　A vat should not run longer than 3 months.
Source: Mary Ann Gill's Receipt Book
Canterbury
1857

General Rule for Shaping Knit Drawers

The following pattern gives instructions for drawers as they were made for sale in the Church at Canterbury. The original broadside is at the Library of the United Society of Shakers, Sabbathday Lake, Maine.

The size may be varied generally by casting on more or less stitches.

Middling size

Cast on 72 stitches, knit 24 rounds seam; then widen 2 or 4 stitches at first leaving the seams; say 2 for middling size drawers and 4 for larger ones.

Then widen each side once in 10 rounds until
    5 tens are done, then
    7 eights,   10 sixes,   11 fours,
    4 threes,   13 twos.

Whole length 248 rounds on the leg.
    Narrow in the seat.

Back part	*Fore part*
3 sixes	11 twos
3 eights	2 threes
4 tens	2 fours
3 eights	2 sixes
3 sixes	1 eight
6 fours	

which makes 56 rounds. Then knit the same number of rounds without narrowing on the fore part, which in all makes 112 rounds in the seat, binding off the seat. Bind off 20 stitches, then 10, 9, 7, 5, and then 4 until it is done except about 10 or 12 stiches, then bind them off and it is completed.

Making a Poplar Box

Poplar cloth box 1
  Warp: fine white cotton sewing thread.
  Warp setting: 10 e.p.i.
  Threading:

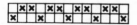

Weaving: 5 rows tabby with poplar strip weft.
        4 rows tabby—alternating one shot wood, one shot cotton
        thread.
Box construction

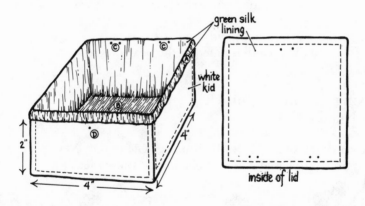

Poplar cloth is glued to cardboard. It is also nailed at 1-inch
intervals.
    Green silk lining is sewn in at top (A), and folded over the box in
a ¼-inch rolled hem. It is slightly gathered at the bottom. A separate 4-inch square is fitted in over the bottom of the box (B). The
lid is attached with two ribbons in the back. Each goes through
a pair of holes (C) on the lid and the back of the box and ties in a
bow on the top of the lid. In the front of the box, a piece of elastic
is attached to another bow. This attaches to a ceramic bead (D),
which is fastened through the front of the box with a metal clip.

Poplar cloth box 2
Warp: fine white cotton sewing thread.
Warp setting: 12 e.p.i.
Threading:

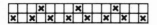

Weaving: 9 rows tabby with poplar strips.
6 rows tabby—sweet grass alternating with white cotton:
1 row light colored sweet grass
1 row cotton
1 row light colored sweet grass
1 row cotton
1 row dark colored (dyed) sweet grass
1 row cotton
9 rows tabby with poplar strips
(This cloth is glued to the box sideways.)

Making a Bonnet Thimble
and Needle Case

(Pattern courtesy of Gladys B. Amos of Glenmont, New York, after an original purchased at New Lebanon or Watervliet.)

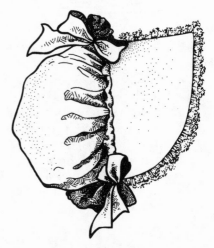

1. Cut one piece of cloth 9 by 7¼ inches for body of bonnet.
2. Cut 4 pieces cardboard—pattern piece A.
3. Cut 4 pieces of cloth—pattern piece B.
4. Cut 2 double pieces of flannel or felt (cut on fold)—pattern piece C. Pink indicated edges. This should be able to open up into a semicircular shape.
5. Glue cloth pattern pieces B to cardboard pieces A. Clip edges and mitre corners. Sew together with lace or rickrack trim.
6. Fold bonnet cloth (9-by-7¼-inch rectangle) in half. Fold under hems on all sides, press. Leaving about ½ inch at the top and 1 inch at the bottom, whip-stitch edges to cardboard pieces, gathering the cloth back on itself to form a ruffle. Gather the top and bottom of the cloth.
7. Stitch flannel pieces to the inside of the cardboard "wings": fold the flannel in half, and sew down along the fold and over the cotton/cardboard seam.
8. Trim with ribbon bow at top and bottom.

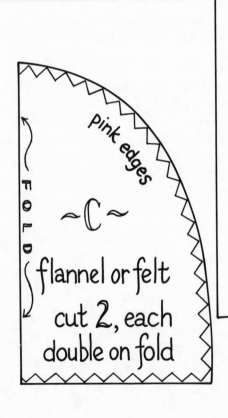

~ B ~

cotton cloth

cut 4

pink edges

FOLD

~ C ~

flannel or felt

cut 2, each
double on fold

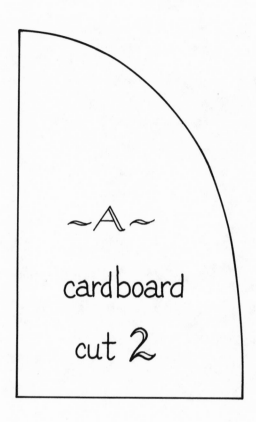

~A~

cardboard

cut 2

Appendix V
Items Purchased in the
Enfield, Connecticut, Fancy
Goods Store, 1910

CATEGORIES	QUANTITIES
Postcards	
with photograph	c. 800
with engraved pictures	c. 600
sewing and household accessories	
holders	28
dusters (presumably wool)	22
needlebooks	4
Shaker spools	3
cushions	35
straw cushions	5
trays	15
baskets, various sizes	13
face cloths	4
rugs (some "secondhand")	12
match scratcher	1
pieces wax	4
silk bags	4
watch cases	1
penwipers	c. 55
(dolly penwiper most popular)	
pillow tops	1
handwoven cloth:	

1 blanket
1 homemade linen sheet
4 pieces "home linen"
miscellaneous cloth, 15 yards

reins	15

doll clothes

bonnets	56
togues	5
tam o'shanters	4
cloak and capes	4
hats	1
sacks	5
robes	1
shoes (pairs)	1
jackets	1

edibles and apothecary items

packages of nuts	c. 1200
packages of nuts, flag root, orange, and apple peel	c. 600
packages of dried corn	c. 260
bottles of wine	35
bottles of helloline	13
jars of jelly and jam	8
packages of wintergreen	7
soap (homemade)	4

clothing

aprons	24
hoods	3
jackets	2
slumber sox	2
baby socks	4
shoes	2
belts	2
neck piece	1

miscellaneous household items and furniture

chairs	15
candlesticks	4
scales	1
tables and chests	4
powder flask	1
bellows	1
mortar and pestle	1
pewter basin	1
teapots	2
pitcher	1
bowls	4
pails	2
bottles	4

Notes

2. The Textiles Overall

1. Andrews, *Community Industries*, p. 184. For full references see References, below, p. 291.
2. Andrews and Andrews, *Shaker Furniture*, p. 116.
3. Millennial Laws, Part II, Section X.
4. Damph, Record of Girls Work, 1845.
5. Williams, Journal.
6. Bushnell, Dyers Journal.
7. Neal, *By Their Fruits*, p. 103. See also Williams, Journal, July 25, 1835.
8. Ibid.
9. Reed, Diary, 1872.
10. Bates, Journal, October 15, 1833.
11. Andrews, *Community Industries*, p. 191.
12. Ibid., p. 179.
13. Millennial Laws, Part I, Section IV.
14. Account Book, Articles Purchased in Hartford, 1849.
15. Zieget, "Our Shaker Adventure," p. 6.
16. Information about this process is from personal correspondence with Eldress Bertha Lindsay and personal conversation with Theodore Johnson.
17. Reed, Diary, December 13, 1872.
18. See Blinn, "Journey to Kentucky" (Summer 1966), p. 58.
19. Babbitt, Daily Record, May 1859.
20. Inventory: Catalogue of Articles. The particular items quoted here were given to Jane Leonard on November 7, 1849.
21. Babbitt, Daily Record, April 29, 1857.
22. See Cooper, *Invention of the Sewing Machine*, pp. 1–16.
23. Personal correspondence with Eldress Bertha Lindsay, July 1976.
24. See Babbitt, Daily Record, September 29, 1857; Reed, Diary, February 4, 1873; Journal, unidentified Canaan, New York sister, July 1855.

25. Record and Journal of Sisters, Watervliet.
26. See in particular Blanchard, Journal.
27. Andrews, *Community Industries*, pp. 209–211.

3. Production of Textiles

1. For a good detailed description of flax processing see Earle, *Home Life in Colonial Days*, pp. 166–187.
2. Williams, Journal, March 15, 1845.
3. Record and Journal of the Sisters, Watervliet, 1837.
4. Percy, *Valley of God's Pleasure*, p. 127.
5. Ibid., p. 127.
6. Young, "Concise View," p. 262.
7. Journal of the Hand Labor of Sisters, Watervliet.
8. Andrews, *Community Industries*, p. 256.
9. From personal conversations with Eldress Bertha Lindsay and Sister Gertrude Soule, August 1976.
10. Andrews, *Community Industries*, pp. 148–151.
11. David Meacham, Patent for Clothier Shears.
12. Andrews, *Community Industries*, p. 151.
13. See for example Percy, *Valley of God's Pleasure*, p. 138.
14. Blinn, Journal, quoted in Ott, *Hancock Shaker Village*, p. 34.
15. "Instructions for the Information and Benefit of Domestic Manufacturers."
16. Personal conversation with Theodore Johnson, November 1976.
17. Young, p. 264.
18. Personal conversation with Theodore Johnson, November 1976.
19. Young, p. 265.
20. Joseph Meacham, Holy Orders, Section 7.
21. Young, p. 261.
22. Young, pp. 261–262.
23. Colin, *North Union Shaker Story*, p. 100.
24. Neal, *By Their Fruits*, p. 102.
25. Neal, "Shaker Industries in Kentucky," p. 610.
26. Percy, *Valley of God's Pleasure*, p. 141.
27. Ibid.
28. Moore, Diary.
29. Ibid.
30. Neal, "Shaker Industries in Kentucky," p. 610.
31. Filley, *Recapturing Wisdom's Valley*, p. 51.

32. Percy, *Valley of God's Pleasure*, p. 141.
33. For a good description of processing silk see Mattera, "A History of Silk," pp. 24–30.
34. Andrews, *Community Industries*, p. 42.
35. Morrell, "Journey to the West," p. 52.
36. Ibid., p. 55.
37. Andrews, *Community Industries*, p. 252.
38. Diary of an unidentified sister, Mount Lebanon, March 24, 1891.
39. Reed, Diary, December 20, 1872.
40. See Andrews, *Community Industries*, p. 285.
41. This description is taken from Phelps, "The Making of a Shaker Bonnet," pp. 1, 6. Phelps is a former member of the Shaker society at East Canterbury.
42. This claim is made by Becker, in his untitled typewritten article. Becker made a film about the Shakers in 1944.
43. McCool, "Shaker Woven Poplar Work," pp. 56–59.
44. Becker, untitled article, n.p.
45. McCool, p. 57.
46. Sprigg, *By Shaker Hands*, p. 138.
47. Domestic Journal kept by the Ministry, Mount Lebanon, December 17, 1791.
48. Young, pp. 263–265.
49. Morrell, "Journey to the West," p. 58.
50. Blinn, "Journey to Kentucky" (Summer 1968), p. 183.
51. Ott, *Hancock Shaker Village*, p. 36.
52. Blinn, ibid.
53. Diary, unidentified sister, Mount Lebanon.
54. Young, p. 245.
55. Knight, "The Reverend William Bentley Visits the Shakers," pp. 7–8.
56. Andrews, *Community Industries*, p. 172.
57. For background information on American handweaving see Burnham and Burnham, *Keep Me Warm One Night*, and Atwater, *American Handweaving*.
58. This is the opinion of the curatorial staff of Shakertown at Pleasant Hill.
59. West, "Shaker Dress," p. 63.
60. Personal conversation with Theodore Johnson, November 1976.
61. Andrews, *Community Industries*, pp. 187–188.
62. Ibid., p. 189.
63. Ibid., p. 191.
64. Young, pp. 245–246.
65. Ott, *Hancock Shaker Village*, pp. 34–36.

66. Andrews and Andrews, *Shaker Furniture*, p. 38.
67. Ibid., p. 39.
68. Ibid., p. 41.
69. Pennington and Taylor, *American Spinning Wheels*, p. 63.
70. For descriptions of this type of textile equipment see Pennington and Taylor, pp. 63–71, and Channing, *Textile Tools*.
71. Pennington and Taylor, p. 63.
72. Andrews, *Community Industries*, p. 42.
73. For a good discussion of dyeing in early America see Adrosko, *Natural Dyes in the United States*.
74. Lovegrove, Journal.
75. Ibid.
76. Record and Journal of Sisters, Watervliet.
77. Klamkin, *Hands to Work*, p. 77.
78. These all appear in Bates, Journal.
79. Quoted in Andrews, *Community Industries*, p. 216.
80. This is in the manuscript which bears Eliza Ann Taylor's name at the beginning; however, the last pages were written by Elizabeth Lovegrove.
81. Andrews, *Community Industries*, p. 253.
82. See Sprigg, *By Shaker Hands*, p. 185.
83. Spencer, "Next Door to the Angels," p. 133.
84. Hulings, "Shaker Days Remembered," p. 8.

4. Household Textiles

1. Inventory: Catalogue of Articles.
2. See Orlofsky and Orlofsky, *Quilts in America*, pp. 271–279.
3. Millennial Laws, Part II, Section XII.
4. Millennial Laws, Part II, Section X.
5. See Little, *Floor Coverings in New England*; Roth, *Floor Coverings in Eighteenth Century America*.
6. Record and Journal of Sisters, Watervliet.
7. Account Book, Groveland, New York.
8. Babbitt, Daily Record, December 9, 1859.
9. Babbitt, Daily Record.
10. Reed, Diary, November 28, 1872.
11. Nordhoff, *Communistic Societies*, p. 137.
12. Millennial Laws, Part II, Section X.
13. Andrews and Andrews, *Shaker Furniture*, p. 1117.

14. See Burnham and Burnham, *Keep Me Warm One Night*, p. 84.
15. See Kopp and Kopp, *American Hooked and Sewn Rugs*, pp. 37–53, and Kent, *The Hooked Rug*, pp. 1–49.
16. See Kopp and Kopp, *American Hooked and Sewn Rugs*, pp. 28–34.
17. Ibid., p. 53; Walker, *Homecraft Rugs*, p. 292–296; Laury, *Handmade Rugs*, p. 31.
18. Joel and Kate Kopp, proprietors of "America Hurrah" Antiques and authorities on American folk art, are among the dealers who think this may be the case.
19. Also printed in *The Illustrated Catalogue and Price List of Shakers' Chairs*.
20. There is a good discussion of the use of tapes in Gehret, *Rural Pennsylvania Clothing*, pp. 242–243.
21. Record and Journal of Sisters, Watervliet.
22. Record of the Children's Order, Watervliet.
23. Account Book, Groveland, New York.
24. Zieget, "Our Shaker Adventure," p. 6.
25. Andrews, *Community Industries*, p. 248.
26. Blinn, "Journey to Kentucky" (Summer 1965), p. 44.
27. Andrews, *Community Industries*, p. 211.
28. Centennial Catalogue of the Shakers' Chairs.

5. Clothing and Personal Accessories

1. Young, "Concise View," p. 334.
2. Blinn, "Historical Notes," p. 2. All subsequent references to Blinn in this chapter are from this source.
3. Blinn, p. 2.
4. Ibid.
5. Reed, Diary, April 27, 1872.
6. Reed, Diary, August 5, 1872.
7. Bates, Journal, February 28, 1835.
8. Williams, Journal.
9. See for example Young, p. 335.
10. "Fifteen Years a Shakeress," p. 32.
11. Faith Andrews, "The Shaker Manner of Dress."
12. Finch, *An Englishwoman's Experience in America* (London: R. Bentley, 1833), quoted in Pearson et al., *The Shaker Image*, p. 41.
13. Bremer, Fredericka, *The Homes of the New World* (New York: Harper and Brothers, 1853), quoted in Pearson et al., *The Shaker Image*, p. 41.
14. Priscilla Wakefield, 1806; James Silk, 1841; and Seth Chandler, *The*

Berkshire American, 1850; quoted in Faith Andrews, "Shaker Manner of Dress."

15. Sarah Orne Jewett quoted in Faith Andrews, "The Shaker Manner of Dress"; and Nordhoff, *Communistic Societies*, p. 136.
16. "The Shakers," *Harpers*, p. 164.
17. Andrews, *Community Industries*, p. 170.
18. Proper for Sisters' Wearing Apparel.
19. Andrews, *Community Industries*, p. 170.
20. See for example Babbitt, Daily Record, September 29, 1857.
21. Tailor's Measurements, Mount Lebanon.
22. Sprigg, *By Shaker Hands*, p. 34.
23. Diary, unidentified sister, Mount Lebanon, 1891.
24. Young, "Concise View," pp. 304–307.
25. See Gehret, *Rural Pennsylvania Clothing*, pp. 33–34.
26. Young, pp. 310–311.
27. Young, p. 312.
28. Young, pp. 312–313.
29. Young, p. 315.
30. Young, pp. 313–314.
31. Blinn, p. 2.
32. Young, pp. 326–327.
33. Blinn, p. 2.
34. Elkins, *Fifteen Years*, p. 29.
35. Young, p. 328.
36. Young, p. 331.
37. Milbern, *Shaker Clothing*, n.p.
38. Quoted in Faith Andrews, "Shaker Manner of Dress."
39. Young, p. 329.
40. Blinn, p. 2.
41. Ibid.
42. Ibid.
43. Ibid.
44. Gehret, *Rural Pennsylvania Clothing*, p. 33.
45. Young, pp. 311–312.
46. Young, pp. 329–330.
47. Elkins, p. 29.
48. Reed, Diary, April 23, 1872.
49. Reclus, "A Visit to the Mount Lebanon Shakers," p. 29.
50. Young, pp. 316, 331–332.
51. Andrews, *Community Industries*, pp. 202–205.
52. Elkins, p. 30.

53. Personal conversation with Sister Elsie McCool, November 1976.
54. Blinn, p. 2.
55. Andrews, *Community Industries*, p. 284.
56. For a discussion of early American footwear see Earle, *Two Centuries of Costume in America*, pp. 359–388.
57. Young, p. 313.
58. Blinn, p. 2.
59. Reed, Diary, February 19, 1872; June 12, 1873.
60. Young, p. 315.
61. Elkins, p. 30.
62. Young, p. 306.
63. Young, p. 309; Blinn, p. 3.
64. Young, pp. 307, 317.
65. Young, p. 308.
66. Young, p. 318.
67. Young, p. 320.
68. Quoted in Faith Andrews, "The Shaker Manner of Dress."
69. Young, p. 320.
70. Elkins, p. 29.
71. Young, p. 317.
72. Young, pp. 318–320.
73. Blinn, p. 3.
74. Young, pp. 322–323.
75. Blinn, p. 3.
76. Ibid.
77. Ibid.
78. Ibid.
79. Andrews, *Community Industries*, pp. 252–253.
80. Blinn, p. 3.
81. Young, p. 326.
82. Blinn, p. 3.
83. Young, p. 325.
84. Young, p. 325.
85. Young, p. 324.
86. Gehret, *Rural Pennsylvania Clothing*, p. 180.
87. Fennelly, *Garb of Country New Englanders*, p. 46.
88. Charles Daubenny, "Journal of a Tour through the United States and Canada" (Oxford, 1843); quoted in Colin, *North Union Shaker Story*, p. 141.
89. Gehret, *Rural Pennsylvania Clothing*, pp. 192–194.
90. Hall, "Various Industries of the Mount Lebanon Shakers," p. 40.

91. Blinn, p. 3.
92. Milbern, n.p.
93. Blinn, p. 3.
94. Inventory: Catalogue of Articles.
95. Filley, *Recapturing Wisdom's Valley*, p. 40.
96. Young, p. 333.
97. Faith Andrews, "Shaker Manner of Dress."
98. Filley, *Recapturing Wisdom's Valley*, p. 41.
99. "Fifteen Years a Shakeress," p. 193.
100. Ibid., p. 193.
101. Millennial Laws, Part II, Section XVII.
102. This document is also excerpted in Andrews, *Community Industries*, p. 218.

6. Fancywork

1. Millennial Laws, Part III, Section IV.
2. Fancy Goods Catalogue, Hart and Shepard, East Canterbury, New Hampshire. n.d. [c. 1920].
3. Personal conversation with Eldress Bertha Lindsay, August 1976.
4. Miscellaneous newspaper clippings in the Emma King Library, Old Chatham.
5. See in particular miscellaneous correspondence with Frances Hall in the Andrews collection at Winterthur, and Zieget, "Our Shaker Adventure," p. 6.
6. Personal conversation with Sister Elsie McCool, November 1976.
7. McCool, "Shaker Woven Poplar Work," p. 57.
8. Vance, Journal, April 28, 1878.
9. McCool, p. 57.
10. Ibid., p. 58.
11. Braisted, Store Records, 1908.
12. Hulings, "Shaker Days Remembered," p. 8.
13. Zieget, "Our Shaker Adventure," p. 6.
14. Braisted, 1911.
15. Vance, Journal, November 22, 1877; December 18, 1878.

References

My most important source for both information and inspiration has been the textiles themselves. Shaker textiles of all sorts—potscrubbers, blankets, carpets, clothing—have been examined closely. Many have been found in museums (Hancock Shaker Village; The Shaker Museum at Old Chatham, New York; Shakertown at Pleasant Hill; Shakertown at South Union, Kentucky; Shaker Village at Canterbury; The Shaker Museum at Sabbathday Lake; The New York State Museum, storage collection; Western Reserve Historical Society; and Shaker Heights Historical Association). Some have been found in private collections.

I have also used other types of primary sources extensively. Most of the 150 original Shaker manuscripts studied are in the libraries of the Western Reserve Historical Society and the Winterthur Museum (Andrews Memorial Shaker Collection); others are in the Shaker Museum at Sabbathday Lake, Hancock Shaker Village, The Shaker Museum at Old Chatham, and the Kentucky Museum Library at Bowling Green. Many citations are from manuscripts quoted in one or another of Edward Demings Andrews' books about the Shakers, or from various articles in the *Shaker Quarterly* and *The World of Shaker*. Personal interviews and correspondence with Shaker sisters have been helpful in gleaning information about twentieth-century textiles. I have also consulted such original documents as the Shaker *Manifesto*, the Millennial Laws, Shaker broadsides, catalogues of sale goods, and other advertisements. Eyewitness accounts by visitors to Shaker communities and personal reminiscences by people who have lived for a time with the Shakers have also been helpful.

I welcome inquiries about specific textiles, manuscript references, or other sources. Any additions, corrections, or clarifications would be happily received.

Manuscripts are keyed to their locations as follows:

HSV   Hancock Shaker Village Library

KML   Kentucky Museum Library, Bowling Green, Kentucky

OC   Emma King Library, The Shaker Museum at Old Chatham, New York

SDL   Library of the Shaker Museum at Sabbathday Lake

WRHS   Western Reserve Historical Society, Cleveland, Ohio

WT   Edward Deming Andrews Memorial Shaker Collection, Henry Francis DuPont Winterthur Museum, Winterthur, Delaware

Account Book: Cloth and Other Articles Purchased in Hartford. Community unidentified, 1845–1850. WRHS.

Account Book. Groveland, New York, 1838–1848. WRHS.

Account Book kept by the Trustees. Poland Springs (Sabbathday Lake), Me., 1876–1916. SDL.

Adrosko, Rita J. *Natural Dyes in the United States*. Washington, D.C.: Smithsonian Institution Press, 1968.

Andrews, Edward Deming. *The Community Industries of the Shakers*. New York State Museum Handbook 15. Albany: New York State Museum, 1933; reprinted Charlestown, Mass.: Emporium Publications, 1971.

————. *The People Called Shakers: A Search for the Perfect Society*. New York: Oxford University Press, 1953; reprinted, new enlarged edition, New York: Dover Publications, 1963.

Andrews, Edward Deming, and Andrews, Faith. *Shaker Furniture: The Craftsmanship of an American Communal Sect*. New Haven: Yale University Press, 1937; reprinted New York: Dover Publications, 1964.

Andrews, Faith. "The Shaker Manner of Dress as Prescribed for Mother Ann's Children," typed manuscript, n.d. WT. (Also published in revised form in *New England Galaxy*, Spring 1965.)

Atwater, Mary Meigs. *The Shuttle-craft Book of American Handweaving: Being an Account of the Rise, Development, Eclipse, and Modern Revival of a National Popular Art, Together with Information of Interest and Value to Collectors, Technical Notes for the Use of Weavers, and a Large Collection of Historic Patterns*. New York: Macmillan Company, revised edition, 1951.

Babbitt, Sister Mary. Daily Record. Harvard and Shirley, 1856–1862, 1866–1869. WRHS.

Bates, Sister Betsey. Journal. New Lebanon, begun 1833. WRHS.

Becker, Stanton. Untitled typewritten article about Shaker poplar cloth. n.d. HSV.

Blanchard, Elder Grove. Journal of the Ministry. Harvard and Shirley, 1839. WRHS.

Blinn, Elder Henry C. "Historical Notes About the Change of Dress Among Believers," copied from Blinn's journal at Shaker Village, Inc., Canterbury, New Hampshire, by Eldress Bertha Lindsay, *The World of Shaker*, Winter 1974.

———. Journal, quoted in John Harlow Ott, *Hancock Shaker Village: A Guidebook and History*. Pittsfield, Mass.: Shaker Community, Inc., 1976.

———. "A Journey to Kentucky in the Year 1873," ed. Theodore E. Johnson, *The Shaker Quarterly*. Vol. 5, no. 6 (1965) to Vol. 7, no. 1 (1967).

Braisted, Sister Alice. Record of Sales in the Store, Enfield, Connecticut, 1908–1911. WT.

Broadside: Shaker Capes. West Pittsfield (Hancock), Mass., n.d. WRHS.

Burnham, Harold B., and Burnham, Dorothy K. *Keep Me Warm One Night: Early Handweaving in Eastern Canada*. Toronto: University of Toronto Press in cooperation with the Royal Ontario Museum, 1972.

Bushnell, Sister Sally. Dyers Journal. New Lebanon, n.d. WT, OC.

Catalogue of Fancy Goods. Alfred, 1908. SDL.

Centennial Catalogue of the Shakers' Chairs, Foot Benches, etc. New Lebanon, 1876. WRHS.

Channing, Marion L. *The Textile Tools of Colonial Homes: From Raw Materials to Finished Garments before Mass Production in the Factories*. Marion, Mass.: n.p., 1969.

Church Family Recipes. Unidentified community, n.d. WRHS.

Clark, Thomas D., and Ham, F. Gerald. *Pleasant Hill and Its Shakers*. Pleasant Hill, Kty.: Shakertown Press, 1968.

Conlin, Mary Lou. *The North Union Story: A Shaker Society, 1822–1889*. Shaker Heights, Ohio: Shaker Heights Historical Society, 1961.

Cooper, Grace Rogers. *The Invention of the Sewing Machine*. Washington, D.C.: Smithsonian Institution Press, 1968.

Crossman, Sister Abigail. Dye Receipts. New Lebanon, n.d. WRHS.

Damph, Sister Catherine, Caretaker. Record of Girls Work. Watervliet, N.Y., 1845. WRHS.

Diary, Unidentified sister. Hancock or New Lebanon, 1866. WT.

Diary, Unidentified sister. Mount Lebanon, 1891. WRHS.

Domestic Journal kept by the Ministry. Mount Lebanon, Vol. 1, 1780–1841. WT.

Eades, Brother Hervey L. Tailor's System for Cutting Shakers' Garments. Union Village, Ohio, 1849. WRHS.

Earle, Alice Morse. *Home Life in Colonial Days*. New York: Grosset and Dunlap, 1898; reprinted Stockbridge, Mass.: Berkshire Traveller Press, 1974.

————. *Two Centuries of Costume in America, 1620–1820*. New York: Macmillan, 1903; reprinted New York: Dover Publications, 1970.

Elkins, Hervey. *Fifteen Years in the Senior Order of Shakers: A Narration of Facts Concerning That Singular People*. Hanover, N.H.: Dartmouth Press, 1853.

Fancy Goods (catalogue). East Canterbury, N.H.: Hart and Shepard, n.d. [c. 1920]. SDL.

Fennelly, Catherine. *The Garb of Country New Englanders, 1790–1840: Costumes at Old Sturbridge Village*. Sturbridge, Mass.: Old Sturbridge Village, 1966.

"Fifteen Years a Shakeress." *The Galaxy*, January–April 1872. WRHS.

Filley, Dorothy M. *Recapturing Wisdom's Valley: The Watervliet Shaker Heritage 1775–1975*. Albany: The Town of Colonie and the Albany Institute of History and Art, 1975.

Gehret, Ellen. *Rural Pennsylvania Clothing*. York, Pa.: George M. Shumway, 1977.

Giles, Janice Holt. *The Believers*. Boston: Houghton Mifflin, 1957.

Gill, Sister Mary Ann. Receipt Book. Canterbury, 1857. SDL.

Godey's Lady's Book (Godey's Magazine). Published monthly in Philadelphia, 1830–1898.

Hall, Sister Frances, miscellaneous correspondence to and from. New Lebanon, 1950's. WT.

Hall, William Bradford. "Various Industries of the Mount Lebanon Shakers," *The Pegboard* (Lebanon School, New Lebanon, N.Y.), Vol. 4 (June 1936), "First Shaker Number," reprint, [n.p., Darrow School, 1966].

Hendrickson, Sister Rosetta. Receipt Book. Unidentified community, 1844–1854. WRHS.

Hinds, William Alfred. *American Communities*. Oneida, N.Y.: Office of the American Socialist, 1878; reprinted Secaucus, N.J.: Citadel Press, 1973.

Hulings, Martha. "Shaker Days Remembered." *The World of Shaker*, Spring 1973.

The Illustrated Catalogue and Price List of Shakers' Chairs Manufactured by the Society of Shakers, Mount Lebanon. New York: R. M. Wagan and Company, n.d. [c. 1875]; reprint, 1972, available HSV.

"Instructions for the Information and Benefit of Domestic Manufacturers in Woolen Cloths," extract from an advertisement for the fulling mill operated by the Shakers in South Union, Kentucky, September 19,

1815. The document was given to me by Julia Neal of Shakertown at South Union, Kentucky.

Inventory: Catalogue of Articles of Clothing, etc. delivered to those who have left our society. Watervliet, New York, 1827–1864. WRHS.

Journal of the Hand Labor of Sisters. Second Family, Watervliet, New York, 1845–1850. WRHS.

Journal of an Unidentified Canaan (New Lebanon), New York, sister, 1855–1866. WRHS.

Kent, William Winthrop. *The Hooked Rug: A Record of Its Ancient Origin, Modern Development, Methods of Making, Sources of Design, Value as a Handicraft, the Growth of Collections, Probable Future in America, and Other Data*. New York: Dodd, Mead and Company, 1930.

Klamkin, Marian. *Hands to Work: Shaker Folk Art and Industries*. New York: Dodd, Mead, 1972.

Knight, Russell W. "The Reverend William Bentley Visits the Shakers." *The Shaker Quarterly*, Spring, 1964.

Kopp, Joel, and Kopp, Kate. *American Hooked and Sewn Rugs: Folk Art Underfoot*. New York: E. P. Dutton, 1975.

Laury, Jean, and Aiken, Joyce. *Handmade Rugs From Practically Anything*. Philadelphia: Countryside Press, 1971.

"Letters on the Condition of Kentucky: Mineral Springs at Harrodsburg— Epsom Salts—Particular Account of the Shakers, Communicated for the [Richmond, Virginia] Enquirer," Tuesday, May 3, 1825. Mimeographed reprint provided by Shakertown at Pleasant Hill.

Little, Nina Fletcher. *Floor Coverings in New England Before 1850*. Sturbridge, Mass.: Old Sturbridge Village, 1967.

Lovegrove, Sister Elizabeth. Journal. Church Family. New Lebanon, 1840. WT.

McCool, Sister Elsie. "Shaker Woven Poplar Work." *Shaker Quarterly*, Summer 1962.

Mattera, Joanne. "A History of Silk." *Shuttle, Spindle and Dyepot*, Spring 1977.

Meacham, Brother David. Patent for Clothier Shears Adapted to Shearing Machines. New Lebanon, 1797. WT.

Meacham, Father Joseph. "Holy Orders of the Church." New Lebanon, 1841. WT.

Method of Colouring Blue Practiced by the Society of Believers in Kentucky. n.d. WRHS.

Milbern, Gwendolyn. *Shaker Clothing*. Lebanon, Ohio: Warren County Historical Society, n.d. [196–].

Millennial Laws or Gospel Statutes and Ordinances adapted to the Days of Christ's Second Appearing. Given and established in the Church for the protection Thereof by Father Joseph Meacham and Mother Lucy Wright the Presiding Ministry, and by their Successors, the Ministry and Elders. Recorded at New Lebanon August 7, 1821. Revised and reestablished by the Ministry and Elders October, 1845. Reprinted in Andrews, Edward Deming, *The People Called Shakers*. Oxford: Oxford University Press, 1953; reprinted New York: Dover Publications, 1964.

Moore, Eldress Nancy E. Diary. South Union, Kty., 1863. KML.

Morrell, Prudence. "Account of a Journey to the West in the Year 1847," edited by Theodore E. Johnson. *Shaker Quarterly*, Summer, Fall, 1968.

Neal, Julia. *By Their Fruits: The Story of Shakerism in South Union, Kentucky*. Chapel Hill: University of North Carolina Press, 1947.

———. "Shaker Industries in Kentucky." *Antiques*, March, 1974.

Nordhoff, Charles. *The Communistic Societies in the United States: From Personal Visit and Observation*. New York: Harper and Brothers, 1875; reprint ed. New York: Hillary House Publishers, 1960.

Orlofsky, Patsy, and Orlofsky, Myron. *Quilts in America*. New York: McGraw-Hill, 1974.

Ott, John Harlow. *Hancock Shaker Village: A Guidebook and History*. Pittsfield, Mass.: Shaker Community, Inc., 1976.

Pearson, Elmer R., Neal, Julia, and Whitehill, Walter Muir. *The Shaker Image*. Boston: New York Graphic Society with Shaker Community, Inc., Hancock, Mass., 1974.

Pennington, David A., and Taylor, Michael. *A Pictorial Guide to American Spinning Wheels*. Sabbathday Lake, Me.: The Shaker Press, 1975.

Phelps, Florence. "The Making of a Shaker Bonnet." *The World of Shaker*, Summer 1975.

Piercy, Caroline B. *The Valley of God's Pleasure: A Saga of the North Union Shaker Community*. New York: Stratford House, 1951.

Pratt, Sister Zeruah. Book of Receipts for Coloring. Tyringham, 1834. WRHS.

Products of Dilligence and Intelligence. New Lebanon, n.d. [c. 1905]. Original WRHS; copies also in SDL, HSV, WT.

Proper for Sisters' Wearing Apparel. Unidentified eldress. Hancock, 1840. Typescript HSV.

Reclus, Elie. "A Visit to the Mount Lebanon Shakers in 1878." *Shaker Quarterly*, Spring 1971.

Record of the Children's Order (Girls Work and Caretaker), Watervliet, New York, 1846. WRHS.

Record and Journal of Sisters, First Order, Watervliet, New York, 1830–1841. WRHS.

Reed, Sister Polly Ann. Diary. New Lebanon, 1872–1873. WRHS.

Roth, Rodris. *Floor Coverings in Eighteenth Century America*. Washington, D.C.: Smithsonian Institution Press, 1967.

Second Family Receipts. Tyringham, n.d. WRHS.

Shaker Image.

Shakers, miscellaneous newspaper clippings relating to. OC, HSV.

"The Shakers." *Harpers New Monthly Magazine*, June–November 1857.

Spencer, Sylvia Minott. "Next Door to the Angels—My Memories of the Shakers." *Shaker Quarterly*, Winter 1970.

Spiritual Dresses for the Families, January 1, 1842. Concerning the Robes and Dresses that are prepared for all such as go up to the Feast of the Lord or attend to her Holy Passover. Hancock. WRHS.

Sprigg, June. *By Shaker Hands*. New York: E. P. Dutton, 1974.

Springer, Pauline. "The Weaver's Ready Reckoner." Alfred, n.d. SDL.

Tailor's Measurements. Mount Lebanon, 1838–1842. WRHS.

Taylor, Eliza. "A Brief Memorandum of the Work done at the Wash-house in the colouring line, the colour, quantity and quality of the wool yarn, cloth, etc." Begun May, 1842. WT.

Vance, John. Journal. Alfred, N.Y., 1876–1878. SDL.

Walker, Lydia Le Baron. *Homecraft Rugs: Their Historic Background, Romance of Stitchery and Method of Making*. New York: Frederick A. Stokes Company, 1929.

West, Eugene. "Shaker Dress." *The Pegboard*, First Shaker Number. New Lebanon: The Darrow School, 1937.

Williams, Sister Anne. Journal. New Lebanon, 1832–1855. WRHS.

Young, Elder Isaac N. "A Concise View of the Church of God and of Christ on Earth Having its Formation In the Faith of Christ's First and Second Appearing." New Lebanon, 1856. WT.

Zieget, Irene. "Our Shaker Adventure." *The World of Shaker*, Fall 1973.

Personal Correspondence and informal interviews:

Eldress Bertha Lindsay, Canterbury, New Hampshire, July and August 1976.

Sister Gertrude Soule, Canterbury, New Hampshire, August 1976.

Theodore E. Johnson, Sabbathday Lake, Maine, November 1976.

Sister Elsie McCool, Sabbathday Lake, Maine, November 1976.

Sister Mildred Barker, Sabbathday Lake, Maine, November 1976.

Further Reading

Abbey, Barbara. *The Complete Book of Knitting*. New York: Viking Press, 1971.

Account Book of Bonnets, baskets, etc. Watervliet, New York, 1836–1857. WRHS.

Andere, Mary. *Old Needlework Boxes and Tools: Their Story and How to Collect Them*. New York: Drake Publishers, 1971.

Bemis, Elijah. *The Dyer's Companion*. New York: Evert Duychinck, 1815; reprinted New York: Dover, 1973.

Birrell, Verla Leone. *The Textile Arts, A Handbook of Fabric Structure and Design Process: Ancient and Modern Weaving, Braiding, Printing, and Other Textile Techniques*. New York: Harper and Row, 1959.

Bogdonoff, Nancy Dick. *Handwoven Textiles of Early New England: The Legacy of a Rural People, 1640–1880*. Harrisburg, Pa.: Stackpole Books, 1975.

Bolton, Ethel Stanwood, and Coe, Eva Johnston. *American Samplers*. Boston: The Massachusetts Society of the Colonial Dames of America, 1921.

Book of the Busy Hours. Hancock. Commenced March 1 and June 23, 1877. HSV.

Chair Order Book. New Lebanon, 1881–1885. WT.

Channing, Marion L. *The Magic of Spinning: How to Do It Yourself, with the Emphasis on Wool, the History of Spinning, and Other Facts*. Marion, Mass.: n.p., 1966.

Cooper, Grace Rogers. *The Copp Family Textiles*. Washington, D.C.: Smithsonian Institution Press, 1971.

Desroche, Henry Charles. *The American Shakers from Neo-Christianity to Presocialism*. Amherst, Mass.: University of Massachusetts Press, 1971.

Dillmont, Thérèse de. *The Complete Encyclopedia of Needlework*. Paris, France: D.M.C. Company, n.d.; reprinted Philadelphia: Running Press, 1973.

Early Book of Records of the Hancock Church Family, 1789–1801. OC.

Emery, Irene. *The Primary Structure of Fabrics—An Illustrated Classification*. Washington, D.C.: The Textile Museum, 1966.

Fennelly, Catherine. *Textiles in New England, 1790–1840*. Sturbridge, Mass.: Old Sturbridge Village, 1964.

Gallagher, Constance Dann. *Linen Heirlooms: The Story and Patterns of a Collection of 19th Century Handwoven Pieces with Directions for Their Reproduction*. Newton Centre, Mass.: Charles T. Branford Co., 1968.

Groves, Sylvia. *The History of Needlework Tools and Accessories*. London: Country Life, 1966.

Harbeson, Georgiana Brown. *American Needlework: The History of Decorative Stitchery and Embroidery from the Late 16th to the 20th Century*. New York: Coward-McCann, 1938.

Hart, Sister Emmeline. Journal. Enfield, N.H., n.d. WT.

Journals of the Ministry, Harvard, Mass. Written in the Years 1884, 1845, and 1847. WRHS.

Katzenberg, Dena S. *Blue Traditions: Indigo Dyed Textiles and Related Cobalt Glazed Ceramics from the 17th through the 19th Century*. Baltimore: Baltimore Museum of Art, 1973.

Lane, Rose. *Woman's Day Book of American Needlework*. New York: Simon and Schuster, 1963.

Lee, Sister Polly. Journal. Groveland, New York, beginning 1843. WRHS.

Lichten, Frances. *Decorative Art of Victoria's Era*. New York: Charles Scribner's Sons, 1950.

Little, Frances. *Early American Textiles*. New York: The Century Company, 1931.

Merrimack Valley Textile Museum. *Wool Technology and the Industrial Revolution: An Exhibition*. North Andover, Mass.: Merrimack Valley Textile Museum, 1965.

Montgomery, Florence M. *Printed Textiles: English and American Cottons and Linens, 1700–1850*. New York: Viking Press, 1970.

Order Form for Cloaks. Unidentified community, n.d. WT.

Reath, Nancy Andrews. *The Weaves of Hand-loom Fabrics: A Classification with Historical Notes*. Philadelphia: The Pennsylvania Museum, 1927.

Receipt Book. Unidentified Community, n.d. SDL.

Recipes from South Union and Mount Lebanon, 1835–1837. WRHS.

Ries, Estelle H. *American Rugs*. Cleveland: World Publishing Company, 1950.

Seligman, G. Saville, and Hughes, Talbot. *Domestic Needlework: Its Origins and Customs throughout the Centuries*. London: Country Life, 1926.

"A Short Treatise on the Process of Cutting by the Square and plumb rule with some general observations on the business of tailoring." Probably New Lebanon, December 1828. SDL.

Sister's Diary. Hancock, 1854. WT.

Sober, Marion Burr. *Chair Seat Weaving for Antique Chairs*. Plymouth, Mich.: Balch Printing Company, 1964; reprinted, 1968.

Warren, Geoffrey. *A Stitch in Time: Victorian and Edwardian Needlecraft*. New York: Taplinger, 1976.

Workwoman's Guide. London: Simpkin, Marshall. 1838.

Figure Credits

All photographs not otherwise credited were taken by the author.

1: Paul Rocheleau, Richmond, Massachusetts.
3: Courtesy Shakertown at Pleasant Hill, Harrodsburg, Kentucky.
6: Paul Rocheleau, Richmond, Massachusetts.
7: Original by Louis H. Frohman, Bronxville, New York; Courtesy Shaker Community, Inc., Pittsfield, Massachusetts.
8: Courtesy Ron Emery, Darrow School Archives, New Lebanon, New York.
9: David Serette; original in the Library of the United Society of Shakers, Sabbathday Lake, Maine.
11: Paul Rocheleau, Richmond, Massachusetts.
12: Courtesy *The Shaker Image*, published by the New York Graphic Society.
14: Courtesy Shaker Community, Inc., Pittsfield, Massachusetts.
18: Original in the Library of the United Society of Shakers, Sabbathday Lake, Maine.
19: Original in the Library of the United Society of Shakers, Sabbathday Lake, Maine.
20: Lee's Studio of Photography, Chatham, New York; Courtesy Shaker Community, Inc., Pittsfield, Massachusetts.
25: Original in the Edward Demings Andrews Memorial Shaker Collection, Henry Francis DuPont Winterthur Museum, Winterthur, Delaware.
27: Paul Rocheleau, Richmond, Massachusetts.
28: Paul Rocheleau, Richmond, Massachusetts.
29: Paul Rocheleau, Richmond, Massachusetts.
30: Original at Shaker Community, Inc., Pittsfield, Massachusetts.

32: Philip Lief, Great Barrington, Massachusetts.

36: Paul Rocheleau, Richmond, Massachusetts.

38: Paul Rocheleau, Richmond, Massachusetts.

40: Paul Rocheleau, Richmond, Massachusetts.

42: Paul Rocheleau, Richmond, Massachusetts.

47: Paul Rocheleau, Richmond, Massachusetts.

48: Linda Cobleigh, New Paltz, New York.

49: Linda Cobleigh, New Paltz, New York.

50: Linda Cobleigh, New Paltz, New York.

51: Noel Vicentini; Index of American Design, Smithsonian Institution, Washington, D.C.

53: Gail Giles, Lebanon Springs, New York.

55: Paul Rocheleau, Richmond, Massachusetts.

56: Paul Rocheleau, Richmond, Massachusetts.

60: Gail Giles, Lebanon Springs, New York.

62: Gail Giles, Lebanon Springs, New York.

63: Linda Cobleigh, New Paltz, New York.

64: Linda Cobleigh, New Paltz, New York.

65: Courtesy Shakertown at Pleasant Hill, Harrodsburg, Kentucky.

67: Courtesy Shakertown at Pleasant Hill, Harrodsburg, Kentucky.

68: Courtesy Shakertown at Pleasant Hill, Harrodsburg, Kentucky.

69: Original in the Library of the Western Reserve Historical Society, Cleveland, Ohio.

71: Paul Rocheleau, Richmond, Massachusetts.

72: Paul Rocheleau, Richmond, Massachusetts.

73: Original in the Emma King Library, The Shaker Museum at Old Chatham, New York.

75: Linda Cobleigh, New Paltz, New York.

77: Index of American Design, Smithsonian Institution, Washington, D.C.

79: Paul Rocheleau, Richmond, Massachusetts.

81: Gail Giles, Lebanon Springs, New York.

82: Gail Giles, Lebanon Springs, New York.

83: Private Collection, Courtesy Elmer Ray Pearson, Chicago, Illinois.

84: Paul Rocheleau, Richmond, Massachusetts.

86: Paul Rocheleau, Richmond, Massachusetts.

87: Original in the Library of the Western Reserve Historical Society, Cleveland, Ohio.
89: Paul Rocheleau, Richmond, Massachusetts.
91: Courtesy George Shumway, York, Pennsylvania.
93: Original in the Emma King Library, The Shaker Museum at Old Chatham, New York.
95: Original at Shaker Community, Inc., Pittsfield, Massachusetts.
96: Paul Rocheleau, Richmond, Massachusetts.
97: Paul Rocheleau, Richmond, Massachusetts.
98: Original in the Emma King Library, The Shaker Museum at Old Chatham, New York.
100: Original in the Emma King Library, The Shaker Museum at Old Chatham, New York.
101: Original in the Library of the United Society of Shakers, Sabbathday Lake, Maine.
102: Eugene Mitchell, Pittsfield, Massachusetts; Courtesy Shaker Community, Inc., Pittsfield, Massachusetts.
104: Gail Giles, Lebanon Springs, New York.
105: Original in the Emma King Library, The Shaker Museum at Old Chatham, New York.
106: Original at Shaker Community, Inc., Pittsfield, Massachusetts.
108: Paul Rocheleau, Richmond, Massachusetts.
109: Original in the Library of Shaker Village, Inc., Canterbury, New Hampshire.
110: Original at Shaker Community, Inc., Pittsfield, Massachusetts.
111: Courtesy *The Shaker Image*, published by the New York Graphic Society.
112: Courtesy *The Shaker Image*, published by the New York Graphic Society.
113: Original in the Emma King Library, The Shaker Museum at Old Chatham, New York.
116: Paul Rocheleau, Richmond, Massachusetts.
117: Paul Rocheleau, Richmond, Massachusetts.
118: Original at Shaker Community, Inc., Pittsfield, Massachusetts.
119: Paul Rocheleau, Richmond, Massachusetts.
121: Paul Rocheleau, Richmond, Massachusetts.
123: Paul Rocheleau, Richmond, Massachusetts.

126:   Paul Rocheleau, Richmond, Massachusetts.

127:   Paul Rocheleau, Richmond, Massachusetts.

128:   Paul Rocheleau, Richmond, Massachusetts.

130:   Paul Rocheleau, Richmond, Massachusetts.

131:   Gail Giles, Lebanon Springs, New York.

136:   Gail Giles, Lebanon Springs, New York.

137:   Original in the Emma King Library, The Shaker Museum at Old Chatham, New York.

Appendix I: Courtesy Shaker Community, Inc., Pittsfield, Massachusetts.

Appendix II: John Harlow Ott, Pittsfield, Massachusetts.

142 (poplar box construction):   Gail Giles, Lebanon Springs, New York.

143 (Shaker thimble and needle case):   Gail Giles, Lebanon Springs, New York.

144 (patterns for 143):   Gail Giles, Lebanon Springs, New York.

All color plates are from photographs taken by the author.

Glossary

ALEPPO GALLS (p. 76). A type of gall (an infection on a tree, caused by the gall wasp, with a high tannic acid content); used for dyeing gray and drab colors.

ALUM (pp. 26, 76). Potassium aluminum sulfate (or ammonium aluminum sulfate) used with cream of tartar as a mordant, or setting agent, in natural dyeing.

ANILINE DYES (pp. 15, 80–81). Broadly, a synthetic dye from an organic source; the first synthetic dyes.

ANNATO (pp. 76, 79). A reddish dyestuff derived from the orange-red outer covering of the seeds of a tropical shrub.

ANTIMACASSAR (pp. 145, 243). A doily-like cover used to protect the back or arms of upholstered furniture, particularly from Macassar hair oil. *See also* TIDY.

ARMSCYE (pp. 166, 167). The armhole, or place where the sleeve is set in, in a garment.

BALANCED WEAVE. *See* FIFTY-FIFTY WEAVE.

BASKETWEAVE (p. 135). A weave similar to plain weave, but all warps and wefts are in pairs—i.e., two weft threads go over and under two warp threads, alternately.

BERTHA (pp. 150, 170). Generally, a collar covering the shoulders. Shaker berthas, in use from about 1875, replaced the neckerchief as the bodice covering.

BIFOID (pp. 212, 221). A Shaker poplar cloth box with two semicircular bulges, each with its own independently opening lid.

BIRD'S-EYE WEAVE (p. 52). A small diamond twill pattern, usually with all diamonds about the same size, sometimes other diamond patterns. *See also* GOOSE-EYE WEAVE.

BISHOPRIC (p. 5). An administrative division of the Church made up of several communities in a relatively coherent geographical area.

BOAT SHUTTLE (pp. 71, 72). A boat-shaped shuttle used in weaving for carrying weft yarns back and forth through the web.

BRAID. *See* TAPE.

BRAKE, BREAK (pp. 23, 35, 37). In flax processing, to break the softened flax stalks so that the outside fibers are not damaged. Also called SWINGLE. *See also* FLAX BREAK.

BRAZILWOOD (pp. 76, 79). A source of red dye—from several different trees, mostly common to Brazil. *See also* CAMWOOD.

BREECHES (pp. 188–189). Short trousers which cover the hips and thighs and fit tightly at the lower edges just below the knee. Worn with long stockings.

BUTTERNUT (pp. 75–76). A rich reddish brown dye from the bark of the butternut tree.

CAMBRIC (pp. 25, 26). A fine white linen fabric, or sometimes, a cotton fabric that resembles linen cambric.

CAMWOOD (p. 76). A dyestuff from the west coast of Africa, used for reddish colors; related to BRAZILWOOD.

CAPE. 1. (pp. 185, 214, 246–247). A cloak. 2. (pp. 160, 179, 180). The piece of fabric which is attached to the bottom of a Shaker bonnet or coat and covers the shoulders. *See also* CURTAIN.

CARD, CARDER. *See* HAND CARDS.

CARDING (p. 38). The process of aligning (combing) woolen, cotton, or tow fibers to prepare them for spinning.

CARRIER (pp. 227, *234, 235*). An open wooden box with a wooden handle, usually lined, either rectangular or oblong.

CASKET (pp. 212, 221). A large poplar cloth work box with smaller boxes or pockets on the lid or sides.

CATCHETU (CATECHU) (p. 76). A brown dyestuff from the Acacia catechu tree, also known as CUTCH.

CATERPILLAR (p. 112). A fabric strip sewn through with a running stitch which is pulled tight to create a gathered or shirred ruffle. *See also* SHIRRED RUG.

CHEMISE (p. 184). A loose, one-piece woman's undergarment; a slip.

CHENILLE RUG. *See* SHIRRED RUG.

CHIP (p. 180). Usually, small pieces of straw or palm leaf, already woven, used in bonnets and hats. Occasionally, the straw itself.

CHIP HAT (p. 179). A fabric-covered braided straw hat worn by women prior to 1805. *See also* CHIP.

CLOCK REEL (pp. 64, *66*). A frame on which to wind skeins of yarn, with a counting device ("clock") built in. Most clocks were numbered from 1 to 40, and the needle, or hand, advanced one number for each complete revolution of the reel.

COCHINEAL (pp. 57, 76). One of the most important red dyestuffs, taken from the dried bodies of an insect native to Latin America.

COPPERAS (pp. 26, 76, 79). Ferrous (iron) sulfate, used as a mordant or setting agent in natural dyeing.

COTTON GIN (p. 40). A machine that mechanically removes the seeds and foreign matter from the cotton boll.

COUNTERBALANCE LOOM (p. 67). A foot-powered loom in which all harnesses are interdependent: i.e., moving one harness affects all harnesses.

CRAZY QUILT (pp. 90, *91*, *92*). A patchwork quilt, popular in Victorian times, with small, irregular patches pieced together in a "crazy" fashion. Usually, there were elaborate stitches over the seams and appliqued designs on the patches.

CURTAIN (p. 149). A bonnet cape.

CUTCH. *See* CATCHETU.

DEACON, DEACONESS (p. 5). A temporal leader, in charge of the internal workings of the community.

DIAPER (pp. 26, 52, 93). Any fabric with small, all-over patterns, but usually a cloth with a small diamond-shape twill weave.

DISTAFF (p. 67). A stick or frame on which to hold unspun fibers during spinning.

DOLLAR MAT (pp. 114–118, *115*, *122*). A rug made from dollar-sized circles of wool folded and sewn in an overlapping (scaled) design to a backing fabric. Also called a SCALED RUG.

DOROTHY CLOAK (pp. 185, *186*, 214, 247). A popular hooded, armless, silk-lined cloak, named after its designer, Eldress Dorothy Durgin of Canterbury.

DOUBLE WEAVE (p. 104). A pattern weave which produces two layers of cloth, one on top of the other, usually attached to one another with binding threads.

DRAB (p. 15). A grayish yellow color.

DRAWERS (pp. 184, 194). An undergarment for the lower half of the body, with a sewn-in crotch; underpants.

DRAWING-IN (Appendix). Threading the loom; drawing the warp threads through the heddle-eyes.

DRESSING SACK (p. 250). A loose jacket worn while dressing or lounging.

DRUGGET. 1.(p. 61). A fabric with a linen, or, more often, cotton warp and wool weft. 2. (p. 104). A rug, generally striped, with a cotton warp and a wool weft.

DUSTER. 1.(p. 185). A cloak-like, armless outer garment used to protect clothing from dust when "motoring" in open cars. 2. (pp. *234*, 238). Household items used for dusting: feather duster, wool duster made from unspun wool, and duster mitt worn over the hand.

DYER'S CHAMOMILE. *See* WELD.

DYER'S MIGNONETTE. *See* WELD.

DYER'S MULBERRY. *See* FUSTIC.

DYER'S WEED. *See* WELD.

ELDER, ELDRESS (p. 5). A spiritual leader, appointed by the ministry. Each family had two elders and two eldresses.

EMERY (pp. 30, 224–226). A small pouch (often in the shape of a strawberry) used to keep needles sharp and rust free. It is filled with emery powder, a dark, granular corundum which helps grind and polish the needle when it is drawn through it.

FAMILY (p. 4). A self-contained, financially independent group of Believers, living together in one dwelling—the smallest unit of organization in the Church.

FANCY GOODS, FANCIWORK (pp. 21, 205). Small, decorative, "fanciful" items for adorning the home or person, popular in the Victorian and post-Victorian periods.

FASCINATOR (pp. 249–250). A knitted or crocheted head covering with long ties that came down over the ears and tied under the chin.

FIFTY-FIFTY WEAVE (p. 132). A weave in which there are the same number of warp and weft threads in each inch, or in which the warp and weft are of equal importance in the design. Also called BALANCED WEAVE.

FLAX (pp. 35–37). The plant or fibers from which linen yarn is made. *See also* TOW.

FLAX BREAK (pp. 35, 37). The device that separates the fiber from the stalk of the flax plant. *See also* BRAKE.

FLAX WHEEL (p. 67). A small treadle wheel on which flax is spun, often having a distaff built on it.

FLY-SHUTTLE LOOM (pp. 64, 71). A loom equipped with a device that propels the shuttle across the shed so that the weaver does not have to throw and catch it by hand after each shot. Also called SPRING-SHUTTLE LOOM.

FOOTING (pp. 22, 199). The bottom (foot) part of a sock or stocking.

FOUR-HARNESS LOOM (p. 67). A loom with four shafts, or harnesses, through which warp threads are drawn. The harnesses can be raised in any sequence or combination, so that more elaborate patterns are possible than on a two-harness loom.

FROCK (pp. 25, 61, 194, *195*). A smock-like garment with long, loose sleeves, worn by the brethren. Most frocks slipped over the head.

FULLING (p. 39). The process of washing, cleaning, bringing up the nap of and brushing a woven woolen fabric. In the Shakers' time, the fabric was beaten in the presence of heat and moisture.

FUSTIC (p. 76). A source of yellow dye, used in the form of wood chips.

Also known as YELLOW WOOD or DYER'S MULBERRY.

GAITERS (p. 183). A leg covering or legging, held in place by a stirrup-like strap that fit over the sole of the shoe.

GLAUBER'S SALTS (p. 26). A colorless sodium salt used as a leveling agent in dyeing.

GOOSE-EYE WEAVE (p. 52). A weave closely related to BIRD'S-EYE WEAVE.

GOWN (pp. 160–169). A woman's dress.

GREATCOAT (p. 197). A warm, woolen overcoat for men, having a shoulder cape and wide cuffs, which fit over all other clothing.

GREAT WHEEL. *See* WOOL WHEEL.

GRENADINE (pp. 24, 78). A plain or figured open-weave fabric; made of various fibers.

HABIT (p. 152). Riding habit or outfit.

HACKLING, HATCHELING, HECKLING, HETCHELING (pp. 35, 36, 75). The process of drawing flax (or hemp) fibers through the teeth of a HACKLE, a comb-like device, to straighten or comb them and separate them from remaining particles of the inside stalk.

HAND CARDS (pp. 34, 38). Two pieces of wood, each with hooked wire teeth set into a leather backing mounted on it, and each with a long wooden handle. Used for carding wool.

HANDKERCHIEF (p. 163). As used by the Shakers, sometimes a NECKERCHIEF, large enough to drape around the neck and cover the shoulders; also a "NAPKIN," equivalent of a present-day handkerchief.

HECKLE. *See* HACKLING.

HIGH WHEEL. *See* WOOL WHEEL.

HOLDER (p. 238). A potholder, teapot holder (cozy), or iron holder.

HOOKED RUG (pp. 112, 123, *125*). A rug made by bringing strips of woolen fabric or wool yarn from the bottom of a backing fabric up through to the top by means of a hook, forming loops on the upper surface.

HUCKABACK (pp. 52, 93). A specific weave with a highly textured surface, or the linen towelling commonly made in this weave.

INDIGO (pp. 26, 52, 76, 78). A blue vat dye derived from the indigo plant— generally a dark, grayish blue, but the shade can vary.

JACKET (pp. 188, 190, 192–193). A vest; a waistcoat.

KITCHEN SISTER (p. 149). A sister assigned to work in the kitchen for a specific period of time.

KNITTING PIN (p. 81). A very fine knitting needle.

LAWN (p. 178). A fine, sheer, plain-weave fabric of either linen or cotton.

LIST, LISTING. *See* TAPE.

LOGWOOD (pp. 76, 79). An important dyestuff, in wood-chip form, used in various ways to produce black, blue and purple.

MADDER (pp. 26, 57, 76). The orange-tone red dye derived from the root of the madder plant.

MINOR'S HEAD (p. 67). Device on a wool spinning wheel that helps the spindle turn faster.

MITTS (p. 185). Fingerless gloves worn on dressy occasions in the warmer months.

MONK'S BELT (pp. 8, *9*). A weaving pattern that produces small, rectangular areas of color.

MORDANT (p. 76). A substance (usually a metallic salt) that acts as a fixing or setting agent in dyeing.

M'S AND O'S (pp. 52, 93). A weaving pattern with a textured surface. The pattern areas can appear in "M" and "O" shapes.

NAPKIN. *See* HANDKERCHIEF.

NATURAL DYES (pp. 15, 76). Dyes made from sources which occur in nature—usually plants and plant materials.

NECKERCHIEF (pp. 150, *192*). The kerchief worn around the neck. Women's neckerchiefs were large enough to cover the complete bodice; men's were like bandanas.

NEEDLE BOOK, NEEDLE FOLDER (pp. 34, 227, *230*, *231*). A needle holder made of several pieces of flannel or felt, folded and sewn into the shape of a book.

NICWOOD (p. 80). Nicaragua wood, a form of BRAZILWOOD, used as a yellow dye.

NIDDY NODDY (p. 71). A simple device for winding yarn spun into skeins, made of one long vertical stick with two transverse sticks set at right angles to each other and to the central stick.

ORDER (p. 5). A level in the Church: for example, novitiate, junior, senior, or children's.

OVERSHOT (pp. 52, 87, *88*). A group of weaving patterns in which weft threads pass (float) over two or more warp yarns.

PANTALOONS (p. 189). Trousers.

PARKER MIXED (pp. 58, 148). Cloth made of yarn spun from 90 percent indigo-dyed wool and 10 percent white (natural) wool; named after Brother David Parker of Canterbury.

PENWIPE, PENWIPER (pp. 238, *241*). A piece or pieces of absorbent cloth used to wipe excess ink from fountain pens.

PETTICOAT (pp. 162, 164, 165). An outer skirt worn by women and girls (not an undergarment).

PICK. *See* SHOT.

PINAFORE (p. 200). A low-necked, sleeveless apron, usually worn by a young girl.

PIN FLAT, PIN TRAY (p. 224). A round or oblong uncovered tray of poplar cloth or tin, used to hold sewing pins.

PLAIN WEAVE. *See* TABBY.

PLAIT (pp. 164, 166, 167). Pleat.

PLUSH MAT or CUSHION (pp. 135–142). A mat (cushion) with a short, dense woven wool pile.

PLYING (pp. 51, 58, 96–97). The process of twisting two or more strands of yarn together to make a thicker, stronger yarn—hence, two-ply or four-ply yarn.

POCKET (pp. *29*, 30). In eighteenth-century usage, a small scallop or trapezoidal shaped pouch which tied around the waist and was worn by women under their petticoats. Used for holding sewing and personal accessories, as well as money.

POPLAR CLOTH (pp. 45–48, 212, 216–223). Cloth woven with very fine strips of poplar wood, usually with a cotton warp and a poplar weft. Primarily used to cover boxes of various shapes.

QUATREFOID (QUADRIFOID) (pp. 212, 221, *223*). Shaker poplar cloth box with four semicircular bulges, one on each side, each with its own independently opening lid.

QUILL (pp. 22, *73*). 1. A paper or wooden cylinder used in a boat shuttle to hold yarn; a bobbin. Feather quills were originally used for this purpose. 2. To wind quills with yarn.

QUILL WHEEL (p. 67). A bobbin winder.

RAG RUG (pp. 90–103). A woven rug made with rag strips in the weft.

RAVELED YARN (KNIT) RUG (p. 126). A rug made with a surface pile of unraveled knit yarns.

RECEIVER (HAIRPIN RECEIVER) (p. 246). A small tray for holding hairpins or hatpins, usually made of poplar cloth.

REED (p. 71). The part of the loom devised to separate the warp threads and keep them spaced evenly apart. Originally made of reed, later of bamboo, and now usually of steel.

REEL (pp. 42–43). In silk processing, to unwind the silk filament from the cocoon of the silkworm and wind it with several other filaments on a winding frame, or reel.

RETICULE (pp. 212, 246). A woman's small purse, often with a drawstring closing.

RETTING (pp. 26, 35). The process of decomposing, or rotting, the stalk of flax (hemp) plants, so that the fiber can be separated from the stalk.

RIBBON. *See* TAPE.

RIGID HEDDLE LOOM. *See* SLOT-AND-EYE LOOM.

SCALED RUG. *See* DOLLAR MAT.

SCARNE (pp. 64, *65*, 71). A large upright spool or bobbin holder.

SERGE (p. 75). A strong, twill-weave cloth with a shiny surface and a pronounced diagonal rib.

SEWING CHAIN (p. 229). A long yarn chain, probably crocheted, worn draped around the neck, with scissors or other sewing accessories attached to the ends.

SEWING STEPS (p. 27). A set of two or three free-standing steps used to rest the feet on when sewing, making it unnecessary for the sewer to cross her legs.

SHAG MAT (p. 125). A mat or rug with a long, coarse nap or pile on the top surface.

SHIRRED RUG (pp. 112, *119*, *122*). A rug made by sewing cloth CATERPILLARS to a backing fabric. Also called CATERPILLAR RUG, or CHENILLE RUG.

SHORTGOWN (pp. 162, *163*). A short gown with three-quarter sleeves, worn over a petticoat in the eighteenth and early nineteenth centuries.

SHOT (p. 98). One row of weft. Also called PICK.

SKEIN WINDER, SKEIN REEL (pp. 34, 64, 71). A device used to wind skeins of yarn after spinning; usually a revolving frame with a series of pegs.

SLOT-AND-EYE LOOM, SLOT-AND-HEDDLE LOOM (p. 67). A frame with alternating slots, or open spaces, and slats with small holes (eyes) in them. Yarn is threaded through both slots and eyes; those in the eyes are in a set or rigid position, and those in the slots are free to move above and below them, creating two distinct spaces that the weft threads can move through. A kind of RIGID HEDDLE LOOM.

SPINNING JENNY (p. 48). An early multiple-spindle device for spinning wool or cotton yarn.

SPLASH CLOTH (pp. 20, 95). A small cloth (usually blue and white check) hung on the wall behind a pitcher and wash basin in a retiring room.

SPRING-SHUTTLE LOOM. *See* FLY-SHUTTLE LOOM.

SQUIRREL CAGE (p. *74*). A type of skein winder with two movable drums, placed one above the other.

STOCK (pp. 162, 192). A stiff, narrow collar band that fastens in the back; a cravat.

STRUCTURAL DESIGN (p. 10). Design which emerges from the inherent characteristics of the materials, shapes, or processes used, without additional embellishments.

S-TWIST YARN (p. 98). Yarn spun or plied in a counterclockwise direction.

SURTOUT (pp. 61, 197). An overcoat; perhaps synonymous with GREATCOAT.

SWIFT (pp. *33*, 34). An adjustable reel, usually used to unwind yarn from skeins (but also usable for winding skeins). Umbrella swifts are expandable lath-like devices that clamp to a table.

SWINGLE. *See* BREAK.

TABBY (pp. 52, 132, 135). The basic weave, with each weft thread going over and under alternate warp threads; plain weave.

TAPE (pp. 22, 130–135). A narrow woven band. Also called BRAID, RIBBON, or LISTING.

TAPESTRY CLOTH (pp. 222, 226). Heavily textured commercial woven cloth or wallpaper, used after 1940 as a substitute for poplar cloth.

TEMPLATE, TEMPLE, TEMPLET, TENTERHOOK (p. 71). A weaving accessory which keeps the woven cloth taut and prevents it from pulling in during weaving. Usually made of two pieces of wood with sharp teeth on the edges, designed to catch in the cloth selvedges.

THRONE (p. 26). A platform about one foot high, placed under a window. By sitting on a throne, one could be closer to the daylight from the window.

TIDY (pp. 84, 243). A knitted or crocheted cloth that sat on the arms of chairs or under vases or lamps. *See also* ANTIMACASSAR.

TOMATO CUSHION (pp. 209, 212). A pincushion the size and shape of a tomato; usually red.

TOW (pp. 35, 37, 75). 1. The short, rough flax (hemp) separated from the long fibers in the hackling process; used for rough garments and sacking, and for mops. 2. The cloth made from the tow fiber.

TRUSTEE (p. 5). A temporal leader who handled legal, financial, and business matters, and dealt with the people of the outside world.

TUCKER (p. 165). A narrow collar of fine cloth attached to a chemise.

TWILL (pp. 26, 52, 135). A basic weave with a regular sequence of weft threads, usually "over one and under three" warp threads, creating a diagonal effect. Reverse twills can form herringbone and diamond effects.

TWISTING MACHINE (p. 51). A spinning wheel or mechanical device used to ply yarns together.

TWO-HARNESS LOOM (p. 67). A loom with two shafts, or harnesses, through which warp threads are drawn. Each harness is raised alternately.

VEIL BOX (pp. 212, 246). A poplar cloth box, 10 by 6 inches, used to hold veils.

VITRIOL (p. 76). Probably blue vitriol, or copper sulfate, used as a mordant or setting agent in natural dyeing.

WAISTCOAT. *See* JACKET.

WALKING WHEEL. *See* WOOL WHEEL.

WALL CLOTH (pp. 20, 95). A large cloth hung on the wall around the beds in a retiring room, to protect the wall from moisture and dirt.

WARP (pp. 52, 132, 142, 216). The set of threads (usually vertical) that are stretched on the loom for the weft threads to be woven into.

WARP FACE (pp. 107, 152). A fabric in which the weft is completely covered by the warp.

WARPING BOARD, WARPING REEL (p. 71). A frame on which the warp yarns are measured and counted out before they are put on the loom.

WAX BALLS, WAX CAKES (pp. 226–227). Small, molded pieces of beeswax used to coat sewing thread to prevent it from becoming twisted or damaged.

WEFT (pp. 57, 132, 142, 216). The threads—usually the horizontal or cross-wise threads—that are woven individually into the warp threads. Also called WOOF.

WEFT FACE (p. 152). A fabric in which the warp is completely covered by the weft.

WELD (p. 76). A yellow dyestuff, also called WOLD, DYER'S WEED, DYER'S CHAMOMILE, and DYER'S MIGNONETTE.

WOAD (pp. 76, 79). A blue dyestuff, related to indigo but less powerful and dependable. Often used as a "helper" in indigo dyebaths.

WOLD. *See* WELD.

WOOF. *See* WEFT.

WOOL WHEEL (p. 65). The large wheel used for spinning wool yarn. The spinner must turn the wheel by hand and walk back and forth while spinning; there is no treadle. Also called GREAT WHEEL, HIGH WHEEL, and WALKING WHEEL.

WOOLEN (p. 38). Yarn or cloth made from carded, rather than combed, wool.

WOOLEN MILL (p. 39). In Shaker usage, a mill in which the processes of carding, spinning, weaving, and fulling might all be carried out.

WORKBAG (pp. 227, *235*). A tall cloth sewing bag, usually with a drawstring closing, set into a round, firm bottom made of cardboard or a scallop-shaped needle case.

WORK BOX (pp. 212, *222*). A box, usually of poplar cloth, for holding sewing tools, accessories, and projects.

WORSTED (pp. 38, 75, 152). Yarn or cloth made of long wool fibers, combed rather than carded, so that the fibers run parallel to the finished yarn, and tightly twisted in spinning.

WRISTER, WRISTLET (p. 250). A knitted tube that slips over the wrist. Worn (at least in the world) when the sleeve of a jacket or coat was relatively short.

YELLOW WOOD. *See* FUSTIC.

Z-TWIST YARN (p. 98). Yarn spun or plied in a clockwise direction.

Index

Library of Congress Cataloging in Publication Data

Gordon, Beverly.
Shaker textile arts.

Bibliography: p.
Includes index.
1. Textile fabrics, Shaker. I. Title.
NK8912.G67 746'.0974 78-69899
ISBN 0-87451-158-5